# [THE
[UNDECLARED]
war]

## Class Conflict in the
Age of Cyber Capitalism

# James Laxer

VIKING

VIKING

Published by the Penguin Group

Penguin Books Canada Ltd, 10 Alcorn Avenue, Toronto, Ontario, Canada M4V 3B2

Penguin Books Ltd, 27 Wrights Lane, London W8 5TZ, England

Penguin Putnam Inc., 375 Hudson Street, New York, New York 10014, U.S.A.

Penguin Books Australia Ltd, Ringwood, Victoria, Australia

Penguin Books (NZ) Ltd, cnr Rosedale and Airborne Roads, Albany, Auckland 1310, New Zealand

Penguin Books Ltd, Registered Offices: Harmondsworth, Middlesex, England

First published 1998

10 9 8 7 6 5 4 3 2 1

Copyright © James Laxer, 1998

Printed and bound in Canada on acid free paper ∞

CANADIAN CATALOGUING IN PUBLICATION DATA

Laxer, James, 1941–
    The undeclared war

ISBN 0-670-87660-7

1. Social Classes – Canada. 2. Social classes. 3. Social conflict – Canada. 4. Social conflict. 5. Capitalism – Canada. I. Title.

HN110.Z9S6 1998    305.5'0971    C97-932755-5

Visit Penguin Canada's web site at www.penguin.ca

*To the memory of Gwyn Jones*

# Acknowledgements

I WISH TO express my gratitude to those who have helped me in researching and writing *The Undeclared War*.

I am grateful to the staff of the Organization of Economic Cooperation and Development in Paris for their assistance in locating a long list of publications for me. Ethan Poskanzer, Kate Laxer, Hugh Mackenzie and Paul Brannigan generously offered their time and helped me solve problems encountered in writing the book. At Atkinson College, Louise Jacobs often kept the world at bay so I could get on with the job. I owe many thanks to Joyce Nobel, Linda McQuaig, Gord Laxer and Gerry Caplan, who read the manuscript and offered invaluable suggestions and criticisms.

In April 1997, my good friends Gwyn Jones and Muriel Guy appeared at the door of my apartment in France, having made the long trek from their home in Bath, England. Gwyn had loaded up the trunk of their car with books he thought would help. Gwyn has been the source of many intellectual and human adventures in my life over the past decade. When he passed away in November 1997, I lost a uniquely generous friend.

Everyone at Penguin has been strongly supportive, as they were with my last book. Just the thought of getting out on the road with Scott Sellers to publicize the book pushed the writing along. My wonderful editor Jackie Kaiser was full of inspiration and ideas and was kind enough to time the birth of her baby perfectly and thus was able to complete an edit of the first draft. Meg Taylor, who took over for Jackie, was energetic, intelligent and endlessly helpful in seeing the project to completion. Alison Reid did a great job copy editing the book.

Thanks to Emily and Jonathan for putting up with a father who was usually leashed to a computer or notebook. Sandy, my spouse, was a kind, generous and thoughtful companion during the many months when this project was on the boil.

## Contents

## Chapter 1

# Fields of Combat

Wars are no less vicious for being undeclared. Such is the case with the conflict that now rages between the social classes. This is a civil war, and by definition civil wars are not declared. The conventional wisdom is that the Cold War has been followed by an era of peace in the industrialized world. In fact, the Cold War has been followed by the class war, which, like its predecessor, is also international in scope.

Today's class war is not hidden—although it is rarely named for what it is. It is there wherever we look—in factories, offices, schools, in the global restructuring of multinational corporations, in stock and bond markets, in the policies of central banks and in the deliberations of governments. And its effects resonate for citizens worldwide.

Just ask Canadians how things are going for them in the late 1990s and their answers will differ radically. Put the question to an investor or corporate manager, and you will likely be told that these are very good times indeed. The public sector deficit has been wrestled down, inflation is low, the economy is growing, corporate profits are good and a lot of money has been made in the stock market. We're on the right track and should stay the course. These days the billionaires who are the exemplars of investors are amassing wealth on an unprecedented scale. Assuming he worked sixty hours a week and took a two-week vacation,

Microsoft president Bill Gates made about US$7 million dollars an hour in 1996–97.

Ask the same question of a man who works for a salary or a wage, and the response is sure to be far less buoyant. Between 1974 and 1994, the earnings of the average male Canadian worker, in constant 1994 dollars, declined from C$31,242 a year to C$31,087. During this period, women's real incomes did increase, but they stayed well below those of men. Between 1974 and 1994, the earnings of the average female worker, in constant 1994 dollars, increased from C$14,813 to C$19,359.[1]

Wage and salary earners are the survivors of years of downsizing. They're working harder than ever to cover the duties of those whose jobs have been axed. And the anxiety that they may be cut in the next round of job shedding never really leaves. They know all too well that just because their employer makes a profit doesn't mean that their jobs are secure. Here are two typical examples. In 1995, General Motors Canada increased its profit by 36 percent and reduced its workforce by 2,500. The same year, the Bank of Montreal reported a 20 percent increase in its profit and downsized its workforce by 1,428.

If the person you speak to is under thirty and has children, and he or she does not have a university education, the odds are that you have encountered someone who is really up against it. Young families headed by mothers and fathers without university degrees have seen their real incomes plunge over the past two decades.

Should you put the question to someone working part-time but who wants full-time work, you will probably hear about real economic need. In 1994, the median income of a part-time worker in Canada was C$7,425.[2] The number of Canadians who work part-time but would prefer full-time work has increased sixfold over the past two decades.

If you talk to someone who has been out of work for a long time or is living on welfare, you are almost certainly face-to-face with real desperation. Not since the Great Depression of the 1930s has it been as terrible to be poor as it is now. Today the poor are scapegoated by business leaders, intellectuals and politicians. They are held to be responsible for their plight by a society that has opted for a war on the poor in place of a war on poverty. A central precept of the Common Sense Revolution of Ontario's current Conservative government is that welfare payments keep the poor hooked to government handouts and stop them from searching for a job. In October 1995, only four months into office, the Ontario Conservatives cut the income of a family with two children living on welfare from c$1,549 a month by c$335 a month.

Thirty percent of the children in Toronto—the city picked by the United Nations as the best place in the world to live—are subsisting below the poverty line. Taking into account the cost of living in Toronto, Statistics Canada in 1995 reckoned the "low income cut-off" for a family of three at a pre-tax amount of c$26,232.[3]

In the summer of 1997, I returned from a six-month stay in France, where I regularly saw homeless men and women and unemployed youths staking out busy intersections in cities and towns to ask for money from drivers caught in traffic. In Toronto, there are more people than I can ever remember sitting on the sidewalk on downtown streets waiting silently for a little consideration from passersby. Others are more aggressive, coming up and asking for money.

In July 1997, Woolworth's announced that it will shut down almost all of its stores in the United States. Nine thousand people are to lose their jobs. Following the announcement, Woolworth's stock rose sharply.

One of the certitudes of the so-called new economy is that labour disputes are becoming a thing of the past. Wage and salary earners have quietly accepted their place alongside the new millionaires and billionaires.

But things do not go according to the script. In the mid-summer of 1997, 185,000 workers at United Parcel Service in the United States went on strike. It was the biggest American strike in decades. Well over half of the strikers were part-timers, making about us$11 an hour. They wanted full-time work and aspired to the pay of the full-time ups drivers, about us$20 an hour. The ups workers and their representative, the Teamsters Union, insisted that they should keep control of their pension fund in order to determine how it is invested. ups, which made a profit of over us$1 billion in the year before the strike, wanted to manage the pension fund.

The American public supported the strikers, not ups. Ten days into the strike, 55 percent of those polled by Gallup said they were on the side of the strikers, while only 27 percent supported UPS. In the end, UPS agreed to create ten thousand new full-time jobs and to raise the wage rates of part-timers from US$11 an hour to more than US$15 an hour over the five-year life of the contract. And the union kept control of the pension fund.

Hostilities commenced in today's class war in the mid-1970s, and the struggle has been growing in intensity ever since. The outbreak of hostilities between the social classes brought an end to the long truce that prevailed, despite numerous lapses, in the decades following the Second World War.

And there is no doubt about who has taken the offensive. Sensing the opportunity to forge more advantageous arrangements for itself, business started the fighting. And as the early battles were easily won, business and its political and intellectual champions have revelled in their newfound power. Early hesitations have been put aside. Now they are solidly committed to tearing up the terms of that post-war truce. Like previous wars between the social classes, the current one is certainly about economics, but it is also about politics, culture and ideology.

The assertion that we live in an age of class war will immediately set some alarm bells ringing. For many analysts and commentators, the very notion of social class is archaic, a leftover from decades ago, with little relevance for these post-modern times. In this age of identity politics and revolutionary technology, does it make sense to think of society as divided between a class that is dominant and classes that are dominated?

The idea that we live in a new age is not misguided. Cyber capitalism is certainly different from capitalism in the days of Henry Ford. Today, there is a powerful tendency to stress the discontinuities, the fractured identities that are at the surface in this post–Cold War historical moment. But the fact of discontinuity does not dissolve the need to analyze global capitalism as a system and to draw conclusions about who has power within it and who does not.

I contend not only that social classes do exist but that the best way to make sense of the issues that confront us at the dawn of the new millennium is to understand this as an age when an intense power struggle is under way between those who own and control capital on one side, and wage and salary earners on the other. Later I will examine what social classes are and what the power relations between them mean for society. In this chapter, we will tour the fields of battle on which the new class war is being fought. Throughout the industrialized world, the conflict comes into full view when we consider the immediate issues around which it rages:

*The income gap between the rich and everyone else has been widening rapidly.* When the Harvard economist Robert Reich stepped down as U.S. labor secretary at the end of President Bill Clinton's first term in January 1997, he issued a blunt warning: "From the 1950s through most of the 1970s the income of the poorest fifth of Americans grew faster than the income of the top fifth. Between 1950 and 1978 the inflation-adjusted family income of the bottom quintile grew by 138 percent, while the real income of the richest 20 percent of families grew by 99 percent."[4] However, between 1980 and 1995, the earnings of those in the highest bracket, adjusted for inflation, rose by 10.7 percent, while the median wages for a worker declined by 3.6 percent. Meanwhile, the real incomes of those in the lowest bracket fell by 9.6 percent. And as Reich pointed out, wealth is "even more unevenly distributed than income. Not only does the richest 20 percent of the United States hold the bulk of the total wealth, but over the period from 1983 to 1992 this group received some 99 percent of the total gain in wealth."[5]

And the economic recovery of the mid-1990s did not stop the income gulf between rich and poor from continuing to widen. *Pulling Apart*, a study released by the U.S. government's Center on Budget and Policy Priorities in December 1997, showed how dramatically the income gap had increased from the mid-1970s to the mid-1990s. In the period from 1994 to 1996, the average income of the top fifth of families with children was us$117,499, 12.7 times as much as the income of the bottom fifth of families with children, us$9,254. In forty U.S. states in 1994 to

1996, the income gap between the top and bottom 20 percent of families was greater than it had been in any state in the mid-1970s. In no U.S. state in the mid-1970s was the income of the top fifth of families with children more than ten times as great as that of the bottom fifth of families.[6] The most extreme case was that of Washington, D.C. There, the income of the top fifth of families with children reached us$149,508, twenty-eight times as much as the bottom fifth of families, at us$5,293.[7]

In Canada, the situation was similar. A Statistics Canada study published in December 1997 revealed that during 1996 the average income of the poorest fifth of families declined by 3.1 percent, to c$17,334. Meanwhile, the richest fifth of Canada's families saw their average inflation-adjusted incomes increase by 1.8 percent in 1996 to c$114,874.[8]

Even this evidence of a widening income gap fails to paint the picture in colours that are sufficiently stark.

The wealthiest three Americans—Bill Gates, Warren Buffett and John Walton (and family)—have combined assets worth us$94 billion.[9] The bottom fifty million Americans have combined assets of just over us$90 billion, and this includes the equity they have in the ownership of their homes. If you include only people's financial assets, Gates, Buffett and Walton have combined assets worth as much as the financial assets of the poorest hundred million Americans.[10] And the us$94 billion in assets owned by Walton, Gates and Buffett are their personal holdings alone. We are not even talking about the much wider corporate assets they control. Three people on one side of the ledger, 100 million people on the other. Welcome to cyber capitalism, American-style.

*Footloose corporations are leaving wage and salary earners in the lurch.* Because they can now threaten to move anywhere on the globe to find the labour conditions they desire, corporations enjoy enormous leverage with their employees. And they are acting on their advantage. Developments in microelectronics have enhanced the ability of firms to operate on a global scale. Today, companies can source raw materials, machinery, parts, components, final assembly, industrial research and marketing in different parts of the world.

In the first half of the 1990s, United Technologies, a conglomerate producing aircraft components, automotive parts, elevators, etc., eliminated 33,000 jobs in the United States and created 15,000 jobs in other countries. In late 1996, a survey of 7,500 German companies undertaken by the German Industry and Trade Federation revealed that German business was planning to create at least 300,000 jobs outside Germany, most of them in low-wage locations in Eastern Europe. Decisions to shift jobs abroad on a huge scale came when German unemployment had hit 4.1 million or 10.8 percent of the workforce.

Moreover, the latest plans to shift jobs abroad have simply amplified recent practice. Between 1992 and 1994, German businesses created 237,000 jobs outside Germany.[11] Siemens, the giant electronics company that is the largest private employer in Germany, has led the way in moving jobs to Eastern Europe.[12] Steep labour costs at home are invariably cited as the major reason for the decision to establish operations and jobs elsewhere.

*Businesses are reshifting from full-time to part-time work.* In all the advanced countries, business has taken advantage of high unemployment to create a more flexible workforce, tailor-made to meet its needs. Part-time workers can be paid lower wages and salaries. They don't receive as many benefits, and employers are not legally required to give as much notice when their jobs are terminated.

In Canada, the number of part-time workers who would prefer full-time work has increased dramatically over the past two decades. If the official unemployment rate in Canada reflected the number of hours of work lost by these part-timers because they can't find full-time work, it would be significantly higher. In 1995, when the official unemployment rate was 9.7 percent, counting the hours lost by part-timers desiring full-time work would have pushed the jobless rate up to 12.7 percent.[13]

In Britain, whose economic performance has been applauded by commentators in the English-speaking world in the mid-1990s, two-thirds of the jobs created between 1992 and 1997 were part-time. During that half decade, Britain created only 388,000 jobs, including part-time jobs, with a workforce of approximately 25 million. Half of the new full-time jobs were temporary.

Indeed, part of the island kingdom's so-called economic miracle was due to the fact that Britain's official statistics sharply undercounted the number of those unemployed and failed to use internationally approved methods for calculating unemployment. When Britain's official unemployment rate was declared to be 6.2 percent in February 1997—by far the lowest rate in any major European country—an independent report from Sheffield Hallam University in the U.K. calculated that the real number of British unemployed was twice the 1.8 million officially acknowledged. That's because British counting methods left out those among the unemployed who were ineligible for benefits, those on government programs, many long-term jobless and many listed as having retired early or as permanently sick.[14]

In the United States, as elsewhere, part-time workers are less well paid than their full-time counterparts. In 1994, while only 3.1 percent of full-time workers were paid as little as US$4.25 an hour or less, 15.5 percent of part-time workers were paid at these low rates.[15]

In a report issued in 1996 by a fact-finding group set up by the government of France, the negative effects of part-time employment on young workers were clearly documented. In France between 1990 and 1996, the proportion of young workers (aged fifteen to twenty-nine) involved in various types of part-time employment increased from 18.1 percent to 22.6 percent. And of those working part-time, the number of young workers who would have preferred full-time work increased from 6.6 percent to 10.6 percent. Overall, between 1989 and 1994, the average income of French workers aged twenty to twenty-four declined from 5,600 francs a month (about US$1,400) to 4,700 francs (about US$1,175). And the number of households designated as poor whose breadwinners were under thirty increased from 11.2 percent of those in that age group in 1989 to 18.5 percent in 1994.[16] In France, the shift to part-time work, especially among the young, is clearly representative of the widening gap between rich and poor.

These days business gurus are frank in advising corporations to move to a structure that keeps full-time work to a strict minimum. One such guru is Charles Handy, a well-known British broadcaster and business consultant. To succeed today, Handy says corporations need to acquire the contours of a "shamrock"—the three-sided Irish clover leaf. As Handy puts it, "The shamrock's three leaves represent: the core workforce, the contractual fringe, and the flexible labour force."[17] Writing in the cheery style that has made him popular, Handy says that because the members of the core workforce "are expensive . . . there are fewer of them. Every successful business has quadrupled its turnover in the last ten years yet halved its core workforce . . ."[18]

The second group, the contractual fringe, is hired through what is called "outsourcing." As Handy bluntly says, "There is, after all, no sense in giving the high rates of pay and the privileged conditions of the core, to people and tasks which can be equally well done by people outside the organization."[19] Exactly this reasoning motivated General Motors of Canada to outsource some of its production by selling off a number of its plants in the mid-1990s. Outsourcing was the issue on which the Canadian Auto Workers (CAW) mounted a three-week-long strike against GM in September 1996. The CAW challenged the right of a highly profitable company, which GM certainly was, to outsource without negotiating a deal on this crucial question with its employees.

Then comes the third leaf in the shamrock, the flexible workforce. Handy says that "it makes no economic sense to have your core workers doing extra to cover the peak periods of activity, nor to store up enough workers to be able to cope with any peak without overtime. . . . Cheaper by far . . . to hire in occasional help, part-time or temporary, at lower rates.

"That has the sound of exploitation about it, of getting labour cheap. It can be . . ."[20] Handy isn't worried about the risk of exploitation because he believes there are plenty of workers who like part-time work. What he does not say is that in an era of chronic underemployment, corporations are taking the advice of consultants like him and pushing workers out of the core workforce against their will, forcing them to take part-time work when they would prefer full-time employment.

But Handy does understand the fundamental shift in capitalism that is occurring: "The way things are going it may well be that there will be

more people working outside the core than *inside* it by the end of the
century."[21] It was precisely to avoid being pushed outside the core workforce that UPS drivers waged their crucial strike in the summer of 1997.
And most Americans sympathized with the strikers because the issue of
part-time versus full-time work resonated with them.

*Tax reforms lighten the burden borne by the rich, while penalizing wage and
salary earners.* Everywhere in the industrialized world, high-income earners and those who control capital have been fighting to have their share
of the tax burden reduced. And they have been hugely successful. In 1979,
Americans with incomes of US$1 million or more paid 47 percent of their
incomes, on average, in federal taxes. By 1994, these very high income
earners were paying, on average, only 32 percent of their earnings in federal taxes.[22] As a consequence of the hefty tax cuts of the Reagan era, the
wealthiest Americans were handed a handsome bonus, which they could
use to live more luxuriously or to amass larger pools of capital.

About a decade after the Reagan tax cuts in the United States, the
people of Ontario were the recipients of an income tax cut whose major
beneficiaries were also the affluent. At the core of the Conservative
Party's Common Sense Revolution platform was an eventual 30 percent
cut in the provincial income tax. For the average income earner, the
income tax cut was to amount to a few hundred dollars a year, but for
someone making C$100,000 a year, the fully implemented cut promised
a tax rollback of about C$4,600. A partner in a major law firm who makes
C$200,000 a year could expect a tax cut of about C$11,200.

In the United States in the 1950s, corporations paid 39 percent of
U.S. income taxes, while individuals paid the other 61 percent. By the
1980s, corporations had reduced their share of income taxes to 17 percent and individuals were required to pay the other 83 percent.[23]
Between 1980 and the early 1990s, corporate taxes were reduced as a
proportion of overall taxes in almost all major industrialized countries
including Canada, the United States, Germany, France, Britain and
Japan. (Italy was an exception; Italian corporate taxes increased as a
proportion of overall taxes paid.)[24]

*Private corporations and the public sector are shedding jobs.* Everywhere in the industrialized world, corporations are striving to "do more with less." Profitable companies, even highly profitable ones, have joined the rush to downsize.

Canadians have experienced this kind of corporate bloodletting on a massive scale. During the 1988 federal election campaign, spokespersons for corporate Canada promised that after the Canada–U.S. Free Trade Agreement (FTA) went into effect—it did in 1989—more and better jobs would be created in Canada. Having promised one thing, Canada's major corporations proceeded to do the exact opposite. Between 1988 and 1996, large Canadian companies shed tens of thousands of employees. Abitibi Price cut its workforce by nearly 8,000, Alcan shed 11,000 jobs, Imperial Oil cut 4,000 jobs, and Stelco dropped almost 5,000 from its payroll. A study done by the Canadian Centre for Policy Alternatives (CCPA) found that thirty-three major companies slashed their combined employment by 216,000 jobs between 1988 and 1996, for a collective cutback of nearly 35 percent of the number they employed. And this huge slashing of jobs occurred at the same time as the combined revenues of these thirty-three companies increased by more than C$40 billion, from C$117.8 billion to C$158.2 billion.[25]

On the other side of the ledger, a few major corporations have expanded their workforce. For example, between 1988 and 1996, the Montreal-based distiller Seagram's added 15,000 employees to its payroll. However, of the forty-seven large companies studied by the CCPA since the FTA went into effect, only eleven increased the number they employed. These eleven companies added 28,000 jobs to their collective payroll, a small number when weighed against the 216,000 jobs shed by the thirty-three large companies mentioned above.[26]

In the United States between 1991 and 1995, nearly 2.5 million workers lost their jobs because of corporate restructuring.[27] And American corporate executives are keen to apply their job-shedding techniques outside the United States as well, whenever they are given the chance. One case that got them into trouble was in the aftermath of the merger between the Swedish and American pharmaceutical companies Pharmacia AB and Upjohn Inc., to form Pharmacia and Upjohn. The first priority of the American executives of the new US$7-billion giant, with headquarters in Britain, was to draft a plan to slash US$500 million in costs and to turf 4,000 workers from the company's payroll of 30,000 in the first year.[28] Their approach horrified the Swedish executives, who regarded the Americans as lacking any sensitivity to the labour–management environment in Europe. Dick Brown, the American who was temporary chairman of the merged firm, admitted in an interview in April 1997, "In retrospect, we might have been a bit aggressive about the extent of cost savings in the first year."[29]

This American job-slashing approach has been felt elsewhere in Europe as well. David Hermann, the American chairman and chief executive of Adam Opel AG, a General Motors subsidiary based in Frankfurt, believes German production costs are too high. He commented that "52 years of social peace is . . . linked to the now clearly overblown social system and worker benefits." Between 1992 and 1997, he cut the company workforce in Germany from 57,500 to 45,000.[30]

In Canada, many highly profitable companies have been laying workers off, as the following cases from 1995 illustrate: Inco, profits up 3,281 percent, decrease in employees 1,963; CP Rail, profits up 75 percent, decrease in employees 1,500; Canadian Imperial Bank of Commerce, profits up 14 percent, decrease in employees 1,289; Shell Canada, profits up 63 percent, decrease in employees 471; Imperial Oil, profits up 43 percent, decrease in employees 452; and Toronto Dominion Bank, profits up 16 percent, decrease in employees 354.[31]

In this class war, the aggression is not all one way. Increasingly, workers have been resisting. In Paris in January 1997, hundreds of white-collar employees of Crédit Foncier de France S.A., a major quasi-public mortgage bank, occupied the offices of the bank to protest a restructuring program being undertaken by management—with the approval of the government—that put more than 3,300 jobs at risk. Established in 1852 by Napoleon III, Crédit Foncier, though a private bank listed on the stock market, provides mortgages for social housing projects backed by the government, which is why the government had a say in its fortunes.[32]

During the worker occupation, the bank's governor (his job title),

Jérôme Meyssonnier, was kept barred in his gilt-ceilinged office, where he spent his days eating pâté.[33] The workers were especially incensed by the fact that Crédit Foncier had recovered from a loss in 1995 to make a profit in 1996. Patrick Kronenbitter, one of the strike's leaders, noted that the occupation involved all categories of workers from the lowest to some in upper management. In response to a question about the propriety of occupying offices and holding the boss against his will, Kronenbitter observed that in France "occupation of a business is a tradition."[34]

Interviewed by the Paris newspaper *Libération*, employees explained why they felt driven to resort to the occupation of the offices of Crédit Foncier. Françoise Savé, aged thirty-five, a communications assistant with twelve years' experience with the bank, who made a salary of 12,000 francs net a month (about US$3,000), answered the charge that Crédit Foncier's employees were privileged: "We are fighting to save our jobs, not our privileges. We are all ready to adapt, to make sacrifices." Jacques Duhéron, aged fifty-five, a middle-level manager with thirty years at the bank, who made 15,000 francs net a month (about US$3,750) said: "I am not yet old enough to be interested in early retirement. I am worried because I have two children, aged 14 and 15." And Sabine Tooby, twenty-seven, a junior employee making 7,200 francs net a month (about US$1,800) commented, "I was one of the last hired. The future is black and makes me afraid. It's been three years since the problems began, but no one could have imagined this."[35]

The occupation went on for three weeks, although the governor of the bank was released from his office sooner. It was ended only when Crédit Foncier's officers decided to keep the bank going for another two years, while reconsidering its future. The Crédit Foncier occupation was noteworthy because it revealed militancy in a formerly quiescent segment of the workforce—the white-collar financial sector. And in France it was not an isolated case. In the winter of 1997, there were other instances of occupations of white-collar workplaces by salaried employees.

*Major corporations run Third World sweatshops, whose existence has begun to shock the public in the advanced countries.* The most notorious case has been that of the apparel industry. Following reports of inhumane conditions at

13

Central American plants producing garments for Wal-Mart under the trademark of the television personality Kathie Lee Gifford, the Clinton administration set up a presidential task force whose goal was to get industry representatives, trade unionists and human rights advocates to come up with a set of minimum standards for the operation of apparel factories, both inside and outside the U.S.[36]

The spotlight on factories, where clothing and shoes are manufactured, has revealed appalling conditions that include the use of child labour; work in unsafe and unhealthy workplaces; miserably low wages; excessive hours of work; and sexual abuse and beatings meted out to employees by their supervisors.

Big-name companies represented on the presidential task force were Liz Claiborne, L.L. Bean and Nike. Although the task force members were able to agree on such matters as sexual harassment, the beating of employees and the banning of child labour (under fourteen), there were two sticking points: minimum wages, and maximum hours of work. The corporations on the task force insisted that paying minimum wages in any given jurisdiction ought to be good enough, while labour and human rights advocates pressed for the right of workers to a "living wage," making the point that minimum wages often left workers and their families mired in abject poverty. On the hours question, labour and human rights advocates took the position that workers should not be forced to work more than forty-eight hours a week, but the companies insisted that they should be allowed to demand up to sixty hours a week from their employees.[37]

Within the presidential task force, the apparel companies held the whip hand. If they failed to agree with what were to be no more than voluntary guidelines, the task force's efforts would lead nowhere. It was a case of the soft-liners urging the hard-liners to be a little more humane in an industry with a notorious reputation. The ministrations of the softs were not unlike the appeals of the medieval Church to the nobility of the day to be a little kinder to the serfs—well intentioned, to be sure, but probably not very effective.

And while the polite debate about the ethics of the apparel industry droned on, stories about the truly appalling behaviour of the major companies continued to appear. On April 1, 1997, the *International Herald Tribune* carried a *New York Times* column by Bob Herbert that told how Nike pays its workers in Vietnam—90 percent of whom are girls or young women aged fifteen to twenty-eight—wages so low that "hunger follows them like a shadow." Thuyen Nguyen, an American businessman who interviewed workers in Nike's plants in Vietnam, reported that the workers were paid only US$1.60 a day, but that three meagre meals, consisting of rice, a little vegetable and some tofu, cost US$2.10 a day. Even if they spent their entire incomes on food, these workers would go hungry. But they also had to pay for rent, at least US$6 a month, and for other things such as clothing and an occasional bar of soap.

A report by Nguyen on conditions in the factories, issued in March 1997, stated: "Thirty-two out of 35 workers we interviewed told us they had lost weight since working at Nike factories. All reported not feeling good generally since working at the factories. They complained of frequent headaches as well as general fatigue." The conditions of work described in the report were little better than those of slaves, featuring corporal punishment and a rigidly controlled work schedule. Punishments for poor workmanship or the most minor acts of insubordination included supervisors hitting women over the head, workers being forced to kneel with their hands in the air for extended periods and workers having their mouths taped for talking. In other cases, women were forced to stand in the broiling sun and to write down over and over again the mistakes they had made. The report also cited instances of women being molested by their supervisors.

Herbert concluded that the "beauty of the Nike formula is that the cost of the labour to make the product is next to nothing and the price at which the product sells is astonishingly high. That's how the athletes-pitchmen Michael Jordan and Tiger Woods get to make their Nike millions, and Phil Knight, the shrewd and combative Nike chairman, his billions."[38]

The Clinton task force wrapped up its deliberations with the promulgation of a U.S. Workplace Code of Conduct at a ceremony at the

White House in April 1997. The code, endorsed by such major apparel companies as Nike, Reebok, Liz Claiborne and Nicole Miller, was long on rhetoric and short on the enforcement of a clear set of rules. Ostensibly, the code banned forced labour and the employment of children under fifteen and required the companies to pay the minimum wage as established under local laws where the companies operated. It recognized the right of workers to form unions and to bargain collectively, and prohibited physical and sexual harassment or abuse.[39]

But reference to a "living wage" was not included in the code. The notion that workers in the Third World ought to have a right to a wage to reasonably support themselves and their families was just not on. In those Third World countries where a minimum wage even exists, it is so low as to condemn those who receive it to poverty. The result: even if the code were implemented to the letter, apparel workers in the Third World would still be the victims of extreme exploitation.

A *New York Times* editorial described the code as "littered with loopholes."[40] The code merely recommended, but did not require, independent local monitoring of working conditions and public disclosure of infractions. It even allowed companies to exceed the sixty-hour weekly work limit in "extraordinary" circumstances.

What the companies got out of the code was the right to stitch No Sweat labels on their garments, coveted at a time when much of the public is disgusted by accounts of the practices of the apparel companies in the Third World. But desperate apparel workers are unlikely to see any real improvement in their working conditions or wages.

Although the apparel industry is notorious for the way it has made spectacular profits on the backs of Third World workers, it is by no means alone. Royal Dutch Shell, the world's largest oil company, became infamous for its behaviour in Nigeria, where it worked hand in glove with the country's military dictatorship in oppressing people, while extracting millions in profits. In Ogoniland, Shell went so far as to finance the purchase of weapons for the local Nigerian security forces. In one case in 1990, the oil giant asked for assistance from the security forces. Following an incident in which a policeman was killed, the security forces massacred eighty people and burned 495 houses.[41]

In 1995, when many human rights activists and governments were pressuring Nigeria on behalf of the writer Ken Saro-Wiwa and his comrades, Shell refused to use its considerable influence with the dictatorship to seek clemency for those who had been condemned for speaking out in opposition to the regime of Mobutu Sese Seko. Just before Christmas, Saro-Wiwa and eight others were hanged.

After being lambasted by human rights protests in many countries, Shell finally issued a set of business principles in 1997 that included an undertaking to respect human rights. The company said it would consult local groups before embarking on sensitive projects.[42] Of course, the issuing of a statement of principles is one thing, while actions are quite another.

*Trade deals stack the deck in favour of business.* Under the terms of the North American Free Trade Agreement (NAFTA), in effect since 1994, if an enterprise in Canada shuts down and moves its operations to the United States or Mexico, wage and salary earners at the Canadian plant can apply to follow their jobs to the new location. But the chances are that they won't be granted the right to work in the U.S. or Mexico. On the other hand, if the managers of a company moving from one NAFTA country to another apply to move along with their company, it is almost certain that they will be granted the right to take up residence and the right to work in the country to which the business is migrating.

The rights of capital take precedence over the rights of labour in the NAFTA agreement. In fact, to call NAFTA a trade deal is misleading. The three-country agreement has much more to do with differentiating between the rights of social classes than with liberalizing trade. What NAFTA does is to guarantee mobility of capital in North America. It achieves this through the concept of "national treatment," a provision stipulating that government regulations established by member countries must treat companies from all three member countries in the same way.

NAFTA also guarantees the right of business in the member countries (subject to minimal restrictions) to acquire businesses in the other member states. Above all, the agreement ties the hands of member states—at the national and sub-national levels—limiting their ability to treat domestic business differently from business based in the other member countries, and nullifying their power to prevent takeovers of domestic enterprises by those based in the other member states.

Rather than calling NAFTA a trade agreement, it would be more accurate to describe it as a Magna Carta for business, or even more accurately as a constitutional document setting out the inalienable rights of capital. And just as NAFTA ensures the rights of capital, it restricts the powers of member states, whose constitutions entrench the rights of citizens. The same will be true of the Multilateral Agreement on Investment (MAI), which is now being negotiated among the advanced countries.

Ironically, the transferring of jobs from the U.S. and Canada to Mexico as a consequence of NAFTA has not made most Mexicans winners in the process. To qualify for a free trade deal with its northern neighbours, Mexico was forced to make a whole series of internal reforms, most of which directly hurt millions of its own citizens. Mexico, which formerly enforced rules against ownership of companies on its soil by foreigners and which used state ownership and government support for domestic companies to build its economy, has been forced to abandon such practices as the price for entry into NAFTA. The collapse of the Mexican currency, the peso, in 1995, reduced millions of Mexicans, including many in the middle class, to economic desperation. Today many Texans and Mexicans correctly see NAFTA as a threat to their jobs.

*The drive is on for more "flexible" labour markets.* Everywhere in the industrialized world, business is pushing for what it calls a more "flexible labour market." The term sounds innocuous, even forward-looking. It is actually a euphemism for a series of changes highly advantageous to business and disadvantageous to labour. The changes include the reduction or even the elimination of the minimum wage; the easing of restrictions on increasing the number of hours worked and on mandatory overtime; the reduction of payroll taxes paid by employers to finance unemployment insurance, publicly managed pension plans and health-care systems; the easing of measures that restrain companies from sacking employees; and the elimination of regulations that bar the use of replacement workers during strikes.

Pro-business economists and journalists have kept up a constant rhetorical offensive in favour of flexibility, arguing that such measures are essential if countries are to adapt to the tough new conditions of the globalized economy. These advocates are adept at playing countries off against one another, urging those countries that maintain strong pro-labour regulations to give them up in the name of flexibility. European countries, such as France and Germany, where minimum wages and benefits are high and workers enjoy strong job protection, are urged to follow in the footsteps of Britain and the United States, where workers' wages, benefits and protection are inferior.

The advocates of flexibility argue that high wages, social benefits and labour protection are barriers to job creation. To reduce unemployment, they urge, corporations must have a higher incentive to invest. And they will invest, given the choice, in countries where labour is cheaper and pro-labour regulations are absent.

In July 1997, a report issued by the Organization for Economic Cooperation and Development (OECD) challenged the validity of these nostrums. The report issued by the twenty-nine-nation OECD concluded that the effect of Britain's often-touted flexible labour market is to trap workers in poorly paid jobs. According to the report, the existence of unions and a high level of union activity do not impede economic performance and do not lead to higher unemployment and fewer jobs. In Britain, research over a six-year period for the OECD report revealed that workers who began their employment at a wage under the poverty threshold set by the European Union (EU) stayed there on average for more than four years. In this regard, the British record was the worst for any OECD country apart from the United States.[43] The OECD report directly contradicted the claims made by the British Conservative governments of Margaret Thatcher and John Major, in power from 1979 to 1997, that scrapping workers' employment rights and eliminating the minimum wage had led to more job creation and better pay prospects for British workers.

The push for flexibility has not gone unopposed. In South Korea in

January 1997, a huge working-class movement erupted in opposition to proposed government changes to labour legislation. For three weeks, over a quarter of a million workers staged daily walkouts and confronted police in clashes that were often violent. The new labour law was intended to make it easier for companies to dismiss workers, to extend hours worked and to hire replacement workers during strikes.44 The confrontations, the most serious in the history of the South Korean labour movement, forced the government to back down. After South Korea had sustained US$3 billion in production losses, the government of then-president Kim Young-sam announced that it would reconsider the labour law and that it would suspend arrest warrants that had been issued against the key strike leaders.45

Just as the Paris occupation of offices by bank workers broadened the range of employee militancy, so too did the strikes in South Korea. Until they occurred, it was assumed that South Korea's workforce, which had enjoyed a huge increase in its living standards over the past couple of decades, would not engage in a tough confrontation with a still-authoritarian government over such a broad concept as employee rights. The new toughness demonstrated by South Korean workers came as a shock to many financial analysts who assumed that the workforce in the so-called Asian tigers was still placid.

*Under the watchful direction of the United States, the International Monetary Fund (IMF) and the World Bank use their muscle to open up Third World countries to foreign investment.* Very high on the list of U.S. foreign policy objectives is to win the global struggle for its version of free enterprise. To win long-term foreign credits, to receive foreign aid, to be entitled to the best multilateral trade terms under the World Trade Organization (WTO)—the successor to the General Agreement on Tariffs and Trade (GATT)—Third World countries are forced to privatize publicly owned corporations, to open up their domestic economies to foreign competition and their firms to takeovers by multinational corporations. They are also compelled to reduce social benefits.

It was bitterly ironic that at the same time as the Clinton administration task force was investigating the abuse of Third World workers by apparel companies, Washington was putting pressure on Vietnam to proceed more rapidly toward economic "liberalization." When the U.S. treasury secretary, Robert Rubin, visited Hanoi in April 1997 (the highest-ranking U.S. official to do so since the end of the Vietnam War), his purpose was to warn that the United States would make a trade deal with Vietnam (the key to admission to the world trade system) only in return for a more wide-open regime for U.S. companies operating there.[46] While American liberals tut-tutted about the exploitation of the Vietnamese, the Clinton administration was tightening the screws to win even wider access for the Nikes of this world to countries like Vietnam.

*Two-tier health-care systems are on the rise.* In the autumn of 1996, there was a knock at my door in Toronto. It was a long-time acquaintance whom I hadn't seen for many years, a retiree of modest means, now eighty years of age. I was struck, as always, by how much younger than his age he looked. But, as he informed me, he had developed angina, a heart condition for which he was taking medication. He told me that his doctors believed his quality of life—he suffered from pain and shortness of breath—would certainly be improved if he underwent cardiac bypass surgery, but that his angina could not be regarded as life threatening. Because of his age and the non-life-threatening nature of his ailment, doctors would not grant him the bypass operation. If he had C$40,000, he told me, he would go to the U.S. and pay privately for the surgery.

Any public health-care system has to decide what it will cover and what it will not. But the tendency in the Canadian, British and European systems is increasingly to ration what is covered. Two things are happening simultaneously—fiscal belt tightening, and the rapid development of new and often expensive medical procedures. The consequence is that two-tier systems are emerging, one where the highest quality care is being purchased by the affluent, and one where everyone else makes do with a lower standard of care. (In the U.S., where forty million people have no health coverage at all, and tens of millions of others have limited coverage, even the two-tier health-care systems that are becoming evident in Canada and Europe would be a giant step forward.

President Clinton's attempt in 1993–94 to move the U.S. toward a universal health-care system was defeated by a powerful conservative lobby.)

There is little doubt that a wealthy person faced with the predicament of my acquaintance would travel to the U.S. and pay for the bypass surgery. While the Canadian public system is narrowing its scope, the private American system is available to wealthy Canadians.

Also in the fall of 1996, another friend in Toronto was undergoing chemotherapy for cancer. She had been suffering rather severe side effects from the medication that was part of the treatment. After this had gone on for a couple of months, her doctor switched her to another drug that caused her far fewer problems. The doctor admitted that she had known from the start that the second drug was preferable, but that it was much more expensive and that she was required under the guidelines of the Ontario Health Insurance Plan (OHIP) to prescribe the second drug only if it was absolutely essential. The rich don't hesitate to purchase the best drugs for themselves right from the start.

In November 1997, I had firsthand experience of the onset of a two-tier health-care system in Ontario when I accompanied my mother to a doctor's office in suburban Toronto to have a cataract on her eye removed. "Do you have your money order or certified cheque?" asked the woman behind the desk before my mother had removed her coat. Knowing that the C$150 fee was to be charged for a part of the procedure that is not covered by the province's health-care plan, I had brought cash. "The corporation does not accept cash," the woman behind the desk informed us. "Tomorrow when you come back for your post-procedure check-up, you will have to bring the money order or certified cheque."

In southern France, the administrative secretary of a small municipality told me that in her area, not far from Avignon, poor children were displaying dental problems not encountered for decades, which resulted from substandard diets and hygiene.

The creation of state-financed medical care systems to make high-quality health-care available to all citizens was one of the great egalitarian transformations of the post-war decades. In Britain, Western Europe and Canada, such systems were in place by the end of the 1960s. Although they differed in the details of their financing and in the services they provided, for the first time in history, they delivered first-class, publicly funded medical care to the whole population. Today, the universal systems in Britain and Canada, and to a lesser extent in Western Europe, are under attack. Governments are creating crises through cuts to funding, hospital closings and the laying-off of nurses. In one way or another, two-tier health-care systems, with one tier for the affluent and another for the rest of the population, are fast becoming a reality.

*Industrialized countries are creating one immigration system for the rich and another for everyone else.* The age of globalization is often depicted by its promoters as involving a general freeing of all people to participate as they choose in the new global economy. In fact, while the world is certainly becoming freer and more open for business, it is becoming less free and more closed for labour. As corporations invade the whole world, turning traditional societies upside down, the Third World is going through a gigantic process of urbanization, accompanied by immense strife and frequent warfare. One consequence is that millions of people are on the move, as would-be emigrants or as refugees. A similar process has been at work in Eastern Europe in the aftermath of the demise of the Soviet system.

Millions of people have been clamouring for admittance to the advanced industrialized countries. In response, immigration policies, as they apply to workers and even to middle-class applicants, are being constantly tightened. Under insistent pressure from right-wing extremists, virtually every government in Western Europe has adopted a hard-line opposition to any form of mass immigration. In France, for example, the door to new immigrants has been slammed shut. By 1997, France was admitting only 50,000 immigrants a year, a tiny number for a country with a population of fifty-eight million. And those from non-European Union countries seeking a *carte de séjour*—needed to allow them to work in France—were treated in shabby fashion, a process I have witnessed firsthand. In Nice (where I was applying for a *carte de séjour*, but without the right to work, in the winter of 1997), applications for the right to work are made at the Préfecture de Police, a large fortress-style enclave not far from the city's airport.

The office opens each workday at 9:00 A.M., but there are so many applicants that only those who have lined up outside the compound by eight-thirty have any chance of seeing an official. The lineup pits people against each other. At a few minutes after nine, the police open the gates and allow the several hundred applicants to run about a hundred metres to the building where applications are made. The lucky, the strong and the fit get there first and grab the numbers from the ticket-spitter to entitle them to an interview. Those who are older and not so fit will have to return another day. Meanwhile, those on the inside who have made it to the interviews experience their own nightmare. Many are sent away, having been told to come back with a long list of documents, a list the office does not provide until an applicant makes it through to a potential interview. Others struggle with their poor French and have to sink or swim in their interviews. The whole process is designed to humiliate and block people from even getting a chance to make a case for their right to work in France.

France has not been alone. In the mid-1990s, Germany has been expelling tens of thousands of people, sending them back to the Eastern European countries from which they came during periods of war and political upheaval.

During the nineteenth century and much of the twentieth century, immigration to North America, Australia and New Zealand was comparatively open for Europeans, less so for Asians. For millions who migrated to one new world or another, this was a lifeline to opportunity. In Canada, for instance, between 1901 and 1911, the country's population increased by a dramatic 34.2 percent, by far the most rapid rate of increase for any decade in the twentieth century. During that decade, when hundreds of thousands of people from Europe and the U.S. started farms in the Prairie provinces, 44 percent of the nation's population increase resulted from immigration.[47]

New rules now make it much more difficult for people without substantial means to migrate to Canada. Immigrants must now pay a C$975

Right-of-Landing Fee. The federal government's 1994 immigration plan spelled out a long-term strategy for focusing future immigration on so-called economic immigrants. Economic immigrants are entrepreneurs, investors and those with much-needed skills.[48] Today, as the door for business and freedom of capital is opening, for typical working people the door to migration is being pushed shut.

*New high-tech services and computers benefit the affluent but marginalize many other people.* The revolution in communications technology, a function of microelectronics, is the miracle of our age. One outcome of the innovative technology is new services that improve communications for those who are able to afford them. Cellular telephones have become playthings of the affluent. Telephone service deregulation has been bringing down long-distance charges—of greatest interest to the affluent—while the pressure is on for local rates—of greatest importance to the non-affluent—to increase dramatically.

Computer literacy is now a growing prerequisite for those who covet the best jobs. The proportion of Canadians using computers in the workplace increased from 21 percent in 1987 to 48 percent in 1994.[49] But access to computers, and thereby to computer literacy, is steeply unequal in Canadian society. The top 20 percent of households in terms of income are more than four times as likely to be equipped with a computer as the bottom 20 percent of households—53 percent compared with 12 percent. And there are still relatively few computers in Canadian elementary and secondary schools—one for every fifteen to twenty students in 1995.[50]

In 1994, while 86 percent of those living in households with incomes in excess of C$100,000 a year reported that they could use a computer, only 38 percent of those in households with incomes from C$20,000 to C$29,000 and a mere 28 percent of those in households with incomes below C$20,000 could make that claim.[51]

A Statistics Canada study of computer literacy concluded that unequal access to new technology means that "people with low incomes who might benefit the most from improving their computer skills, such as those who are unemployed and those with limited education, and their children, face the possibility of becoming further marginalized as other Canadians use computers to develop new skills."[52]

In 1994, only 17 percent of Canadians who are computer users had accessed any online services or had logged on to the Internet in the previous twelve months.[53] It is the affluent, who can afford high-tech software and hardware, who are going on-line as e-mail and the Internet transform global communications and information gathering. At its very heart, cyber capitalism is markedly inegalitarian in its impact.

*A neo-Victorian return to servants and masters is under way.* In Britain, where the income gap between rich and poor widened substantially between 1979 and 1997 when the Conservatives were in power under Thatcher and Major, large numbers of the rich and the merely affluent are once again hiring servants. Whereas in the years 1978–80, the top 10 percent of British income earners made 3.8 times as much as the lowest 10 percent of earners, by 1990–91, the ratio had risen to six times as much for the U.K. as a whole and to eight times as much for top earners in London. In fact, during this period the richest 10 percent of British income earners saw their disposable incomes soar by 62 percent, while the poorest 10 percent witnessed a 17 percent decline in their disposable incomes.

As a consequence of rising wealth at one end of the spectrum and deepening poverty at the other, London's fashionable Hampstead and other upmarket districts in the U.K. are once again places where servants are employed in large numbers. For the most part, though, it's not a replay of the television melodrama "Upstairs Downstairs" with butlers and maids living belowstairs. Today's servants—they are usually called household help—usually live in their own accommodations. U.K. servants are paid wages that range from as low as £2.5 an hour (about US$4) to as much as £5 to £6 an hour (US$8 to US$10).

In most cases, the servants' jobs are in the black market economy, since employers wish to avoid paying benefits and employees don't want to pay income tax. On top of it all, the welfare state is a factor in the neo-Victorian rise of domestic labour, since the state provides health care, which makes the whole arrangement more affordable. Although the motive for some of the affluent is to hire nannies, for others it is greater leisure. They now have enough income to pay someone else to cook and do chores.54

*Many top businesses are vigilant to crush any expression of opposition to their activities.* A favourite tactic of business magnates and powerful corporations in our era is to sue anyone who challenges them. Libel chill is an important part of the social landscape of our age. It limits freedom of expression to a significant extent.

In Canada in recent years, writers know that they'd better tread very carefully around certain well-known business moguls, such as Conrad Black and the members of the Reichmann family, who have a reputation for suing anyone who mentions them in an unflattering way. Write about something else and leave these people alone is today's word to the wise. In the eighteenth century, Voltaire had to dress up his attacks on the royalist regime in France so that he could get his tracts past witless official censors. Are we on the way back to this kind of behaviour, as billionaires and corporate giants use their wealth to effectively censor criticism of their activities?

McDonald's, the world's largest fast-food vendor, is a very litigious corporation, as many who have criticized it have discovered. In Britain, this lesson was learned by a small London environmentalist group that had the temerity to challenge the company that has sold billions of Big Macs around the globe. In the late 1980s, London Greenpeace (not affiliated with the well-known Greenpeace International) launched a public campaign in opposition to some of the practices of the fast-food megacorp. McDonald's responded by hiring private detectives to spy on the offending group. Meetings were recorded, offices were entered and agents formed close relationships with the activists. Strong evidence exists that one woman agent established an intimate liaison with one of the leading activists in the group.

Once the evidence had been gathered, McDonald's sued five members of London Greenpeace. Three of those sued backed down and apologized for what they had done, while the remaining two held out. What followed was a libel trial that went on for thirty months at a cost of millions of pounds, the longest court case in British history. McDonald's suit against the two members of London Greenpeace was over a leaflet titled "What's Wrong with McDonald's." The leaflet accused the fast-food giant of promoting unhealthful food, exploiting Third World workers and countries, and damaging the environment.

The willingness of McDonald's to strike back against those who criticize it or allegedly use or misuse its company symbols has certainly not been limited to the members of London Greenpeace. At the libel trial, evidence was presented that McDonald's, during a four-year period, had taken action against forty-five British entities, including newspapers, magazines, universities and the British Broadcasting Corporation.[55]

On June 19, 1997, after 314 days of trial, Justice Sir Rodger Bell found in favour of McDonald's and ordered the two environmental activists to pay the equivalent of us$98,000 in damages. The battle was not over, however. Helen Steel and Dave Morris, the two defendants, were in no position to pay the fine, and they had no intention of giving up the fight. They announced plans to appeal the decision to the European Court of Human Rights, where they planned to argue that multinational corporations should not have the right to sue for libel. As soon as the trial was over, Steel and Morris defiantly distributed the offending leaflets outside the courthouse.[56]

Litigious giant corporations and wealthy individuals are effectively rewriting the rules about what can be published and what can be said in public.

*The United States has the death penalty, but not for the rich.* At 12:02 A.M. on the morning of September 24, 1997, Samuel Lee McDonald, lying strapped to a gurney with a sheet covering him up to his chin, gagged and arched his back. An injection of sodium pentothal, administered remotely, had just hit him. In swift order, this was followed by a dose of pancuronium bromide, which stopped his breathing, and a shot of potassium chloride, which immobilized his heart. The black forty-eight-year-old convicted killer of an off-duty policeman, who was also black, was the twenty-seventh person executed in the lethal-injection chamber at the Potosi Correctional Center in Mineral Point, Missouri.[57]

In the United States, where executions resumed after a hiatus between 1968 and 1977, the application of the death penalty has exhibited an extreme bias with respect to class, race and gender. Only a relatively small number of the approximately 100,000 convicted murderers in American prisons end up being executed—432 between 1977 and January 1998.[58] Thirty-nine percent of those executed between 1977 and 1995 were black, even though blacks constitute only 12.6 percent of the American population.[59] And Americans don't like to execute women. Despite the fact that one in eight of those arrested for murder is a woman, since 1977 only one woman was executed in the United States prior to the execution in Texas of Karla Faye Tucker on February 3, 1998. Tucker's execution became a worldwide media sensation. Despite strong evidence that she had been rehabilitated during her fourteen years on death row, Tucker's execution went ahead on schedule. Tucker's execution broke the taboo against putting women to death and opened the door to further executions of women in Texas and other U.S. states.

In the U.S., those who are executed are chosen through a highly politicized lottery in which some people are much more likely to draw the death card than others. Those who win this unluckiest of lotteries are invariably the poor, the ill-educated and those from broken families. In the U.S., those who are rich or even middle class are not executed. As Christopher Hitchens has written, ". . . nobody who is not from the losing classes has ever been thrust into a death cell in these United States."[60]

*The rich are outliving the rest of us.* Although it may be a commonplace in fiction to recount the miseries of the rich, if life expectancy is taken as an objective yardstick, the highly affluent appear to be thriving. The biggest single factor in determining why some people live longer than others is not genetic inheritance, body weight, diet, fitness or even smoking—it is social class. The higher the social class one belongs to, the longer, on average, one lives. Working with Statistics Canada data, John Frank, a professor at the University of Toronto's department of preventive medicine, says that there are differences in the health and longevity of Canadians according to the social class they belong to.

"The higher up the social ladder, the lower—rung by rung—your disease and death risk," he commented.[61]

A corollary is that societies that have a narrower income gap between those at the top and those at the bottom have a life expectancy that is on average higher than societies where the income gap is wider. On average, the Japanese, the French and the Swedes live longer than Canadians, Americans and the British.[62] (Interestingly, the U.S., which spends 14.1 percent of its Gross Domestic Product on health care, the highest for any major country, has the lowest life expectancy of the countries listed here.[63] The U.S. also has the widest income gap between rich and poor among these countries.)

Studies undertaken in the United Kingdom in the 1980s revealed a clear link between social class and life expectancy. A report titled, *The Health Divide*, prepared by Margaret Whitehead for the British Health Education Council, noted that death rates were highest in the heavily working-class regions of the country, Scotland, north and northwest England, and lowest in the more affluent southeast of England and East Anglia. The report went beyond analysis of broad regional differences to draw this conclusion: "Numerous studies at the level of local authority wards have pinpointed pockets of very poor health corresponding to areas of social and material deprivation. Alongside them, areas with much better health profiles can be detected and these exhibit more affluent characteristics."[64]

Official mortality statistics for Britain reach the same conclusions. Adjusted for the age structure in each region, mortality rates are significantly higher in working-class Scotland (1.349 per 100,000 population) than in the regions of the more affluent south of England (1.044 to 1.066 per 100,000 population).[65]

Those who specialize in analyzing life expectancy have long been aware of the importance of social class. According to Leonard Syme, professor emeritus of epidemiology at the University of California at Berkeley, "Social class is of such overwhelming power that we epidemiologists in our research typically hold it constant so that we can study other things. If we didn't do this, social class would swamp all other factors and we would not be able to see the role of any other issues."[66] This means that to study the specific impact of changes in diet, fitness or body weight on longevity, medical researchers have had to control their studies to negate the impact of the most important factor of all— social class.

Why social class should have such an impact on life expectancy remains something of a mystery. Two factors seem to stand out. First, those who have control over their lives tend to outlive those who do not. Second, a general well-being suffuses the existence of those who occupy an exalted position in the social order. And this well-being apparently translates into health and longevity. If you doubt this, as John Frank says, just ask those who work for life insurance companies. "Every life insurance company in the market place has known this for many decades . . . The higher one's social standing and education the lower one's death risk."[67]

Now we've toured the battlefields in the contemporary class war. It is not that the events and issues I have been discussing have not been covered by the media. What is at issue is the interpretation that is attached to them. In my opinion, what connects the issues I have discussed in this chapter is that they are integral to the contemporary struggle between the social classes.

What caused the outbreak of today's class struggle in the first place? And what exactly are social classes? What does it mean to live in a society that is divided between those who belong to dominant social classes and those who belong to dominated social classes?

## Chapter 2

# Class

In North America, discussions of social class are considered to be in questionable taste, indeed are surrounded by formidable taboos. It is less outré to converse graphically about kinky sex than to suggest that social classes exist, or that their existence has important consequences. To claim that social classes matter is regarded as an indictment of a society that prides itself on asserting that nobody is better than anybody else.

In American society, the individual has always been paramount, leaving little room for the contemplation of social class. The relegation of the idea of class to the periphery in the United States is unique in the industrialized world. In recent decades, as the American perspective has grown ever more ascendant in Canada, the denial of class has grown fashionable among Canadians as well. Since the American societal model is now so influential in Canada, the way Americans sweep the question of class under the carpet matters hugely to us.

The American denial of class is more than a little ironic. Despite its overt egalitarianism, American society has always been marked by profound inequalities. A country with an immense rhetorical stake in the principle of an egalitarian capitalism that serves the interests of the little guy, the United States actually has had the widest income gap between rich and poor of any advanced industrialized country.

And that gap has been widening in recent years. According to the 1996 report of the OECD on the U.S. economy, income inequality in the United States increased over the period from 1973 to 1993. The consequence was that the real family income (adjusted to take account of different kinds of families) of those at the tenth percentile from the bottom fell 21 percent over these two decades, while those at the fiftieth percentile rose 5 percent and those at the ninetieth percentile grew 22 percent.[1]

According to the U.S. Labor Department, median wages for workers, adjusted for inflation, were 3 percent lower in 1996 than in 1979. (Adjusting for inflation, men were paid almost 9 percent less in 1996 than in 1979, while women were paid 7.6 percent more.) And while household income increased in the U.S. by 10 percent between 1979 and 1994, 97 percent of the gains in household income went to the richest 20 percent of households.

At the same time as workers have been living with wages that do not increase and ever-greater job insecurity, their bosses have never had it so good. Top pay for American corporate executives has skyrocketed to about two hundred times the pay of the average worker, compared with only forty times twenty years ago.[2] On top of the income gap between capitalists and workers, there is the more important wealth gap. For it is wealth—the ownership and control of capital and of property—that is the source of capitalist power. The wealth gap is much wider than the income gap. A very small proportion of the population enjoys control of the means of production and of the world's resources. And on the other side, in the industrialized world, there are tens of millions of people who have no assets whatsoever, or who have what economists drily call "negative assets," i.e., those whose debts exceed their assets. Fifty percent of families in the United States have financial assets of less than $1,000.[3]

American capitalism's great leavener has been the opportunity for some individuals to migrate from the dominated to the dominant social class. Perhaps more important than mobility itself has been the idea of mobility. Throughout history, all social systems have involved at least a degree of mobility between the social classes, needless to say in a downward as well as in an upward direction.

The record of the rise of some individuals from lower classes to the ranks of the patricians in Rome or to the ranks of the aristocracy in medieval Europe is indisputable. But what has distinguished capitalism from earlier types of class-divided societies is the theoretical equality of all citizens. There are no legal barriers to upward mobility in a capitalist society, as there were in earlier types of societies. Being born in the lower ranks may result in a person's being kept out of certain exclusive clubs and associations, the preserves of the old rich, but it does not place any legal barriers in the way of a rise to the status of a financial magnate. This difference between capitalism and earlier types of class-divided societies is exceptionally important. It is the fruit of democratic struggles from the seventeenth and eighteenth centuries to the present.

In America, the idea of social mobility has been uniquely potent. At least in white America, everyone grows up being told the story of the rise of some hardworking, lucky, perhaps ruthless, individuals from rags to riches. The idea is that those who have ability and tenacity can fight their way out of poverty, make successful entrepreneurs of themselves and ultimately brawl their way into the establishment. The Horatio Alger myth, the story of the poor boy who makes a fortune—sometimes by marrying the boss's daughter—is deeply embedded in the American consciousness. There have been enough cases, from the rise of the Rockefellers and Carnegies in the nineteenth century to the meteoric advance of cyber capitalists such as Bill Gates, to lend substance to the myth.

In contemporary America, Horatio Alger and the bashing of wage and salary earners go hand in hand. Writing in *Business Week* magazine about how difficult it would be for Europe, with its economic culture, ever to spawn a Bill Gates, Gail Edmonston, an American journalist, tried to imagine the prospects for a would-be young mega-entrepreneur in France. In France, she wrote, a wannabe Bill Gates would encounter workers who hope to retire at fifty-five and who want to be paid a full week's salary for thirty-two hours' work a week. He would run up against employees like those at Crédit Foncier who took the governor of their bank hostage in their fight to save their jobs. And he would encounter young people, half of whom want to work for the state. "To see why so few French youths follow in his footsteps, you need only look at France through Bill Gates's eyes," she wrote.[4] The message: it's the fault of recalcitrant wage and salary earners, with too many rights, that rags-to-riches billionaires don't emerge in France.

(Actually, the rich in France have been doing just fine lately, much like their counterparts in other countries. Lilliane Bettencourt, the richest person in France, owns L'Oréal, the cosmetics giant. Her personal fortune is estimated at 42.1 billion francs [over US$7 billion]. In the single year 1996–97, the five hundred richest persons in France saw their combined personal wealth soar by 28 percent to a very hefty total of 675 billion francs [about US$115 billion].)[5]

The Horatio Alger myth glosses over the hard fact that real-life rags-to-riches stories are highly unusual. In addition to having the widest income gap between rich and poor in any industrialized country, the U.S. also displays a number of other severe and enduring barriers to upward social mobility. A first-rate university education is very costly in the United States, while in some European countries such as France there are no tuition fees. Moreover, upward social mobility in the U.S. is particularly difficult for African Americans and Hispanics, as a consequence of deeply embedded prejudice and discrimination, which result in a social system that displays elements of caste as well as those of class. Between them, African Americans and Hispanics now constitute 20 percent of the American population.

Any attempt at identifying social classes in the United States typically results in pigeonholing the population into statistically based categories, which classify people by income, education and occupation. The standard American interpretation is that people occupy a continuum that extends from less desirable to more desirable occupations and incomes. According to the customary view, society is populated by an endless variety of individuals, some rising in position, others falling, in constant flux. In such a scheme, there is no sharp divide, no qualitative break that places some people on one side of a societal wall and other people on the other side.

According to the most influential interpretation in the United States, the inequalities that do exist in advanced societies are the consequence of what happens when people of differing levels of ability apply dissimilar amounts of energy to the task of getting ahead. The advanced countries, this interpretation has it, have become meritocracies. The social scientist Daniel Bell, an important proponent of this notion, put the position this way: "The post-industrial society, in its logic, is a meritocracy. Differential status and differential income are based on technical skills and higher education, and few high places are open to those without such qualifications."[6]

In this depiction, bank presidents, corporate lawyers, fund managers, billionaires and media tycoons reached their positions by having demonstrated superior merit. They belong where they are, just as auto workers, secretaries, teachers, scientists and the unemployed belong in the positions they have attained.

The implication of the theory that advanced capitalist societies are meritocracies is that power and influence are fairly and legitimately acquired. It doesn't matter all that much how rich your father was, or what kind of family you come from. A further implication is that such a meritocracy is fully consistent with democracy, because no one passes on undue power to their heirs through inheritance, and indeed, no one holds power so disproportionate that it calls into question the very idea of a citizenry with all people being, to an important extent, social equals.

In Canada, Conrad Black's privately acquired power to determine who works and who doesn't, or to influence the way people think just because he owns 60 of the country's 105 daily newspapers,[7] is not seen as meaning that he enjoys power of a qualitatively different sort from that of his fellow citizens.

Remember those celebrated Bank of Montreal television commercials of a couple of years ago with a family sitting on a front porch and wondering if this could be their year? Implying that those who run banks are genuinely concerned with the problems of typical families, the ads concluded with the beguiling question, "Can a bank change?"

In the real world, bank presidents make millions. Their incomes have been skyrocketing in the 1990s. Meanwhile, the incomes of most families have stagnated, and a majority of Canadians fear that they could lose their jobs, or that if they keep their jobs they will have to work harder to do the work formerly done by those whose jobs have been shed. And is it reasonable to believe that bank presidents, fund managers, corporate lawyers and media tycoons don't have much more ability than secretaries, teachers and industrial workers to establish the priorities for our society and to affect the course of state policy? Is it reasonable to suppose that the sons and daughters of bank presidents, fund managers, corporate lawyers and media tycoons are not much more likely to remain wealthy and influential than the sons and daughters of secretaries, teachers and industrial workers?

Putting aside the rags-to-riches myth allows us to turn to a consideration of the actual experience of social class. What barriers are placed in the way of someone who grows up in the home of wage and salary earners, and what benefits exist for someone who grows up in the business class?

Members of social classes do not live their lives in isolation. That is why analyses that seek to reduce social classes to statistical categories are as wrongheaded as attempts to understand living creatures simply by examining the size and shape of their bones.

Essential to the existence of social classes is the presence of other social classes. Every social class lives in an ongoing relationship with other social classes that are either more or less powerful than itself. A social class can never be understood on its own but only in relation to the others. It is always the case that social classes are either dominant or dominated, that they either exercise power over others or they have power exercised over them. Indeed, conflict has always lain at the heart of the interaction between dominant and dominated social classes.

The capitalist and working classes entered the historical process in tandem, in the same epoch, and have been irretrievably linked to each other ever since. Together, they created capitalism and indeed were created by it. As a consequence of their interaction, both classes earn a living. But as a consequence of the relationship between these two classes, there is an enduring disparity of power between them. In a capitalist society, there can be no capitalist class without a wage-and-salary-earning class. Equally, there can be no wage-and-salary-earning class without a capitalist class. Without workers who sell their labour to earn wages or salaries, those with capital to invest could not make a profit.

In contemporary capitalism, the most consequential societal fault line falls between those who control capital and those who work for a wage or a salary. This is true for two reasons: the lives of those on one side of the fault line are qualitatively different from those on the other side of the line; and migration from the class of wage and salary earners into the capitalist class is no easy thing.

More important than the high standard of living enjoyed by those who control capital is that capital is able to reproduce itself through the employment of labour. In our society, capital is magical. It opens the door to the acquisition of the labour of others and to reaping the profits that result from that labour. No wonder capital is so highly prized. As a general rule, the control of capital allows capitalists to maintain their position, and in turn keeps labour locked in its subordinate place.

By expending their labour, employees create value through the production of goods and services. Through labour, and through labour alone, is a profit ultimately realized as a result of the investment of capital. This point needs to be emphasized during the 1990s, a decade when the illusion is abroad that stock and bond markets create value all by themselves. One could even say that extreme forms of this illusion give rise to a kind of psychosis—let's call it market psychosis. The problem with suggesting professional help for those who suffer from this malady is that the condition is so widespread among our society's elites that the prospects for treating individual sufferers seem dim at best.

At a time in the industrialized world when thousands of people have become millionaires by playing the markets, and when billionaires have been expanding their wealth by hundreds of millions or even billions of dollars in a single year, confusion is understandable. What surging stock and bond markets do is to increase the assets of stock and bond holders so they can access goods and services created by expenditures of labour, or so they can invest in the future production of goods and services that will be created by expenditures of labour.

Those playing the stock, bond or foreign exchange markets don't normally think in these terms. They are so caught up in the conflicting advice of bulls and bears, the competing claims of mutual fund managers and contradictory market projections, that they easily forget that without expenditures of labour no value can be created. Without labour, stock and bond markets would amount to no more than your child's game of Stock Ticker. What is true, though—today as in all periods in the history of capitalism—is that those who control capital hold the key to the future. And that is because control of capital carries with it control over labour, which is the key to future production, and thereby of future profits. Upper classes, dominant classes, never constitute more than a small percentage of the population. (I reckon that the capitalist class makes up about 3 to 4 percent of the population in advanced capitalist countries, and I will show how I reach that conclusion in a later chapter.)

The principal activity of those in the dominated classes is to work for, and to produce profits for, those in the dominating classes. In turn, those in the dominating classes benefit enormously from the work done for them by those in the dominated classes. By its very nature, therefore, the essence of the relationship between capital and labour is exploitative. The word *exploitation* sets alarm bells ringing. The claim that the relationship between the social classes is necessarily exploitative has always provoked indignation and denial. In his memoirs, Conrad Black wrote hotly that "it is a myth of the left and one of the well-springs of the pervasive Canadian spirit of envy that the success of a person implies the failure or exploitation of someone else."[8]

Throughout history, the defenders of class-divided societies have passionately denied that at the heart of their particular social order exists systematic exploitation of one class of people by another. They have made the case for their societies in a number of ways: by asserting that a hereditary elite is divinely ordained; by insisting that those who have descended from upper-class backgrounds are groomed to be society's natural leaders; or by arguing that the upper classes are chosen in a competitive contest that ensures that the fittest rise to the top. Contemporary capitalist society finds the first two kinds of arguments—although they were respectable not all that long ago—somewhat embarrassing. It has settled on the third, insisting that the members of current elites got where they are because they have demonstrated their mettle and have left the drones behind.

The orthodox contemporary view is that the relationship between business and labour involves nothing more than buyers and sellers acting in a marketplace where all participants have equal rights. Businesses hire workers at prices set by the market. Workers sell their labour in the same market and according to the same rules. Apparently, we are dealing with nothing more than transparent and straightforward transactions. In theory, all persons enter the market when they have something to offer—their capital or their skills—and they buy and sell in accordance with the laws of supply and demand.

This conventional understanding of the relationship between capitalists and wage and salary earners ignores the most important ingredient of all—power. Business and labour occupy positions that are not simply different in degree, but fundamentally different in kind. While the domination of business over the investment and production process is far from absolute, it dwarfs that of labour. Business directs the investment process, the fundamental mechanism that makes the productive system function. It is business that hires labour, not the reverse. During periods when labour has been in short supply, wage and salary earners have certainly enjoyed enhanced bargaining power, but business has always been in the driver's seat. That is because the power to invest or to withhold investment rests with business, never with labour.

The balance of power between capitalists and employees is reflected in the indisputable fact that in all periods in the history of capitalism, business has, on average, enjoyed substantially higher material rewards than wage and salary earners. To an overwhelming extent, the business class establishes the rules under which labour is compelled to exist.

This should not be taken to suggest that the relationship among capitalists is free of strife. Within the ranks of business, there is a constant struggle for survival. As technology advances, as new sources of raw materials are discovered and exhausted, as markets for particular goods and services rise and fall, some businesses thrive, while others perish. The consequence is uneven development: some businesses greatly expand their wealth, and the wealth of others declines or even disappears. But in the midst of all the fury and drama of the successes and failures of particular businesses, the relationship between capital and labour remains the underlying fact on which the whole system is based.

Dominant social classes are populated by those who exercise control over the processes of economic production. And in exercising this control, they require the active backing of the state. In the advanced countries, the state does many things that serve the interest of a wide range of social groups. For instance, the state finances much of the educational and health-care systems. These activities aside, the state always protects the rules of property and the system of production that serve the interests of the dominant classes.

Those who own capital, and those who control capital, are the initiators in our social order. They determine which projects go ahead and which do not. They decide whether investment will favour some communities, regions and countries while bypassing others. They decide which research gets done and which does not. In an age when public sector broadcasting is in retreat in many countries, they strongly influence which cultural offerings will get the nod and which will not. Mega-moguls like Bill Gates preside over ordinary men and women because of their capacity to make these sorts of fundamental decisions.

During the post-war decades, things were a little different. In those days, the public sector offered an alternative source of capital and creative energy in both the economic and cultural spheres. At the dawn of the new millennium, however, that notion has perished. As governments downsize and cut costs, they have lost their role as creative proponents of long-term projects to improve people's lives, to upgrade the nation's infrastructure and to contribute to its artistic and intellectual expression.

In Canada, the culture of nation building, under which social programs were expanded, universities were established and the CBC flourished, has gone the way of the great auk.

As the public sector has diminished not merely in its financial outlays but also in its vision, the democratic notion of a broadening sphere of creativity and decision making outside business has shrunk. In our time, the ascendant idea is that the marketplace is the legitimate arena for making the most important societal decisions. As for the democratic state, whose government is elected by the citizenry as a whole, its role in encouraging social betterment is waning.

The relationship between business and labour enables capitalists to expand their capacity for an enhanced material and cultural existence as a direct consequence of the inferior position of wage and salary earners. Those in dominant social classes are given the chance for cultural self-realization, within the norms of their society, much more than those in the dominated classes. They are liberated, to a very considerable extent, from menial labour. For those in dominated social classes, life's activities centre on the provision of labour, more or less menial, on behalf of those in the dominant classes. Those in the dominated social classes are far less free to develop themselves within the range of cultural and intellectual possibilities that exist in their society.

In the absence of wealth, the vast majority of the population is forced to enter the labour market to seek employment. The terms on which employment is sought vary, depending on many circumstances. Those with valued skills and advanced education fare much better than those with few skills and limited education. Those seeking jobs during an expansionary economic phase or in a booming country or region fare better than those seeking jobs during a recession or in a country or region experiencing economic decline.

The wide range of circumstances faced by those entering the labour market can blind us to what motivates all who do so. Work for a salary or a wage opens the door to an income, and beyond that provides admission to society at large. A wage or salary determines the level of material well-being for the overwhelming majority of the population. That level can range from one of marked affluence to one at or below the poverty line. As for admission to society through employment, one of the features of life in our era that sets it apart from earlier periods is the extent to which one's job defines one's place in the great scheme of things.

It is the job that initiates social discourse, signalling to others a person's essential similarity to or difference from them. The job bestows respectability, standing. Without it—unless you are independently wealthy—you are on the edge. Young men hanging around in the centre of a town—whether in Europe or North America—symbolize a threatening marginality. They do not have work. They are not a part of society and are to be avoided.

Those who work for a salary or a wage, in non-managerial positions, are always vulnerable to the authority of the gatekeepers, those who have the power to hire, fire, promote and demote. This is true, whether you work in the private sector or the public. Unlike the political realm, where citizens have a right to participate and express their views (although money and career politicians have most of the clout), the workplace, with rare exceptions, is not a democracy of any sort. Once you enter the premises, you have to do what you are told (subject to health and safety regulations, and rules that may exist in a collective agreement, if one is a member of a union).

Those at the bottom of the hierarchy in a workplace typically have their dignity denied in distinguishable ways. Secretaries who work in law or accounting firms take great care not to let their private lives intrude on their jobs. Although the partners in such firms feel free, when their schedules permit, to take their children to dental appointments or to care for them when they are sick, secretaries do not. Secretaries are often closely monitored. The frequency of their visits to the washroom and their conversations with fellow employees are often subject to comment and even to restrictions. Of vital concern to wage or salary earners is the level of support from an immediate superior, a fact corroborated by the endless strategic advice offered in popular magazines about how to get along with the boss. Employees must be careful what they say on the job. A careless remark that suggests disagreement with procedures can land an employee in very hot water, perhaps even cost him or her a job. The work world is an authoritarian world.

The minority of the workforce employed in the public sector generally experiences an environment only marginally less authoritarian than in the private sector. Public sector employees, even those who have considerable education, have told me that they work under constraint— opinions are best kept to oneself. (This was particularly true in Ontario beginning in 1995 when the right-wing government of Mike Harris and the Conservatives came to power.)

A feature of both private and public sector employment highly revealing of the true position of employees is the way job terminations are routinely handled. When a wage or salary earner is let go, he or she is typically summoned to the office of the superior. Once the bad news has been broken, the terminated employee is escorted off the premises. His or her belongings, which have already been collected together, are then handed over. The former employee is not allowed to return to the office where he or she worked. By the time the terminated worker is out the door, his or her computer access (if it is that sort of job) has been extinguished. This extraordinary but common personal drama tells salary and wage earners exactly where they stand. They are part of the company "team" for a time, but once that time ends, they are regarded as potential troublemakers; their capacity to hurt the entity for which they worked must be instantly negated, with no regard for their sensitivities. Those let go are not even accorded the dignity of being allowed to return one last time to bid their colleagues farewell. The gates to the work world open for a wage or salary earner when a superior decides they should open. They close when a decision from above determines that the time has come to deny access to the workplace.

None of this is substantially altered by contractual agreements that subject the right to terminate employees to certain limitations, legislation that establishes the right to severance for dismissed employees, and the right of those dismissed to seek compensation through the courts.

These counterweights to the authority of the employer are minor enough. In no way do they negate the fact that employers have the overwhelming power to decide who works for them and for what duration. (One clear exception to this picture has been the case of tenured academics. Universities cannot easily dismiss them, and their working lives involve a much higher degree of collegiality than is the case for almost all other salaried employees. It is not at all coincidental that as the capitalist class fights to increase the sway of the market, a relentless campaign is being waged in many countries to abolish academic tenure.)

It helps to make this idea seem less abstract when you consider your own personal experience. When you think about the offspring of the rich among your acquaintances and the offspring of wage and salary earners, it is not hard to recognize the differences in their life chances. They are so obvious as to be taken for granted. The offspring of the rich I have known in North America and in Europe have always been regarded as people from another planet in comparison with everyone else. Indeed, they *are* people from another planet. Everyone just assumes that it is natural that they don't really have to work for a living like other people. They do from time to time, but by choice. It's just seen as natural that when they're in their twenties their investment income should exceed their salaries, if they bother to work. No one questions the fact that they spend long periods exploring the South Pacific, skiing in the Alps or going off on a moment's notice to New York or Paris. Designer clothing, imported cars and luxury condos are standard, and their nervous breakdowns just mean that it's time to move to another shrink. They're never labelled bums when they aren't working, as other people would be. And when it's time to have a career, as some of them wish to, their families are there with their contacts in business to open doors. For such people, a mediocre record at university presents no serious obstacle.

The rest of the population occupies a different terrain. They have no such support or access to privileges. Failure for them will have consequences that are more or less disastrous. The sons and daughters of working- or middle-class parents are expected to be industrious, to pursue their studies with vigour and to go out and get a job. If they are unsuccessful, they are regarded as dropouts. And should they encounter psychological problems along the road of life, they are judged harshly. A few years ago, when I was writing a weekly newspaper column, I received letters from people who were no longer able to hold a job. A woman living north of Toronto wrote to say that her husband was not technically disabled but could no longer do the hard physical labour that had been his life's work. She explained how difficult it was to live on the c$680 a month the couple received in a welfare payment that has been cut by over 20 percent by the Ontario Conservative government. Not the least problem is maintaining dignity in such circumstances, she wrote.

The benefits of having a parent who is wealthy or successful in business are innumerable. First, and this is not to be dismissed, is access to capital through inheritance, from a partnership with one's relatives or from some other similar arrangement. Some megacapitalists who are depicted as having worked their way up actually started out in very wealthy families. Conrad Black is such a case. The son of a mere millionaire father—in the opening line of his memoirs he describes his parents as "comfortable"—he made a number of shrewd moves that put him in command of a much larger amount of capital than his father controlled.[9] Beyond capital itself, there are the contacts that go with growing up in a wealthy family. Knowing the right people has always mattered, no less so today. There are two planets under capitalism: one for the rich and the other one for the rest.

The material benefits of membership in the dominant classes are obvious to all. In our age, these benefits include spacious housing, the best food, access to the latest communications technology, top-of-the-line sports gear, expensive clothing, superior medical care and the means to afford lessons to acquire a wide range of skills. In the same general category comes wide access to travel, with all the experiential and cultural benefits this bestows. Most important in this list of benefits is that wealth permits control over one's own time.

The hegemony of dominant over dominated social classes is not merely material but also cultural and spiritual. Although they wouldn't put it quite this bluntly, the dominant regard themselves as the only truly human members of their society, dismissing the dominated as lesser beings. In December 1997, I got a sharp reminder of this truth in a conversation I had in Toronto with two Canadian businessmen involved in manufacturing operations in Asia. One of them pays his workers $4 an hour, the other $2 an hour. The latter reflected optimistically that the fall of Asian currencies, as a consequence of the Asian financial crisis, would lower his labour costs, and that he looked forward to increasing his workforce to 500 from 350.

Dominant social classes expound a worldview that makes their rule, their values, their way of life appear natural and therefore legitimate and beyond challenge. And since dominant social classes are always vastly outnumbered by those in dominated social classes, the rule of one class by another depends on such a hegemonic value system in which the threat of force, while present, is normally not the decisive element. In any successful system of class rule, those in the dominated social classes must, to a very considerable extent, buy in to the objectives, interests and way of life of the dominant classes.

In advanced capitalist societies, all citizens are theoretically equal under the law. All enjoy the right to associate with others, to speak and publish freely and to participate in the electoral process as voters or as candidates for office. These rights, and the theoretical equality of citizens, are extremely significant. They ought not to be disparaged or undervalued, particularly at a time like the present when they are under assault. Despite such rights, however, the differences in power between the social classes in capitalist society are immense, indeed are now widening. Capitalism has delivered abstract equality, but it has also delivered material and societal inequality.

## Chapter 3

# The Evolution of
# Class-Divided Societies

The social classes that occupy the terrain of contemporary society were recognizable as long ago as the late eighteenth century, the era of the French Revolution. By then, capitalist precepts had become more germane to the economy and society than the much older system that separated aristocratic landowners from serfs. In place of the old arrangements were the new ones: a society split between the rising bourgeoisie and its labour force, the working class.

We don't need to buy in to a simplistic, monocausal interpretation that all recorded history is an account of class-divided societies, or alternatively that history is driving purposefully toward some predestined goal such as a classless society beyond capitalism, when we make the salient point that class-divided societies have existed for thousands of years. Before the onset of class divisions, as long as four thousand or more years ago, previously existing societies had a wide variety of capabilities and social arrangements, including hierarchies made up of elders or leaders. What was absent, however, was a more or less permanent division of labour between a ruling class and a toiling class.

Crucial economic and technical advances contributed to the transformation of society into dominant and dominated social classes in a context in which material scarcity remained the essential fact of human existence. A process of uneven development thrust power over the productive process into the hands of some while reducing others to the status of labourers. And from the beginning of this development, force deployed by and on behalf of the privileged sustained the societal division between the dominant order and the dominated.

The first such division into distinct social classes likely arose with the development of an agricultural civilization. Agriculture involved a huge organizational change from the hunting and gathering societies of earlier times. It transformed the holding of property into something much more highly defined and permanent than it had been. Although notions of property associated with the territory of a band or tribe certainly had existed, agriculture necessitated the elaboration of fixed rules about who owned a particular piece of land. Because it vastly enhanced labour productivity, agriculture opened the way for a large increase in the number of people who could be supported on a given parcel of land. Greater density of population in turn heightened the necessity for clear codes of land ownership.

This need for rules reinforced the drive for permanent records and therefore for writing, whether this took the form of the carving of petroglyphs or later the use of hieroglyphics and alphabetized script on stone and papyrus. In the establishment of agricultural civilization, new modes of communication were essential to the viability of the new forms of social organization, as shown by Harold Innis, the pioneer Canadian political economist, in his groundbreaking work *Empire and Communications*. Agriculture also created the basis for much larger and more permanent armies than had existed in the simpler warrior societies of the past. And the rise of a military force, differentiated within the society, was central to enforcing the emerging class divisions.

In ancient societies, masters and slaves were the two essential social classes. Although there were plebeian citizen labourers in the Roman republic, most of the labour in ancient societies, whether Persian, Egyptian, Greek or Roman, was carried out by slaves. In the medieval epoch that reached its peak many centuries after the fall of Rome, the pivotal social classes were serfs—they were not slaves but were tied to the land—and landowners, the most important of whom were aristocrats linked through oaths of fealty to princes, monarchs and emperors.

Feudalism evolved into capitalism over many centuries. As long ago as the twelfth and thirteenth centuries, nascent capitalism arose in regions such as the Flemish towns in what is now Belgium, and in Italian city states, where goods were produced for a wider market. In such towns, early capitalism eked out an existence within the confines of feudalism. In those days, the precursors of capitalism were contained by the fact that feudal armies were the ultimate enforcers of political power. Although there was always a market in the feudal economy, it was extremely limited in scope. Feudal society was predominantly self-sufficient, with the vast bulk of food, clothing and construction materials produced and consumed locally. Salt, weapons, jewellery, luxury goods and spices were produced largely for the upper classes and exported to distant markets. During the high Middle Ages, flourishing commercial enterprises managed the trade in these market products over very long distances. By its very nature, however, feudalism was biased in favour of local self-sufficiency.

Contributing to the changeover from feudalism to capitalism were the revival of Greek and Roman thinking embodied in the Renaissance, the Protestant revolt against the Catholic Church and the onset of new technologies, principally gunpowder and the printing press, which opened the way for the consolidation of centralized monarchies able to restrain the power of barons who had previously maintained their own armies. Crucial as well were the scientific revolutions that modified thinking about the natural order and humankind's place in it. Technical developments in such diverse fields as watchmaking, navigation and shipbuilding were eventually responsible for huge changes in societies in Europe and throughout the world.

Of immense importance because they so expanded the scope of emergent Western European capitalism were the global voyages of discovery and conquest that began in the late fifteenth century. As fish, tea, sugar, rum, timber, animal pelts and other commodities became staples of the new commercial enterprises, the market share of total economic activity expanded prodigiously. By the sixteenth century, feudalism was in retreat in parts of Western Europe, such as England, much of France and the Low Countries. In these places and subsequently in the American Thirteen Colonies, the trend was away from self-sufficient local economies to the widening of the sphere of the market. The enclosures movement in Britain—the forced exclusion of small sharecroppers from land previously in common use for grazing and cultivation—contributed to the emergence of a commercial agriculture whose markets were found in the growing towns and cities. The city of London, with its then-unequalled population of one million people, had already become a huge magnet for the products of rural England.

The final transition to capitalism occurred in Western Europe and the Thirteen Colonies in the eighteenth century, with the American Revolution, and even more important, the French Revolution, as momentous, climactic events. It was the French Revolution that consolidated the new and burgeoning capitalist society at the centre of socioeconomic life, tearing down the remnants of feudalism and legitimizing capitalist private property relations. Gone was the privileged hereditary authority of the landed aristocracy over the serfs. Entrenched was the market, which determined a man's social standing by the monetary worth of his holdings. In the new system, all forms of property became mutually exchangeable, with money the universal medium of exchange. The relationship between the capitalist class and the working class was predicated on the ownership of land, raw materials and the means of production by capitalists and on the workers' need for work to earn a living.

Capitalism, whatever its characteristics of particular place and time, always features a society with these two essential classes. In the early days of its evolution, however, the separation between the two classes, so evident in our time, was still imprecise. For centuries, the amount of capital invested in most enterprises was tiny by modern standards. In those early days, in a system that can be called guild capitalism, the differences between masters, journeymen and apprentices had not yet hardened into the sharp division between owners and workers. In the guild system, masters did work that was not wholly different in kind from that of apprentices and journeymen, many of whom eventually went on to become masters. However, as the guild system evolved, it came increasingly to embody the class divisions of mature capitalism. In practice, many apprentices were but poorly paid labourers and those masters who ran large operations evolved into full-time businessmen.

After the eighteenth-century revolutions, the system evolved into the two basic classes we are familiar with, but even then, small-scale production played a key role. Owners of small enterprises often continued to work alongside their employees. In the nineteenth century, North American family farmers—the largest single occupational group—combined the roles of property owner and worker. In its fascinating way, farmer politics oscillated between the conservatism of the property owner and the radicalism of the underdog up against the big capitalists running the railways and the banks. Small business continues to flourish today, although the concentration of capitalist wealth proceeds apace.

The long-term tendency—albeit not in a straight line—has been toward the ever-greater concentration of capital. Over time, capitalism has departed from anything approaching a laissez-faire market, with its ideal of small firms operating in a state of perfect competition, and moved toward oligopolies (the domination of particular markets by a few large firms) and monopolies.

According to John Cavanagh, co-director of the Washington-based Institute for Policy Studies, "the world's top 500 corporations now have sales equivalent to 28 percent of the world's measured economic activity, but they employ well under 1 percent of the world's workers."[1] The principal five hundred corporations in the world have annual revenues at virtually the same level as the combined Gross Domestic Products of the United States and Japan (the world's two largest economies).

The world's leading multinationals have grown so enormous that they bear no resemblance whatsoever to the average person's idea of private companies. Vast agglomerations of private power and wealth, multinationals are not democratic institutions. Their organizational model is top-down, power extending from the command post on high to the minions at the bottom.

Whereas in Europe capitalism had to struggle to prevail over the remnants of feudalism, the seventeenth-century colonies that became the United States were capitalist from the start. Even nineteenth-century American populism, whether rural or urban, was heavily imbued with capitalist values, its central contribution being to propose means to ensure that the market system be accessible to all. Alone among the major industrialized countries, the United States has never been home to a significant social democratic or socialist movement in the twentieth century. Legitimate politics in the U.S. is delimited by the debate within capitalism. Most Americans accept that the private market system is the most efficient and effective way to produce goods and services, and have never considered any possible alternative.

It has always been the case that those who control the means of production and the sources of wealth have enjoyed greater power than the rest of the population. And so this brings us back to the irreducible fact of two social classes at the heart of contemporary capitalism: a capitalist class, and a working class/middle class whose members enter the authoritarian world of work on terms they cannot control. To glibly depict the wealthy and the non-wealthy as "citizens" as though they share a common reality and are in basic respects equal in condition is a gross disservice to the truth. As the British political philosopher Terry Eagleton has put it, "Liberty for some in such conditions is inseparable from unfreedom for others."[2]

If social class is such a central fact of our existence, why is there such a taboo against the recognition of this fact in contemporary culture? There is a widely held belief in our era that socialism is dead, and that with its demise, capitalism as a system has also died. The logic here is that capitalism as a system can only exist in the presence of challenges to it. Some maintain that in the absence of an "other" against which to contend, capitalism loses its systemic character and evolves into a disorganized or chaotic post-capitalism. To me such reasoning smacks of medieval scholasticism, a contemporary version of debates about how many angels can stand on the head of a pin.

Let me address the contention that the whole topic of social class is bogus, a leftover of the modernist age, not appropriate in these days of post-modernism.[3] At the dawn of the new millennium, advanced industrial societies have become much more heterogeneous in character than ever before. And this necessarily affects social classes. Although it is certainly valid to insist on the heterogeneity of the present, it is much too easy and highly misleading to contrast today's heterogeneity with the supposedly simple homogeneity of past societies.

In Canada, for instance, society has been notably heterogeneous for a century. Indeed, the proportion of the population born outside Canada was higher between 1900 and 1910 than it is in the 1990s, Ukrainians, Germans, Irish, Dutch, Central European Jews and many others arriving during this period. Much was said and written at the time to the effect that these immigrants would never fully integrate into Canadian society. Anti-immigrant, nativist sentiment sprang up in various parts of the country during the First World War and in its immediate aftermath, particularly during the sharp recession of 1919.

The novel character of contemporary heterogeneity nevertheless needs to be acknowledged. We live in an age when issues of ethnicity, gender, sexual orientation and lifestyle have captured public and media attention. In post-modernist writings in recent years, it has been voguish to deconstruct the notion of social class as an allegedly outdated narrative of modernist politics. This tendency has been closely tied to the rise of gender and ethnic political consciousness and to the "end of history" notion that following the demise of the Soviet Union, there can be no real alternative to capitalism anyway.

Along the same lines, it is often argued that contemporary consciousness has been fractured in completely new ways as a consequence not only of the rise of ethnic and gender politics, but of the new communications technology that separates physical location from a sort of cultural hyperspace. In the age of the Internet and MTV, some have suggested, the idea of self-conscious social classes is irrelevant. The rising awareness of ethnicity and gender has occurred at a time when it is widely supposed that socialism is dead. In such a setting, it seems to follow logically that the division of capitalist society between the interests of contending social classes has also given way to a new and multipolar landscape in which the crucial fault lines have to do with questions of identity alone.

I quarrel with this for the following reasons. First, I do not equate the demise of the Soviet Union and the crisis of contemporary social democracy with the death of socialism. The Soviet Union's non-socialism was apparent for many decades before the collapse of Lenin's state in 1991. That capitalist triumphalism should issue from such an event was natural enough. That socialists should conclude that the death of a state, long seen by them as on a non-socialist road, means the death of socialism is little short of perverse. Moreover, the crisis of social democracy, a consequence of the new globalizing capitalism with its successful assault on the welfare state, has sharpened class divisions, making these more, not less, important for the future.

I must part company with those who shelter behind the obfuscation that history is at an end and that therefore all inquiries into the nature of capitalist society are pointless. A curious reason why the contemporary war between the social classes has received less analysis than it deserves has to do with the mood of a sizeable number of left-wing intellectuals in the aftermath of the demise of the Soviet Union. Since Marxists have played a seminal role in elaborating a class analysis of capitalism, the fact, as the Cambridge sociologist Anthony Giddens asserts, that many of those "who once chose to call themselves Marxists . . . have turned away sharply from such an intellectual and political affiliation" has had its effect.[4] It ought not to be necessary to point out that whether or not Marxism is dead—a subject I will not address in this book—has nothing whatever to do with whether social classes exist or whether their existence matters.

No observer not locked in a time capsule could fail to recognize the importance of the rise of ethnic and gender issues. For much of this century, the Soviet Union, as the inheritor of the empire of the czars, suppressed the potential conflicts of a myriad ethnic groups. Once the Soviet Union fell apart, these conflicts burst into flame. And as globalization has taken Coca-Cola, McDonald's and the American dream to every corner of the world, there has been an explosive rise of local and nationalist resistance to such intrusions. These developments have led some observers to conceptualize our age as one in which the emerging battle lines are those between civilizations, with the globalizing West on one side and Islam and China in particular increasingly lined up against it. As for gender issues, it is clear that feminism has permanently altered our consciousness, so that the historic subjugation of women is an issue that can never return to the closet. The struggle for women's equality is bound to continue, and those involved in it will not allow the pursuit of their agenda to be stalled in the interest of other struggles. That is as it should be, but in no way does this lessen the reality that we live in a class-divided society and in an age when the battle between the social classes is growing fiercer.

It is true that the collapse of alternatives to capitalism in our age has given capitalism the appearance of a natural condition rather than a system. But the fact that capitalists themselves may be less inclined than in the past to defend their system as a system because they have less need to do so does not mean that capitalism has ceased to be a system. Indeed, as a system, it is now more extensive and more global in character than ever before. More than ever, that requires analysis of how the system works, and how its component parts, principally social classes, are evolving.

The greatest threat to wage and salary earners does not come from the rise of ethnic and gender politics. It comes from the nature of capitalism itself at the dawn of the new millennium and from the intellectual defences erected to fortify capitalism against all basic criticism. The experience of twentieth-century totalitarianism, particularly of the Hitlerian and Stalinist varieties, has powerfully reinforced the tendency of liberal or post-modernist intellectuals to recoil from overarching theories whose long-term effect could be to unleash new totalizing projects onto the human landscape. What they fear is reductionist, simplistic theories and schemes whose ostensible goal is liberation but whose consequence is to open the way for totalitarian parties with leaders who aspire to complete adherence to their doctrines. That messianism and totalitarianism have repeatedly shown themselves to have vast potential in Western thought is evident to anyone who has reflected on the lessons of the twentieth century. An ironic consequence of the way this lesson has been learned is that there are now powerful currents of thought in the West whose effect is to stand in the way of a critical assessment of the capitalism of our age. Anxiety concerning the potential for some new totalizing project becomes the basis for accepting globalizing capitalism as the least of all evils.

In the absence of coherent challenges to the inequalities that are so evidently a feature of capitalism, it is the totalizing tendencies within contemporary capitalism that are being powerfully reinforced. And contemporary capitalism, far from promoting a society of pluralities of the sort that liberals admire, is itself displaying monolithic tendencies. A world in which those who control capital face fewer societal constraints than they have faced since at least the 1930s is not one in which individual choices flourish. In the post-war period of the mixed economy, state policy reflected to a degree the expectations of wage and salary earners. While capitalist magnates enjoyed more power than their employees, they had to pay attention to the aspirations of others.

The danger of a totalizing capitalism arises precisely because the genuine, if limited, pluralism of the post-war decades has given way to a planetary capitalism with a very narrow vision of the road ahead. Liberals fail to recognize the warning signs of totalizing capitalism because they are looking in the wrong direction. While they scan distant horizons on the watch for a would-be Marx or Freud, they misread the implications of the rise of visionary billionaires like Bill Gates. Such mega-entrepreneurs have dreams of power that go far beyond the desire to amass a huge fortune. They aspire to build their empires by reshaping the culture of the world and monopolizing the way the energies of the world's people are used, believing that the power accruing from their enterprises is inherently virtuous.

My motivation in writing this book is to illustrate that the increasing division of society into a dominant class and a dominated class erodes the capacity of people to make significant choices for themselves. Ignoring the fact of social class will not dispel the worst effects of the prevailing influence of the dominant class. There is no short cut to the kind of world I would prefer to live in—one that celebrates individual difference and enables democratic choice. Facing up to the realities of a class-divided society in order to avoid its further entrenchment is a step along the way toward a world in which pluralities can truly flourish and the common good be served.

Although our society is constantly awash in the rhetoric of change, fundamental change is nonetheless exceedingly difficult to imagine. The powerful will always remain powerful, and the dominant will always figure out new ways to stay on top. That is our reflexive point of view, our rational starting point for considering power relationships in society. We know of course that societies do sometimes change with unanticipated swiftness. In 1989, the revolutionary transformation of Eastern Europe and the Soviet Union commenced. By December 1991, the Soviet Union no longer existed.

Before we consider the pressures that are building in today's industrialized world that could lead to fundamental change, let us reflect briefly on the vast transformation that, more than any other event, ushered in the societal assumptions of the modern world—the French Revolution.

Only a few months before the great events of 1789, the idea of a society without an aristocracy that was vested with a completely different legal standing from the rest of the population was inconceivable to all but a tiny number of people who had thought about such matters. There was immense dissatisfaction with the way things were. The third estate in France, which comprised the whole of the population with the exception of the aristocracy (the second estate) and the clergy (the first estate), had grown immensely powerful over the preceding century. As cities and towns had burgeoned and as capitalist enterprise had developed and flourished in what was already an economy with a global trading system, the disjunction between the society and the formal class system and system of government had grown enormous.

When Louis XVI called the Estates General to meet in 1789 to deal with the government's financial crisis, he created a setting where the real power of the third estate could be used to confront the restrictions placed on it by the division of society into three estates. When he convoked the Estates General, the king inadvertently put the combustible elements of French society into explosive proximity. The great historian Thomas Carlyle wrote an extraordinary account of the fateful meeting of the Estates General on May 4, 1789. In his description we see for the very last time the representatives of the aristocracy, the Church and the rest of the population (the third estate) side by side, on the eve of the conflagration that was to break out within a few weeks:

> Behold . . . the doors of St. Louis Church flung wide: and the Procession of Processions advancing to Notre-Dame! . . . The Elected of France, and then the Court of France, are marshalled . . . all in prescribed place and costume. Our Commons "in plain black mantle and white cravate"; Nobles in gold-worked, bright-dyed cloaks of velvet, resplendent, rustling with laces, waving with plumes; the Clergy in rochet, alb, or other best *pontificalibus*. Lastly comes the King himself, and the King's Household, also in the brightest blaze of pomp . . . Some fourteen hundred men blown together from all winds, on the deepest errand.
>
> Yes, in that silent marching mass there is futurity enough. No symbolic Arc, like the old Hebrews, do these men bear; yet with them, too, is a Covenant. They, too, preside at a new era in the history of men. The whole future is there, and Destiny dim-brooding over it, in (their) hearts and unshaped thoughts. . . ."[5]

The royal government had planned for the three estates to meet separately under its own firm direction. But once they met, everything changed. The decisive event came on June 17, when the third estate met on its own and declared itself alone to be the National Assembly. The representatives of the third estate had taken the first revolutionary step. They had broken the rules, proclaimed the third estate to be the nation and then defied the armies of the king. Over the next two months, the revolution accelerated with the storming of the Bastille on July 14, and the full night meeting of the National Assembly on August 4, when thirty decrees were passed whose effect was to abolish serfdom and noble privilege. On August 26 came the Declaration of the Rights of Man. The old order, described by Carlyle, was no more.

## Chapter 4

# The Rich and the Super-Rich

On the eve of the new millennium, the global capitalist class is a vast sprawling entity. Its international members and institutions consort with one another, making deals, squabbling, pushing and shoving, reaching for advantage and savouring a riotous time during which no coherent opposition has appeared on their collective horizon. Some companies fail as new ones are formed. At the centre of global capitalism, a furious process, like that of a volcano spewing molten lava, is at work, as the struggle for power rushes on.

Let's take stock of the contemporary capitalist class.

The leading multinational corporations are like a fleet of aircraft carriers, able to sail to all corners of the globe, self-sustaining, outfitted for survival in any sea. Multinationals have been in the process of formation since the second half of the nineteenth century. It was in the years following the American Civil War that the industrial corporation, producing goods and acting as its own bank by selling shares in the market, came into being.

Industrial corporations took their first steps toward becoming multinational, with Canada as an early proving ground. It was not difficult for American companies to set up shop in Canada, produce for the culturally similar Canadian market and circumvent Canadian tariffs. By 1914, several hundred U.S. corporations had established branch plants in

Canada. Following the First World War, U.S. corporations—the prototypes for today's multinationals—had set up production facilities in many parts of the world in addition to Canada—principally Latin America and Europe. It was in the glory years following the Second World War, when the United States oversaw the rebuilding of the global economy, that American multinationals took over scores of companies abroad and set up new production facilities. In that era, the structure and managerial style of American corporations became the global standard.

In the post-war decades, multinationals mushroomed in other countries as well. While Germany became a formidable contender in this high-end game, from the 1960s on Japan was the launchpad for the largest number of multinationals. Today, while Japan and the U.S. have about the same number of multinationals among the world's top 500, the combined annual revenues of the Japanese giants is larger than that of their American counterparts. In 1995, Japan was home base for 141 of these megacorps, which together had an annual revenue of us$3,985 billion, within striking distance of Japan's GNP, which was us$5.2 trillion the same year[1]; the U.S. had 153 of these multinationals with a combined annual revenue of us$3,221 billion; in third and fourth place were Germany and France with 40 and 42 giants and revenues of us$1,017 billion and us$880 billion respectively.[2]

Some top multinationals specialize in the production of manufactured products, examples being the world's great automobile manufacturers General Motors, Ford, Toyota and Nissan. Then there are the oil giants Exxon, Standard Oil of California, Royal Dutch Shell and the rest. And there are the producers of other commodities, chemicals, pharmaceuticals and so on. Trendiest in the age of cyber capitalism are the new high-tech giants, with Microsoft Corporation leading the pack. Much of the "new money" in today's capitalism has been made by the rising megacapitalists who have founded corporations in the fields of computer software and microprocessing. Among the five hundred leading multinationals are the world's top banks and financial service corporations. Japan is now home to most of these. The colossal revenues of the world's top five hundred multinationals, which exceed

US$10 trillion a year, are equivalent to about 30 percent of the gross economic output of the world.[3] Never in history has there been economic concentration on such a scale.

And there is no halt to the process of further concentration among the leading corporations. The 1990s has been a decade of unprecedented mergers in a whole host of fields. A few representative examples include the acquisition of CNN by Time Warner (for US$9 billion) in the field of communications.[4] Boeing, the aerospace giant, has acquired its only major American competitor, McDonnell-Douglas. In the United States, where deregulation will make it possible for banks to operate on a nationwide basis and in both commercial and investment banking, there has been a wave of mergers among financial institutions. On Wall Street in September 1997, Travelers Group Inc. acquired Salomon Brothers Inc., the bond-trading giant, for about US$9.6 billion in stock.[5] Similarly in Europe, where the single European market allows financial services corporations to operate in all countries in the European Union, there have been mergers and acquisitions among banks. Deutsche Bank, Germany's largest bank, has taken over banks in Spain, Italy and Britain.

The C$40-billion merger between the Royal Bank of Canada and the Bank of Montreal, Canada's largest and third largest banks, was announced on January 23, 1998. This biggest bank merger in Canadian history was revealed to the public by the Royal's chairman, John Cleghorn, and the Bank of Montreal's chairman, Matthew Barrett. Learning about the merger from a television news story only on the morning of its general announcement was the very surprised Finance minister, Paul Martin. So sure were the two banks of their right to do what they liked that they did not even bother to wait for Ottawa's task force on financial services to report (later in 1998) and for the federal government to perhaps alter its policy framework in light of the report. The new merged bank would have assets of C$435 billion. Initial information suggested the merger would lead to the loss of as many as 9,200 jobs.[6]

One consequence of such immense and growing concentration of corporate power is that leading corporations are able to dictate the economic and social agenda to nation-states in a way that was never imagined in the past. The top multinational corporations are the most potent weapons in the arsenal of today's capitalism. Because a genuinely global economic system has evolved for the first time in history, corporate giants that operate in all parts of the world exercise unprecedented leverage against recalcitrant states that try to apply domestic regulations stricter than those in force elsewhere. Not only do they dominate the global economy through the sheer size of their operations, but they also perform what they might regard as a "civilizing" role on behalf of the system, obliterating local opposition, forcing the world's states and peoples to play by a common set of rules.

Below the level of multinational business is the bulk of the private sector, with its innumerable firms, operating in every sphere of national economies, from the smallest businesses to the middle-size, large and very large companies. Tens of thousands of such firms exist even in an economy as relatively small as Canada's, which gives some comparative indication of the size of the five hundred multinationals that directly account for the production of over one-quarter of the goods and services on the planet.

The capitalists below the level of multinational firms constitute a vast throng of people whose life circumstances vary from extreme wealth for the owners and top managers at the high end of national corporations to near-poverty for capitalism's struggling hangers-on in very small mom-and-pop companies and retail outlets. The majority of those who work for a salary or a wage in the developed world are employed by these sub-multinational capitalists who run the businesses responsible for most of the private sector activity within national economies. And it is salutary in an age of rampant globalization to note that most economic activity still takes place within local, regional or national boundaries. Even in a country as dependent on foreign trade as Canada, roughly two-thirds of economic activity is domestic, involving the production in Canada of goods and services for sale at home.

Sub-multinational business operates in every part of the economy. In manufacturing, it supplies parts and components for products assembled by giant firms, as well as producing some goods from start to finish. In the primary sector, small and middle-size firms exist alongside the majors in industries such as petroleum. Although the majors dominate the extraction of oil and natural gas in Alberta or Texas, thousands of smaller firms produce machinery, sell engineering capability and explore for and extract oil and gas themselves.

Small and middle-size firms that operate in the domestic economy (many smaller firms are also involved in exporting and importing goods and services) grow or shrink, depending on what is happening to domestic economic demand, hiring or laying off employees as the economy expands or shrinks. In most industrialized countries, there still is what we can call a dual economy: firms operating in the international sector experience conditions quite different from those of firms whose market is domestic. In Canada and France, for instance, there have been two distinct economies in recent years—an export sector dominated by multinational business, which has been booming, and a domestic sector dominated by sub-multinational business, which has been essentially stagnant.

Sub-multinational capitalists provide the dominant capitalist class with its essential ballast. These are—particularly at the lower echelons—the masses of the business class. They are encountered in every city, town and hamlet. They shape the mood of capitalist opinion and have an enormous influence on politics at all levels. Although government leaders pay attention to multinational business, politicians largely play to the sub-multinational business class.

Most of the hand-to-hand fighting in the class war takes place at the level of business well below the commanding heights of the multinationals. This is where bosses fight workers for every cent of compensation and to keep benefits and payroll taxes low for employers. This is where the war is waged against any increase in the minimum wage. In June 1997, days after the newly elected Socialist government in France announced a 4 percent rise in the minimum wage, local businessmen appeared on television warning that this policy would lead to layoffs, the replacement of French products with imports and perhaps the sale of French firms to foreigners.

Sub-multinational business fights for legislation to make forming unions as difficult as possible and to ensure that governments allow the use of replacement workers during legal strikes. This level also opposes improved environmental standards and more stringent health and safety regulations on the job. This is where the war is waged to abolish affirmative action programs for women, minorities and the disabled, and to prevent equal rights for same-sex couples.

It is also among the ranks of sub-multinational businesses where the struggle for tax benefits for capitalists takes place. This struggle and the others mentioned motivate business at this level to exert pressure to mould the behaviour of the pro-business political parties in the industrialized countries. The British Conservatives, American Republicans, French Neo-Gaullists, Canadian Liberals, Conservatives and Reformers all interface with business largely at the sub-multinational level.

To varying degrees, depending on particular circumstances and traditions, these political parties are essentially unapologetic advocates for business. Indeed, their main task in terms of policy development is to work out an approach that takes into account the possibly contradictory, or at least divergent, interests of segments of the capitalist class from its noisy and sizeable small business segment at the bottom to the multinationals at the top. Typically, quite distinct political groupings in these parties speak for different segments of the capitalist class. Throughout Canadian history, the major political parties have always vied for the support of all elements of the business class. It has been truly rare for the party that has the support of business to lose a Canadian federal election.

Private firms are the capitalist system's crucial institutions. But it is individuals, not firms, who constitute the capitalist class. Using the United States as our example, let's make a broad estimate of how many people in an advanced country should be reckoned as members of the capitalist class.

In 1994, 127 million Americans (of the 260 million population) were classified in official statistics as employees in civilian occupations—in other words, as wage and salary earners. In addition, there were 10.5 million Americans classified as self-employed.7 Overwhelmingly, wage and salary earners constitute the working class/middle class. Among employees, however, there are also corporate managers, including those who are top executives of major corporations. The self-employed category comprises those who earn their income by investing their own capital, but this category also includes a very large number of people such as consultants who sell their skills on a contractual basis and are not classed as employees. It also includes a vast number who operate very small businesses, in some cases involving themselves alone. It would be wrong, therefore, to put wage earners and salaried employees in one class and the self-employed in another. Some of the most powerful capitalists are employees, and some of those living at the bottom end of the income scale are self-employed.

Just who are the capitalists, then? (Needless to say, official statistics do not include a category labelled *capitalist* in their publications.) It is not possible to draw a rigid line between those who ought to be classified as capitalists and those who belong to the working class/middle class. But that does not prevent us from coming up with a reasonable definition of who belongs to each of these classes and estimating how many people are in each.

The best basis for deciding who belongs to which social class is according to the roles they perform in the economic and social system. Since the wheel on which the economy turns is the investment of capital and the making of profit as a consequence of that investment—all else in a private market economy is a means to that end—the most useful definition of social class has to do with the role people play in the ownership and control of capital. When we analyze capitalist society from this perspective, two social classes emerge. Numerically the largest class by far comprises those who work for a wage or a salary in non-managerial positions. The much smaller, but socially dominant capitalist class, is made up of those who earn their living by investing their own capital and who derive their income from the profits, dividends and interest payments that accrue from that investment.

In the purest sense, those who own and invest their own capital and who realize their principal income from that ownership constitute the capitalist class. But this definition is incomplete. In some ways it is even misleading. This definition certainly includes, and quite properly, Bill Gates, Conrad Black and the guy in Etobicoke who owns a small candy factory, but it leaves out the executives of major national and multi-national corporations and the managers of vast investment funds. A definition of the capitalist class that omits the CEOs of major banks and the managers of huge investment funds is incomplete.

A full reckoning of who the capitalists are has to include those who manage major corporations, banks and investment funds, as well as those who own and invest significant amounts of capital. In practice, these two aspects of what it is to be capitalist—the ownership and investment of capital on the one hand, and the management of capital on the other—tend to converge. The managers of major national and multi-national corporations are paid high salaries, although in many cases most of their income derives from stock options and other benefits. Some executives have access to arrangements to hold back a portion of their salaries, which is invested in their companies to grow until the person retires. And corporate managers, whose incomes have been exploding while those of their employees have stagnated, are quickly accumulating large sums of capital. Top corporate managers, even if they start out with little or no capital of their own, are en route to acquiring enough capital that their future incomes will depend much more on dividends, profits and interest payments than on salaries. Such managers are moving from managing other people's assets to the more desirable position of having their own substantial assets to invest. The capitalist ideal, which is to acquire capital of one's own, dominates the dreams of every manager and would-be manager. The manager knows that to achieve this goal, he or she (usually he) will have to serve the interests of others reliably and assiduously in the hope of acquiring the power and the wealth to achieve genuine independence.

When we add together these two groups of people, those who own and invest capital as the principal means by which they earn their income and those who are senior managers of national and multinational firms, we come up with about 3 or 4 percent of the adult population of a country like the United States or Canada. In the United States in 1989, 3.4 million persons had gross assets of US$600,000 or more. This wealthiest sector of the population had a combined net worth of $4.8 trillion.[8] But just as the holding of assets within American society as a whole is markedly unequal, so too is the holding of assets within the capitalist class. The 3.4 million wealthiest Americans form a steep pyramid stretching all the way from those on the edge of the capitalist class to its stratospheric peak among a handful of multibillionaires.

First, let's eliminate the small-timers among the wealthy, those whose net assets are less than US$1 million each. This leaves us with 1.262 million persons. Most of these, 945,000 of them, have net assets that range between US$1 million and US$2 million. Then we move on to the 208,000 persons with net assets between US$2.5 million and US$5 million. At this point, we are still only in the foothills of the capitalist class, which moves upward from here to the real peaks. There are only 73,000 individuals with net assets between US$5 million and US$10 million. And of our original 3.4 million wealthy persons, just over 1 percent of them are left—36,000 persons—with net assets higher than US$10 million. These 36,000 have combined personal net assets worth US$492 billion. But US$10 million would hardly impress Bill Gates as personal wealth of any note. So our 36,000 individuals—1 percent of the wealthy—are the apex of the pyramid, where we encounter the truly super-rich.[9]

Before going on to consider the super-rich, let's look first at the managers, of great importance both because they steer the major corporations and because being hired as a manager is the most important career step taken by those who are not yet capitalists but aspire to be.

It has been recognized for decades that a managerial elite is essential to run enterprises, and that though the day of the great mogul is far from over, most large corporations are run by top managers rather than directly by owners. Most managers today, particularly in the Anglo-American world, have risen through the ranks following their education, typically as accountants, lawyers or graduates of business administration programs.

The odd example still exists of the manager who started on the factory floor and made it all the way to the stratospheric levels of upper management in a giant multinational, but such cases are increasingly rare.

The way corporate managers are selected is indicative of whether advanced capitalist societies are actually meritocracies. In an earlier chapter, we noted that influential analysts like Daniel Bell assert that the advanced countries are meritocracies, meaning that talent and hard work rather than family background and social connection are the road to the lucrative managerial jobs. Is this true? Do the best managerial jobs go to the most talented and dedicated? Or does a great deal have to do with who your parents are, how much they are worth, who you know and what kind of socialization you received?

The British sociologist John H. Goldthorpe has examined this subject extensively. According to him, empirical studies undertaken in the 1960s and 1970s that investigated the relationship among social origins, level of education and status destinations in the United States and Britain did lend some support to the idea that merit was becoming more important. But recent studies, Goldthorpe has written, carried out in Britain and Sweden in the 1990s have pointed in exactly the opposite direction, indicating that the relationship between social origins and status destinations may actually be strengthening.[10]

Respected analysts have made the case that if there were to be a growing weight given to educational attainment in determining status destinations, this would still be a dangerously flawed indicator of the existence of a meritocracy. These analysts reason that people in positions of power understand how important it is for their offspring to earn a degree in business administration, law, economics or accounting. High-income families do not leave such matters to chance.

Critics call this phenomenon "credentialism," which is not at all the same thing as meritocracy. One such critic, the Massachusetts Institute of Technology economist Lester Thurow, has called the increased spending by high-income families on higher education a "defensive expenditure" to protect their "market share" of the best jobs.[11] In his study of the meritocracy question, the sociologist A.H. Halsey suggests that education is "increasingly the mediator of the transmission of status between generations." He concludes from the evidence, however, that in this intergenerational process there has been no reduction in the influence of the family and the extent to which "ascriptive forces find ways of expressing themselves as achievement."[12]

As if resorting to credentialism on the part of high-income families were not enough to undermine the case that a meritocracy exists, there is evidence that educational attainment is far from being the only thing that counts when managerial appointments are made. Social skills rather than education appear to play a major role in determining eligibility for desirable positions. Upper classes have always understood the value of grooming their offspring to excel in social encounters. Indeed, Goldthorpe argues that participation in "human resources management programmes" has become increasingly important in assessing potential managers. These programs used to select recruits emphasize a candidate's personal qualities, placing considerable weight on such attributes as loyalty, commitment, adaptability and capacity for teamwork. Moreover, these criteria for screening applicants are often used even before educational attainment is considered.[13]

It is not surprising, then, that a very considerable number of the desirable positions promising lofty income and social status go to persons from high-income families. That fact has been acknowledged by an alternative, if virulent, defence of capitalism's fairness that has been mounted by some right-wing thinkers in the United States. These thinkers start from the premise that if a continuing strong correlation between social background and status destination is undeniable, it's useful to come up with an unassailable explanation to show that those getting the best jobs are indeed the fittest. The late American sociologist Richard J. Herrnstein has asserted that within the educational system, reliance on IQ testing has been increasing and selection procedures for entrance have become more merit based. Therefore, he concludes that the inequalities in outcomes in the competition for places in the best schools must be the consequence of differences in genetic endowment.[14] If people from high-status backgrounds are getting into the best schools and later are landing the superior jobs, this line of reasoning claims, they must be innately smarter than those doing less well, and so, this argument goes, the social hierarchy mirrors society's intelligence hierarchy. Those who get the best jobs are the brightest, while those who get the undesirable jobs, or no job at all, are the least bright.

This way of justifying the strong link between elevated social background and the best jobs has ominous implications for the future. If the brightest people are at the top of the hierarchy and the dullest at the bottom, it means that over time social classes are becoming ever more like castes, with less mobility between them. Their populations will be more fixed in place, not by social barriers but by genetically determined barriers.

If controversy continues to swirl about the reasons that certain people get the best jobs, the importance of top managerial positions is readily apparent. Corporate managers are bred for their ability to function in large organizations. Their ability to interact with superiors and inferiors counts more than anything else. Corporations are not unlike the military. They have a top-down command structure and established ranks. Corporate managers know full well that getting along with their own bosses advances their causes. Corporate cultures the world over, despite the differences between American-style bottom-line fetishists and German- and Japanese-style production wonks, regard reliability as the most important attribute in would-be managers. Not wanted are those with an independent cast of mind. A truly creative person, inclined to take a broad view, to consider, for instance, the interests of workers, the local community and the environment, in addition to those of shareholders, could be seen as subversive.

In what could have been an early guide for corporate managers, Shakespeare put these words into the mouth of Julius Caesar: "Let me have men about me that are fat, Sleek headed men, and such as sleep o' nights: Yon Cassius has a lean and hungry look; He thinks too much: such men are dangerous."

For top managers, success is achieved by having dependable junior managers who will not question the overall purpose of the enterprise. The reason dependability is a much more desirable quality for managers than creativity is that a manager forms a link in an organizational chain, a link on whom others must be able to rely. And let us not forget that the job of a manager is to handle the capital of other people, a role suited to the unquestionably ambitious who know how to keep their own personal greed within reasonable bounds.

Over the past four decades, executive compensation has soared, particularly in the United States. In 1953, the equivalent of 22 percent of U.S. corporate profits went to the payment of executives, but in 1987 executive compensation had reached the equivalent of 61 percent of corporate profits. In 1988, the average U.S. CEO was being paid ninety-three times as much as the average manufacturing worker. Only nine years earlier, in 1979, the average CEO was making twenty-nine times as much as the average manufacturing worker.[15] (German and Japanese CEOs, on the other hand, are still paid much less than their American counterparts.) The huge increase in the pay packages of American CEOs results from top management's success at riding the wave of new technology; related productivity gains have meant fabulous incomes for themselves. Their employees, whose average real incomes have not been increasing and who have faced rising job insecurity, have not been so fortunate. In his book about an earlier generation of business moguls, *The Rich and the Super Rich*, Ferdinand Lundberg compared managers to cormorants, Chinese fishing birds sent out to catch fish with a knot tied around their necks to prevent them from consuming the fish. But cormorants, like managers, are rewarded when the knot is occasionally loosened so that they can swallow a fish often enough to keep them interested in the pursuit.[16]

The manager occupies a transitional position within the capitalist class. Do the job well on behalf of others, and someday others will be doing the job on your behalf. It's an extremely attractive bargain, and it involves corporate managers very directly in today's class war. At the centre of the current lean managerial approach has been a drive toward cost-cutting through shedding labour. Managers who make an impact on their corporations and catch the eye of their superiors are the ones who figure out how to maintain corporate output while shedding jobs. Managers who lay workers off are the great corporate "builders" of our age. Indeed, a manager who demonstrates the ability to slash jobs is likely on that account to win a bigger personal remuneration package and to climb the corporate ladder. The ascent to the top is often directly related to having pushed hundreds or thousands of workers into unemployment.

An ideal Canadian example of the kind of top manager who laid off a large number of workers on his way to glory was Victor Young, chief executive officer of Fishery Products International Ltd. In February 1995, the *Financial Times* named Young Canada's CEO of the year for having completely turned his ailing company around. In the process, the *Financial Times* said, "Nearly three of every four FPI employees—more than 6000 in all—were laid off, most of them residents of single-industry Newfoundland towns." For the *Financial Times*, this was a happy story. The company was successfully restructured to the benefit of shareholders. Not a further word was said about those who lost their jobs.[17]

The point has already been made that defining membership in the capitalist class in terms of ownership of capital can be misleading. Lately, there has been a widespread attempt to convince anyone who owns stocks or bonds, who has a registered retirement plan or whose employment entitles him or her to a pension that he or she is an investor and thus a capitalist. In the 1980s, the Thatcher government in the U.K. regarded it as a very significant political victory when the number of Britons owning stocks surpassed the number of trade unionists. If you want to decide whether you're in the capitalist class or in the working class/middle class, just ask yourself which source of income is more important to you—your wage or salary, or your investment income. (Pension funds are a huge source of capital in today's economy. But that does not turn those entitled to a pension into members of the capitalist class.)

If managers are recruits to the capitalist class (some of them have parents who were already capitalists), let us turn our attention to those who are at the very zenith of the class, today's super-rich. But first the indelicate question of inheritance needs to be raised. To what extent does the passing on of wealth from one generation to the next play a part in determining who is wealthy?

Through the inheritance of wealth, there is, of course, a very direct and entirely non-meritocratic mechanism for transmitting influence and power from one generation to the next. Popular accounts of the current ranks of the rich and the super-rich, such as the annual Rich List of the *Sunday Times* in Britain or *Forbes* magazine's list of the richest four hundred people in America, or the magazine *Challenges'* annual list of the wealthiest people in France, like to boast that it is the self-made who are increasingly rising to billionaire status. The *Sunday Times* Rich List for 1997 emphasized that in the vast increase in wealth enjoyed by Britain's millionaire class, "it is the self-made businessmen who are leading the way."[18]

As we have seen, in capitalist society, holding a position in the dominant social class tends to be justified by the supposed merit of those at the top. Those who have made it are held to be the most dynamic and creative people in the society, the ones who have fought their way to positions of supremacy by displaying their mettle. Nothing is more problematic for this notion than the fact of inheritance of wealth, in some cases vast wealth. It is difficult to sustain the argument that those who stand on capitalism's highest peak are the worthiest and fittest when it is perfectly evident that many of the wealthiest people in the world had astonishingly good judgment in choosing their parents.

When we raise the question of inheritance, we unearth an important paradox. Although capitalism is often justified as socially "fair" on the grounds that it has become meritocratic, the fact remains that one of the ideals of the system is that individuals have the right and the opportunity to amass vast wealth and pass it on to their offspring.

If meritocracy were truly desired, it would not be difficult to design a capitalist system that would actually reward the talented and the hardworking while weeding out the free riders. In such a system, education at the advanced levels would be highly competitive, and there would be no tuition for all who could make the grade. The best posts would be available to those who had thus demonstrated their superiority. Top positions would be rewarded handsomely. But there would be a catch: children would not be allowed to inherit fortunes, but instead, at the death of a parent accumulated wealth would be turned over to some socially agreed purpose, perhaps of one's own choice. Offspring would have to make their own way just as a parent did, discovering for themselves how far they could get in life's gruelling contest.

Such a system would be meritocratic. It is noteworthy, however, just how little inclination exists to implement such a system. In contrast to the meritocratic ideal, the real capitalist ethic supports the right to pass on wealth exactly as one pleases. The greedy state should keep its hands off. At its deepest level of aspiration and of practice, contemporary capitalism is profoundly anti-meritocratic.

The super-rich have achieved all there is to realize in the capitalist system. They have wealth, power and independence unrivalled by that of other mortals. To get some notion of how awesome is the wealth of the richest humans on the planet, it helps to remember that the bottom half of American families have assets of less than US$1,000. By contrast, the world's richest ten persons, whose names appeared in the Rich List of the *Sunday Times*, had assets worth a total of US$186 billion in 1997.[19] Their total wealth was about the same as the Gross Domestic Product of Sweden or of Austria.[20] This does not refer to the assets of companies in which these individuals have a share, but simply to the personal holdings of the top ten wealthiest. (Understandably, the Rich List compiled by the *Sunday Times* often differs from other lists, such as that of *Forbes* magazine, in the estimates it makes of the financial worth of individuals.)

In 1997, the richest person in the world was the sultan of Brunei, estimated to be worth about US$49 billion.[21] His personal holdings began in petroleum and have now been diversified into massive foreign investments. Brunei is a tiny state perched on the South China Sea on the northern coast of the island of Borneo. Even in an age of crass and conspicuous displays of wealth by the super-rich, the sultan's ostentation is remarkable. A few years ago, he celebrated his twenty-fifth anniversary on the throne by riding a gilded chariot pulled by forty men through the streets of his capital. For international travel, he has a customized Boeing 747.[22]

There have been allegations that the world's richest man does not limit his eccentric behaviour to escapades with chariots. In 1997, Shannon Marketic, a former Miss U.S.A., charged in an American lawsuit that she had been kidnapped by the sultan to serve as a sex slave in Brunei's 1,788-room royal palace. According to Marketic, when she and six other women arrived in Brunei, having been hired to make speeches and do promotional work, their passports were confiscated. Marketic said she and the others were forced to entertain men. If they were told they were going "to tea," or advised not to wear makeup, these code phrases indicated that the man they were to visit expected to have sex with them. Marketic said she was spared having sex with the regulars at the sultan's parties because his brother, Prince Jefri, wanted her for himself. Although she did not allege that Prince Jefri slept with her, the former beauty queen claims she was forced to perform "physically and morally repulsive acts." The sultan categorically denied the accusations and claimed diplomatic immunity to dodge the suit in a U.S. court. Marketic's allegations are not the first to accuse the sultan of collecting harems. In 1993, hearings were conducted in the Philippines resulting from reports that the sultan was inviting Filipino models to Brunei under false pretences.[23]

The second wealthiest person on the planet, according to the *Sunday Times*, is John Walton, an American whose individual wealth, concentrated in Wal-Mart and other retailing, was estimated at us$24 billion. (Actually, Walton has to share his fortune—which *Forbes* reckons at a much higher us$32 billion—with other members of his family, including his mother and his siblings.)[24]

Following the Waltons, in the number-three spot in the *Sunday Times* Rich List was fellow American Bill Gates, president of Microsoft, with personal holdings worth US$18.8 billion.[25] The *Forbes* 400 list, published in October 1997, six months after the *Sunday Times* Rich List, estimated Gates's assets as a cool US$40 billion, which put him ahead of the combined fortunes of the Waltons, making him the richest American, and the second-richest person in the world, next to the sultan of Brunei. In 1996–97, Gates had a very good year (which partly accounts for the different estimates of the *Sunday Times* and *Forbes*), during which his personal wealth soared by an unimaginable US$21.3 billion.[26]

The other seven men on the list of the world's wealthiest ten include four more Americans. Top among these is Warren Buffett, the investment banker.[27] In 1996, he bet a huge bundle from his personal billions on McDonald's. He reasoned that although McDonald's has been slumping a bit in the U.S., it has enormous potential in the rest of the world, which now accounts for 59 percent of its earnings. The fast-food giant is expected to increase its foreign profits at about 20 percent a year as it expands further into established markets such as Germany and France and plunges into Russia and China in a big way.[28]

The other three Americans are Peter Haas (Levi's blue jeans), Forrest Mars (confectionery—Mars bars and M&M's) and Pierre du Pont (chemicals). In addition to these Americans are Saudi Arabia's King Fahd (oil), Paul Sacher, the Swiss pharmaceutical mogul, and Lee Shau Kee of Hong Kong (real estate).[29]

The origin of the wealth of the top ten compiled by the *Sunday Times* is of interest: two are monarchs, who combine dictatorial power with fabulous personal wealth; five inherited their fortunes—Walton, Haas, Mars, du Pont and Sacher; and three are self-made billionaires—Gates, Buffett and Lee Shau Kee.

Gates certainly did not inherit his fortune, but his father, a highly respected lawyer, may have taught his son important lessons, among them the one that was the key to his success. What launched Gates as a financial power was persuading IBM to leave the legal ownership of his software in his own hands. More than his flair for software, it was Bill Gates's understanding of the value of an ironclad legal contract that opened the way for his rise to megawealth.

Similarly, Warren Buffett did not inherit vast wealth from his family, but he was not exactly born into poverty either. Buffett's father was a stockbroker who became a member of the U.S. Congress. When Warren Buffett started out on his own as an investor in the mid-1950s, he began with US$105,000 borrowed from family and friends.[30] If not from a wealthy background, Buffett certainly came from a privileged family with very good connections.

(The Forbes 400 list positions super-rich Americans somewhat differently than does the *Sunday Times*. *Forbes* agrees that Warren Buffett is next in wealth behind Gates. After Buffett, Forbes ranks the next three megarich Americans as Paul Allen (US$17 billion), the co-founder of Microsoft with Bill Gates; Lawrence Ellison (US$9.2 billion), another software mogul who co-founded Oracle Corp in 1977; and Gordon Moore (US$8.8 billion), co-founder of Intel Corp., the micro-processor giant.)[31]

The wealthiest Canadian is Kenneth R. Thomson, the reclusive heir to the newspaper empire founded by his father, Roy, the late Lord Thomson of Fleet. In 1996, his personal wealth was estimated by the *Financial Post* at C$8.2 billion. Thomson owns newspapers in many countries. After Thomson, a renowned penny-pincher, the second-largest Canadian fortune belongs to the three sons of the late K.C. Irving, Arthur, James and John. Their combined assets—invested in ocean tankers, oil refineries, service stations, forest products, and media outlets—totalled C$7.5 billion. Number three on the list of super-rich Canadians is Charles R. Bronfman, who owns 16 percent of Seagram's. He inherited his wealth, estimated in 1996 at C$2.9 billion, from the late Sam Bronfman, who made his money selling booze in the days of Prohibition in the United States. Then come the Eatons—Frederik, George, Thor and John Craig—whose combined fortune was reckoned by the *Financial Post* in 1996 at C$1.7 billion. The Eatons remain far from destitute, despite the financial problems of their flagship department store chain, whose original store was founded by their ancestor Timothy in 1869. The fifth-largest Canadian fortune, estimated at C$1.4 billion, is in the hands of Ted Rogers, the communications mogul. Rogers, who inherited his fortune from his father, owns Canada's biggest cable TV service. He also controls Maclean Hunter, the giant publishing company, and has major holdings in cellular phone operations.[32] None of those who control Canada's five greatest fortunes is self-made.

Determining who among the super-rich got their start from inheritance and who assembled their fortunes from scratch and just what these fortunes are worth is no easy matter. A few years ago, the *Sunday Times* Rich List named that well-known inheritor of wealth, Her Majesty the Queen, the wealthiest person in Britain. Since then, severely negative revaluations of her property have caused the compilers of the List to drop her to the seventy-third position and to rate her personal wealth at a mere £250 million (about US$408 million). (At number seventy-three, she is tied with upstart Canadian publisher Conrad Black, who is thought falsely in some meritocratic circles to have been born in the modern equivalent of a log cabin.) Before you rush to send Elizabeth Regina a cheque, it should be noted that considerable mystery surrounds her investments. Prior to 1994, when she started paying taxes, a very long bull run on the stock market should have enabled her to amass about £400 million in profits without even counting her other assets. And if you add the royal art collection, which is worth more than US$16 billion, she then leaves Conrad Black in the dust. But the art treasures are held in a charity, the Royal Collection Trust, and including them in the calculation of her personal fortune is not regarded as good form.[33]

Counting the Queen, Britain's richest thousand includes 146 other aristocrats: 11 dukes, 10 marquesses, 25 earls, 11 viscounts, 1 baroness, 39 lords, 13 baronets, 41 knights, 1 dame, and 6 ladies. The wealthiest of the aristocrats, the duke of Westminster, worth £1.7 billion (US$2.8 billion), bases his vast fortune on his ownership of a considerable slice of the exclusive West End of London; as a consequence, he is Britain's number-one landlord. In Britain, the transition from a hereditary aristocracy to modern capitalism is not fully complete, more than two hundred years after the French Revolution, let alone the transition to a meritocracy. (In fairness, it should be noted that one of the 41 knights is the unquestionably self-made pop star, Sir Paul McCartney.)[34]

Among the ranks of the super-rich and the merely rich, we find that a sizeable portion of them in all the advanced countries inherited fortunes. The proportion of the total, including family fortunes dispersed among a number of individuals, is likely in the order of 50 to 60 percent, a little more in some countries, a little less in others. As for the rest, some have made it into the ranks of the super-rich from families that were merely rich, parlaying a family business into a fortune worth hundreds of millions of dollars. Some come from comfortably middle-class families. And some, particularly in entertainment and sports, have made it all the way from the working class or even poverty to fabulous wealth. Mick Jagger is also on the list of the thousand richest Britons. Unlike Sir Paul McCartney, he has not been knighted.[35] The only African American on the Forbes 400 Rich List is the television star Oprah Winfrey, whose assets were rated as worth US$550 million in 1997.[36]

Other entertainers can be expected to turn up on rich lists in the future, as a consequence of their very high rates of pay. In 1996, 133 Hollywood stars had made it into the exclusive club of those who received at least $1 million a film. Among the 96 men on the list, the best paid were Jim Carrey, John Travolta, Mel Gibson and Tom Hanks, at about US$20 million a film. The best paid of the 37 women on the list were Demi Moore and Julia Roberts (US$12 million a film), followed by Sandra Bullock and Michelle Pfeiffer (US$10 million a film).[37]

Throughout the history of capitalism, there has always been a mix of "old money" and "new money." Overall, old money has predominated, as indeed it still does today. It is not surprising in a social system permitting wealth to be easily passed on from one generation to the next that, once established, great fortunes do not tend to be quickly dispersed. The rich are good at hanging on to their money, as they always have been. Today, the existence of a globalized system of finance, which helps keep both individual and corporate taxes low for the wealthy, and the proliferation of tax havens have made it even easier for today's rich and super-rich to keep what they have. Seventy-eight of the richest thousand Britons, for example, are tax exiles who have escaped to places like the Bahamas, where governments don't bother much about taxation.[38]

But there is mobility from below into the capitalist class and even into its upper realms of wealth. This has always been true, and it is a fact of considerable importance for the system, offering hope to the population as a whole that the system is open to new talent, that rags-to-riches stories are not impossible. And even if for the average person this kind of hope is not much greater than winning the lottery, it has worked to legitimize capitalism for the general populace. In addition, mobility from below brings much-needed new talent into the capitalist class. Throughout history, all class-divided societies have required the addition of new recruits from below, because dominant social classes constitute only a small part of the population. Reliance on only their own offspring to advance the interests of the system would pose the severe risk of an attenuation of energy, which can only be prevented by the infusion of new blood. In the pre-revolutionary societies of the late-eighteenth century, new aristocrats came from the increasingly influential urban bourgeoisie. Capitalist societies have always been open, to a greater or lesser extent, to ambitious newcomers from below. John D. Rockefeller and Henry Ford were self-made entrepreneurs who understood new technology and new markets better than their old-money competitors. Such recruits have helped renew capitalism. But of course it is customary for the heirs of innovators, the second, third and fourth generations, to become charter members of the "old money" club.

There is no evidence whatsoever that those who rise into the ranks of the dominant class bring with them compassion for those they have left behind. Indeed, popular wisdom suggests that "new money" capitalists are more savage, if anything, than the scions of long-established wealth. A civilizing effect is thought to occur as new money becomes old, as the second, third and fourth generations of a dynasty acquire education and what is regarded as good breeding. Certainly, John D. Rockefeller and Henry Ford were ruthless characters who displayed little human kindness toward competitors, employees or anyone else.

In 1997, there are still a Rockefeller and two Fords on the Forbes 400 rich list. David Rockefeller Sr., the grandson of America's first billionaire, the oil tycoon John D. Rockefeller, is worth us$1.8 billion.

The Rockefeller family fortune is reckoned at US$7.2 billion.[39] Henry Ford's last surviving grandchildren, William Clay and Josephine, have fortunes worth respectively US$1.4 billion and US$800 million.[40]

The fact of great wealth in the hands of a few poses problems for democratic theory and practice. In principle, all citizens in the advanced capitalist countries are equal in certain basic respects. Supposedly all are entitled to participate and to have their views and interests taken into consideration in the setting of public policy. That theory needs to be weighed against the reality of a social pyramid with fabulously wealthy persons at the top. Exactly what sort of equal citizenship do other Americans share with the Waltons with their US$32 billion? Here is a family with vast power to determine where investments will flow and where they will be cut back. They can decide, subject to the most minimal legal restraints, who will work and who will not. They sit at the apex of an empire over which they rule, for good or for ill, almost entirely as they choose.

Now that we know who the capitalists are, where do they aspire to take us? What is the societal project of contemporary capitalism?

The capitalists of our age have devised a set of rules by which they want everyone to play. These certainly do not take the form of laws like those of nation-states, but the guidelines and values established by the capitalist class have a pervasive effect. In many respects, they matter more than the laws passed by the parliaments, congresses and national assemblies of the leading nation-states. To speak of the societal project of the capitalists may conjure up a conspiracy in the minds of some, but there is no conspiracy at the heart of global capitalism, no secret, decision-making body. There are, however, overlapping circles of influence resulting in a more or less consistent party line.

The British periodical the *Economist* says that the annual global economic forum held each winter in Davos, Switzerland, is attended by "the people who run the world." Davos is one of the venues where the most significant issues concerning the future of capitalism are debated.

In attendance are business moguls, top-flight economists of one orthodox persuasion or another (monetarist, supply-side, rational expectations school and so on), government leaders and media commentators
from around the world.

The values and methodology of Anglo-American capitalism, with its
insistent emphasis on freedom for the market, have predominated at
Davos in the mid-1990s. As a consequence of resumed economic
growth in the United States and Britain in the mid-1990s, the Anglo-
American economic model appears robust in comparison with the more
interventionist European and Japanese models. In Continental Europe,
unemployment rates have been very high—above 12 percent in Germany, France and Italy in 1997. For its part, Japan passed through a
period of economic trouble in the 1990s, with a collapse in land values
and stock prices, and accompanied by scandals involving business and
government.

So at Davos in the mid-1990s, the advocates of British- and American-style capitalism were proselytizing among the Europeans and
Japanese. In the winter of 1997, Bill Gates was the poster boy of American capitalism. His appearances at Davos created greater excitement
than those of heads of governments. Writing from Davos that winter,
the *New York Times* correspondent Thomas Friedman proclaimed that
"the U.S. growth model . . . is in the ascendancy. . . . Globalization is
us. . . . Call me crazy, but I think it merits a little rational exuberance."[41]

At their bastion of capitalism on Front Street in Toronto, *Globe and
Mail* editorialists were also expressing enthusiasm, with some reserva-
tions, for the Anglo-American model. Admitting that the British and
American variety of capitalism had led to a sharp increase in income
inequality, a *Globe* editorial commented that "the difficulty of fixing the
Anglo-American system should not obscure its virtues."[42]

The Anglo-American cheerleaders didn't mention that much of the
American and British success in the 1990s has been due to the steep
devaluation of their currencies against those of their competitors.
Devaluation had restrained their imports and had encouraged their
exports, thus making the Anglo-American recovery much more a matter

of old-fashioned protectionism than its advocates like to admit. At Davos, the lessons drawn from the British and American experiences were that labour costs had to be cut, social spending slashed and job protection for workers reduced. The Anglo-American line favoured a market-centred system with a minimal welfare state and with little government intervention in the economy. The private sector should be left to do the job, essentially on its own.

In addition to Davos, other highly influential centres of capitalist policy making have been extolling the Anglo-American model. The Paris-based OECD has as its members the leading industrial nations in the world. Staffed by orthodox economists from these countries, the OECD publishes reports on the key issues facing the global economy and annual report cards on the performance of the economies of member states. In the mid-1990s, it recommended full speed ahead for globalization and the transition of member states to more market-driven economies. OECD reports backed pro-business changes in the regulation of labour, privatization of state-owned enterprises and cuts to welfare programs.

One of the drawbacks of Davos, or forums like it, is how very public it is. The world's media flock there, and much of what happens takes place under the glare of international publicity. Naturally, at Davos there are countless smaller, informal and private gatherings. Those who run the world at the dawn of the new millennium also like to meet without having the media know just who is meeting who or what is said. In the summer of 1996, for instance, Conrad Black invited some acquaintances to a weekend at an estate in King City, just north of Toronto. The guest list, which was not issued to the media, included members of European royalty, business moguls and Jean Chrétien, the prime minister of Canada.

But even Conrad Black doesn't play in the very top league. Today, the most coveted invitation in the business world is one from Bill Gates, who according to the *New York Times* is now "considered by some the most important man in the world."[43] Not far from Seattle, Washington, Gates has been building a fantastic, futuristic mansion on Lake Washington.

This techno-retreat is designed to be the super-rich man's personal paradise of the twenty-first century.

Indeed, you are never far from electronic magic in the Gates house. In this modern Neroesque dwelling, occupants carry an electronic pin with them. As Jim Cutler, the architect of the Gates house, explained,

> When it's dark outside, the pin will cause a moving zone of light to accompany you through the house. Unoccupied rooms will be unlit. As you walk down a hallway, you might not notice the lights ahead of you gradually coming up to full brightness and the lights behind you fading. Music will move with you as well. It will seem to be everywhere, although, in fact, other people in the house will be hearing entirely different music or nothing at all. A movie or the news will be able to follow you around the house too. Screens will appear at the touch of a hand, ready to accept your instructions or entertain you.[44]

In May 1997, Gates invited a very exclusive gathering of more than one hundred business tycoons and top government officials from twenty-five countries to attend a Microsoft Corporation "CEO Summit." The summit, held in Seattle, where participants discussed how technology is changing the world of business, was an opportunity for Gates to unveil his vision of the future of cyber capitalism to the select gathering. A special event of the assemblage was a dinner at Gates's mansion-in-progress, to which guests were brought by cruise boat. The guest list was to be kept secret, but it was leaked to the media. Gates's guests included the very wealthy Steve Forbes, who is already seeking the Republican presidential nomination for 2000, and Reed Hundt, the chairman of the Federal Communications Commission—a key contact, as Gates constructs corporate alliances linking computer software and broadcasting (he already owns 11.5 percent of the cable operator Comcast),[45] and a long list of Gates's close business allies from around the world.[46] Also in attendance was Al Gore, U.S. vice president.

Events of this kind give a peek into the closed world of the super-rich.

Gatherings of this sort have always been held by those who exercise immense power, but it is now regarded as completely acceptable for top political leaders and government bureaucrats to consort at secret conclaves with billionaires who have evolved their own strategies for acquiring power and wealth. In our era, as the authority of governments elected by the people declines, the power of private empires soars.

The very fact that Bill Gates is now considered by some of the mainstream media to be the most important man in the world reveals just how great the shift has been. In the mid-twentieth century, even a Henry Ford was never seen as more powerful than a Franklin Roosevelt or a Winston Churchill. But at the end of the twentieth century, it seems normal that Conrad Black's significance dwarfs Jean Chrétien's, or Bill Gates's Al Gore's, or that of his boss, Bill Clinton.

The problem that figures like Gates pose for a democratic society is not primarily their aspiration to vast personal wealth but the way they make fundamental decisions that determine the socioeconomic course of the industrialized world. Microsoft, the corporation that Gates co-founded in 1975, provides insight into how the highly ambitious super-rich and their corporations are reshaping the world for their own purposes. The great success of Microsoft was based on Gates's uncanny understanding, which surpassed that of his competitors, that the development of software rather than hardware was the key to the burgeoning computer market.

In September 1983, the company launched Microsoft Word, its word processing application. Two months later came the release of the Windows operating system, which facilitated the company's taking the lead. After that, Microsoft's steady rise pushed its annual revenues to US$2 billion in 1991. In 1996, the company's annual revenues broke through the US$10 billion barrier. On the road to these enormous revenues, the company produced an improved version of Windows. By 1996, Word had a 90 percent share of the world market for personal computer (PC) software applications and Windows enjoyed an 83 percent share of the world PC market for operating systems.[47]

The game Gates is playing is an old one. The difference is that he is playing it with up-to-date materials and on a much wider playing field. The game, which John D. Rockefeller, Andrew Carnegie and Henry Ford knew well, is the planned creation of a monopoly or near-monopoly in the chosen arena of business. Gates wants to control the software applications and operating systems not only for PCs—he's already done this through Word and Windows—but for the corporate computing market as well, through a new system called Windows NT.[48] The new software is designed to allow desktop machines to display Windows software while the software is running on a central computer, as is the case with a mainframe.[49] The objective is to give Microsoft the dominant position in providing software systems for the homes and offices of the future. (Microsoft encountered legal problems in the U.S. in 1997 for allegedly attaching the marketing of its Internet Explorer to that of Windows.) In 1997, Microsoft made a deal with Apple that pushed the one-time serious rival co-founded by Steven Jobs to the margin of Gates's empire.

Gates's strategy extends far beyond technological prowess to include intricate corporate alliances and takeovers to construct an empire and to block other competing empires from being created. The game is played all over the world and involves politicians, states, and the culture of developed and developing countries. Observers have noted that Gates often acts not merely like a businessman but as though he is running for some global political office after the manner of a would-be president of the United States.[50]

In March 1998, Gates was called to testify before the Judiciary Committee of the U.S. Senate. The issue was the allegedly monopolistic practices Microsoft was using to drive competitors out of the Internet software market. Senators tried to pry open details of Microsoft's nondisclosure agreements, which forbid businesses that license Microsoft software from discussing those agreements with outsiders. One rival of Bill Gates—Scott McNealy, chief executive of Sun Microsystems Inc.—told senators that software developers can be fearful of criticizing Microsoft. He said: "Sometimes I wonder why you would go up against the most dangerous and powerful industrialist of our age."[51]

In Gates we have a truly global economic player, operating at the cutting edge of technology, who runs a private empire that is his to command. Some may see his dictatorship as benevolent, but that it is a dictatorship there can be no doubt.

As the state and its elected leaders make fewer decisions that really matter, these private empires, run by super-rich impresarios and corporate managers, are setting the agenda. They decide where investment flows and where it does not. They determine who works and who does not. They calculate which states and political leaders are onside and which are not.

Gates is far from being the only player of such games. For instance, Lou Gerstner, the CEO of IBM since 1993, has been engaged in a life-or-death struggle to bring back the high-tech giant from its near collapse because it failed to understand the desktop computer revolution. Gerstner made the bet that in addition to PCs, there was a future for a new generation of mainframes, the corporate computers, from which businesses and individuals had fled to the PCs. Under his direction, IBM cut its workforce in half, from 406,000 in 1986 to 219,000 in 1994. Whether IBM can make it back to its former position as the dominant high-tech company remains to be seen. By 1997, more than US$40 billion had been added to IBM's market value, from its low point in 1992.[52]

This is an age in which super-rich figures, and not just Bill Gates, are bent on carving out roles for themselves far beyond business in any narrow sense. Well known are the cases of Americans Ross Perot and Steve Forbes, two moguls who decided that their wealth positioned them for political careers. In the 1992 U.S. presidential election campaign, Perot spent tens of millions of his own dollars promoting himself to the electorate. (In 1997, Perot's fortune was estimated at US$3.3 billion.)[53] Unlike those who sought the Democratic and Republican nominations for the presidency, Perot did not raise funds for his independent candidacy or play by the rules that would have entitled him to matching government funds for his campaign. That way, he was absolutely free to seek the country's top political position doing exactly as he pleased, not having to abide by advertising limits and spending restrictions that affected the other candidates. His idiosyncrasies aside—he pulled out of the campaign in the summer of 1992, only to reenter it a few weeks later—Perot proved that vast wealth alone is a sufficient qualification for entering American politics at the top, a presidential election. Winning 19 percent of the vote in 1992, Perot did a great deal to take victory away from the other right-wing contender, the incumbent, George Bush, and to hand it to Bill Clinton, who won with a minority of the vote in a contest in which he would have been very hard-pressed to defeat Bush one on one.

In 1996, Steve Forbes used personal wealth alone—most observers would agree that his gifts for political campaigning were almost embarrassingly meagre—to make himself a significant candidate in the race for the Republican Party's presidential nomination. Forbes's flat-tax proposal, a boon to the wealthy if there ever was one, was an idea that other candidates and the national media had to take very seriously. In the end, though he didn't win the nomination, his campaign helped set the stage for Bob Dole's decision to make tax cuts a key campaign plank. It even influenced the eventual winner of the election, Bill Clinton, to avoid policy proposals that would benefit ordinary Americans but cost money. The Forbes campaign helped create the political setting for Clinton's decision to sign into law a Republican welfare bill that removed the right of the permanently jobless to social assistance, a right they had enjoyed since the New Deal of the 1930s.

Not particularly gifted themselves, Perot and Forbes nonetheless illustrated that a more talented super-rich person could use the circumstances of a future political crisis to make an end run around the American political system to win the presidency. Today's capitalism, with its uniquely powerful super-rich paladins and its weakened states and political leadership, is demonstrably vulnerable to the threat of caesarism. This is particularly so in the United States where presidential elections, with their election of delegates through a system of primaries, allows wealthy individuals to emerge from nowhere into the national limelight in a way that would be more difficult in countries with parliamentary party systems, such as much of Western Europe or Canada.

Even though parliamentary systems make caesarist projects more

# Chapter 5

# Money Men

We live in the age of money. The ground-breaking capitalists of our time are not those who make trains, planes or automobiles but the manipulators of symbols. Bill Gates is a demigod, not merely because of his wealth but because he is the sorcerer, the master of symbols. He produces the very technology that has helped liberate the flow of money in our time. He is the alchemist who fuses the new technology with money. Although money has been around for thousands of years, it is only through microelectronics that it becomes a pure expression of value, a virtual metaphor unencumbered by materiality.

It has often been noted, and I believe truthfully, that this is a dreary age for the arts as well as for the physical and architectural monuments that will be left to posterity. The real monument to our age, if *monument* is the right word, is in the marriage, the fusion, of the electron and the dollar. The marriage between microelectronic technology and money was made in heaven.

The buildings future generations will look back on as the markers of our era will be the shimmering bank towers in the heart of the great cities. Noteworthy because it is so spare, so symbolic, in its profile is the Deutsche Bank tower in Frankfurt, the highest building in the city's financial district, crowned with the starkest of bankers' logos, a single diagonal slash mounted on a background square.

The hegemonic position occupied by money is reflected in the way businesses now run, the travel and telephone industries being two telling examples. Gone are the days of a regular price for a flight from Toronto to Paris. Now a traveller is overwhelmed by choices—ticket deals of various kinds, charters, seat sales and how to use flight-plan points. And no matter what price a ticket costs, someone else invariably offers a different deal at a better price. The same is true of telephone rates. Assorted deals are promoted for lower rates on long-distance telephone calls, or for lower rates for the people called most, or for packages with various kinds of reductions. And you hear stories about people signing up and sometimes having to wait interminably to make long-distance calls through cut-rate servers.

One of the proudest claims of those who defend deregulated capitalism is that today the consumer is in command, able to shop among a myriad airlines or telephone companies to get the best service at the best price. A professor at the University of Michigan Business School has tested the proposition that this is the golden age of consumer satisfaction. In 1994, Claes Fornell created the American Customer Satisfaction Index (ACSI). Based on regular interviews with sixteen thousand customers of two hundred companies in thirty-three sectors, the ACSI revealed a declining level of satisfaction with service in each of its successive quarterly reports from 1994 to 1997.[1] Significantly, over the three-year period, Americans remained just as pleased with the hard goods they were buying, but they were increasingly irritated with service, particularly from companies in deregulated sectors such as airlines and telephones. Air travellers were annoyed with ever more frequent delays, baggage problems and difficulties in getting to speak to an employee rather than a computer-driven answer machine.

Telephone customers complained of lengthening delays in having problems looked after, and even of difficulties getting telephone numbers from operators sitting at computers half a continent away. One man in Kennewick, Washington, who wanted a phone number in Walla Walla, just down the road, was told by operators working in Arizona that Walla Walla was not in their database. Professor Fornell believes the reason consumers are so unhappy can be summarized in three words: downsizing, reengineering and retrenchment.[2] Deregulated industries have not improved their services—cramped, crowded and notoriously late aircraft and rising costs for basic telephone rates are standard. Instead, deregulation has created vastly elaborate markets modelled after the way that brokers operate on the floor of the stock exchange. Supporters of the privatization of electric power companies and water utilities want them to go the same way.

Today the stock market does more than raise capital for productive enterprises. It is also a lottery, a daily scoreboard for the players of the capitalist class and a manifestation of the spirit of the age. The rhetoric of the "new economy" suggests that everyone is now involved in the ownership of stocks and bonds through mutual funds. Although it is certainly true that millions of wage and salary earners in the United States and Canada have modest investments in mutual funds, the ownership of financial assets is shifting ever more to the wealthy. In the U.S., apart from the equity they have acquired through owning their homes, a majority of American families are actually net debtors. As the economic analyst William Greider puts it in his book *One World Ready or Not: The Manic Logic of Global Capitalism*, most families do not have "a mutual-fund nest egg or even net savings of any kind."[3] In the U.S. during the 1980s, the proportion of financial wealth in the hands of the bottom 80 percent of families declined from 9 percent to 6 percent of the total. Meanwhile, the financial assets held by the top 1 percent rose from 43 to 48 percent.[4] From mid-1996 to mid-1997, the rising American stock market increased the wealth of the United States by about US$1.4 trillion. Half of this gigantic new wealth went to families with annual incomes of US$200,000 or more.[5]

Stock and bond markets rise and fall to signal the pleasure and displeasure of investors with economic and political developments. They express displeasure by selling when too many jobs have been created because what is regarded as excessive job creation makes investors fear a return to inflation. The consequence when bond markets fall is that interest rates are pushed up, which in turn has the effect of slowing economic growth, thereby helping ensure that future job creation will also be stalled. Indeed, stock and bond markets hold their own quasi-referenda on every trading day, and government is far more finely tuned to the results of these exercises than to the citizen electorate.

When I conducted a television interview with Robert Reich in Boston in the mid-1980s, he told me that many of the best and brightest of his students in economics at Harvard were not going into manufacturing but into "money." Small wonder that other industries are reconfiguring to exemplify the stock market Zeitgeist.

If multinational corporations have come fully into their own in our era, this is not because the megacorps of several decades ago have simply become larger and more powerful, although in many instances this has been the case. There has been a revolution over the past decade in the ranks of the capitalist class, a revolution centred in the banks and the financial services sector. Globalization's leading edge has been the revolution in the financial sector. Indeed, to a very considerable extent, globalization is the movement toward liberalization of financial services writ large. To see who ranks where in the global capitalist class, we have to understand how "finance capital" has achieved supremacy over "industrial capital."

Following the collapse of the system of fixed exchange rates in the mid-1970s—fixed exchange rates had been established following the Second World War—the advanced countries have liberalized their capital markets. This crucial development, propelled by new technology in conjunction with the drive for government deregulation, has underlain an important change in the nature of contemporary capitalism. Its consequence has been a vast increase in the power of financial markets, banks and other financial services corporations. We have been witnessing a shift that has given financial corporations and those at their helm an unprecedented strategic power within the global economy, more than ever before in the history of capitalism. What has given bankers, fund managers and currency speculators their increased influence is the newfound mobility of capital. In the early post-war decades, countries regulated the amount of capital that individuals and corporations could move in or out of their territories. As recently as the mid-1980s, nations like France still retained significant controls on the movement of capital. Until 1997, Israel maintained capital controls, but the decision to dismantle them led to a bitter struggle within the cabinet and to the resignation of the Israeli minister of finance.

Most people think of deregulation in relation to airlines or telephone services, but the deregulation of capital markets is far more significant. Now that most advanced states have removed the important forms of capital controls, they have lost the ability to oversee the capital accumulated within their borders. Capital shifts in and out of countries as investors choose, and this has a considerable effect on the way governments set their policy. The power to transfer capital at will from country to country directly disadvantages wage and salary earners, exacerbating the leverage of the whole of the capitalist class vis-à-vis its employees. Manufacturers can threaten to relocate production offshore to places with conveniently lower wages and less stringent environmental regulation, and many actually do move their operations. This option effectively tips the balance in the relationship between capital and labour in favour of capital.

Moreover, the newfound free movement of capital has also altered the balance of power within the capitalist class. In the post-war decades, the great manufacturers, automakers and steel producers were at the apex. Ford's Rouge River plant near Detroit was the symbol of American industrial might. Countries were ranked as economic powers according to their capacity to produce steel. Ford and General Motors and other giant manufacturers have not become powerless today, but microelectronic technology permits new giants like Microsoft to play a role in contemporary capitalism not unlike that of the great automakers half a century ago, or the giant railways in the late nineteenth century. But the most significant shift within capitalism benefits those who control highly mobile pools of capital—the banks and other financial institutions, the bond market and mutual funds. Indicative of the change is that governments and central bankers have made inflation the main target of economic policy. The trade-off in this stance is clear: the price of very low inflation has been slower economic growth. Investors prize low inflation, which improves their rate of return. Manufacturers, on the other hand, pay a price in lost sales due to slower growth.

Like all significant shifts in power, this one has forced changes in state regulation. As we have seen, deregulation to facilitate capital mobility has been encouraged to place finance capital at an advantage over industrial capital. But it is a serious error to imagine that state authority has simply diminished. Those who control capital have succeeded in pressing for a global system of regulation by governments that reflects their interests, just as the post-war regulatory system reflected the interests of the big manufacturers.

The new system of regulation, while decreasing the authority of nation-states, has established formidable protection for the international rights of capital. Giving legal legitimacy to the right to move assets from one part of the world to another, while minimizing opportunities for state intervention, have been the objectives of the so-called regional free trade agreements and the World Trade Organization. Much more important than their lowering of trade barriers has been the ability of NAFTA, the European Union and the WTO to assure capital the right to mobility without penalty. NAFTA and the EU explicitly limit the rights of member nations to pursue state-supported industrial strategies, strategies that involve subsidies or tax breaks to benefit domestically owned firms. The rules enshrined in NAFTA, the EU, the WTO and the future MAI, once they are accepted by member states, are no less than constitutional guarantees of the freedom and supreme rights of capital.

One of the key jobs of the WTO is to protect intellectual property globally, to insist that member countries play by the rules enshrined in international copyright law. While the efficacy of an old set of rules applying to the rights of citizens has been sharply reduced, a potent new set has been elaborated. The weakened rules are those on which the power of the nation-state was based. Significantly, these rules, embodied in national constitutions, include the rights of citizens, which are entrenched in such instruments as the Canadian Charter of Rights and Freedoms, and the Bill of Rights in the U.S. Constitution.

The abolition of exchange controls by the newly elected Thatcher government in Britain in 1979 and a similar move by Japan the following year opened the door to the development of today's integrated global financial services sector. The dismantling of exchange controls in Britain, Japan and other countries gave corporations immense scope to seek investment capital outside the countries where they were based. In addition, new information technologies have eroded legal and physical barriers between economic sectors and countries. As cross-border financial transactions have proliferated, the formerly discrete sectors within the financial services industry have become intertwined: banks and non-banks such as securities houses now compete for the same business. In the past, important structural differences from country to country determined the way banks and other financial institutions functioned.

In the United States, for instance, the banking business has been legally separated from the securities business (the partition was legislated by the Glass-Steagall Act of 1933).[6] The separation of banking and securities occurred in the early 1930s, when many banks failed during the Great Depression. The idea was to ensure that bank deposits were not subject to the same risks as those existing as a matter of course in the securities market. By contrast, some other advanced countries—Germany is a noteworthy case—have universal banking systems permitting banks to operate in all the areas of the financial services business, including underwriting, functioning as members of securities exchanges and dealing directly on stock exchanges.

In the United Kingdom, France, Italy and Spain, financial institutions now normally take the form of large groups within which all financial services—banking, securities, leasing—are available, with each of these activities offered by a separate subsidiary.[7] In the United States, though the legal separation between banking and securities remains intact, there has been a growing practical fusion of the two, so that firms on either side of this legal divide can offer products that are highly similar. Moreover, American banks are now able to venture much further into the securities field than in the past. Japan has also allowed banks and securities houses to move into each other's main areas of business.[8] Since

the beginning of the 1980s, the separation of Canada's financial industry into four separate realms—banks, trust and loan companies, life
assurance companies and securities dealers—has been breaking down.
For instance, in June 1987, new legislation made it possible for feder-
ally chartered financial institutions to acquire ownership of securities
firms.[9] Today, Canadian trust, loan and insurance companies can be
owned by other financial institutions, and trust, loan and insurance companies are allowed to engage in consumer lending.

As advanced countries shift toward more similar universal financial
market systems, the differences in the ways investment capital is generated for productive enterprises have tended to erode in favour of a more
integrated model. Still, the historical dissimilarities mattered, and they
have left a considerable imprint on the way the financial sector operates
from country to country.

For small companies in virtually all advanced countries, banks are
the dominant source of capital. The case of medium-size firms is more
mixed, with a diversity of capital-raising arrangements, although banks
are a key source of funds for the financing of new corporate projects.[10]
In all advanced countries, the most important source of capital for large
companies is the retained earnings of the firms themselves. (A firm's net
income is divided into two streams—retained earnings, which are re-
invested in the company, and dividends, which are paid out to shareholders.) To a very great extent, therefore, companies are their own
banks. Beyond that, considerable variations exist from country to country. In Britain, stock markets have played a much more important role
in raising capital for firms than in Japan and Germany, because of the
particular history of industrialization in Britain compared with Japan
and Germany.

British industrialization proceeded slowly over many decades from its
early beginnings in the eighteenth century. By about 1830, Britain had
emerged as the world's first industrial country. Initial industrialization,
particularly in the crucial cotton industry, required little capital, so
family savings and retained earnings largely sufficed. In the nineteenth
century, as regional banks were established in Britain, there was some

lending to industrial firms, but mostly on a short-term basis. Toward the end of the nineteenth century, when a new industrial revolution had spawned industries such as steel, chemicals and electronics, which required much higher levels of capital investment, British firms resorted to selling equity and raising capital on stock markets.[11]

In Germany and Japan, industrialization began much later and progressed more rapidly. In Germany, where initial industrialization was concentrated in sectors such as steel, capital requirements were large from the start, so banks geared to the requirements of industry were established.[12] In both countries, banks rather than stock markets became the principal source of external finance for companies, and a tight relationship grew between banks and the non-financial firms relying on them for capital. A majority of the shares of Japanese and German companies is in the hands of either the individual companies themselves or banks and insurance companies that have a long-term relationship with them.[13] Most Japanese and German firms maintain a close link with one or a few banks, which in Japan are known as "main banks" and in Germany as *hausbanks*. As a consequence, it is quite normal for German or Japanese banks to have a large equity share in manufacturing companies and, through directors appointed to their boards, to have a significant say in their management.

The German case reveals how these connections between banks and industry have worked. German banking is dominated by three enormous private commercial banks—all members of the exclusive club of only fourteen banks in the world ranked AAA by Standard and Poor's, the American credit-rating agency. They are the Deutsche Bank, the Dresdner Bank and Commerzbank.[14] In the late 1970s, a West German government commission, the Gessler Commission, investigated the ties between the Big Three banks and major manufacturing firms, shedding light on the considerable power of the banks in key industrial sectors. In the mid-1980s, the power of the Big Three banks was revealed in their equity holdings in major non-financial companies. In 1986, Deutsche Bank's direct equity ownership in such firms included a 35 percent interest in Phillip Holzmann (construction); over 25 percent of

Daimler-Benz (automobiles); over 25 percent of Hapag-Lloyd (shipping); over 25 percent of Karstadt (department store chain); 18 percent of Horten (department stores); and 6 percent of Alliance (insurance). At the same time, the Dresdner Bank had a direct equity ownership in nonfinancial firms, including 25 percent or more of Hapag-Lloyd; Flender Werft (shipbuilding); Gold-Pfeil (leather); Dortmunder-Union (brewing); and Heidelberg Zement (cement). Similarly, Commerzbank's direct equity holdings in 1986 included more than 25 percent of Karstadt and substantial holdings in Sachs (ball bearings) and Hannoversche Papierfabriken (paper).[15]

In addition to these direct holdings, the Big Three banks have very significant additional influence through the medium of holding companies. The consequence of this direct and indirect ownership is that the banks are able to appoint members to the supervisory boards of a large number of manufacturing companies. (The supervisory boards of German companies hire and fire the company's top managers and make the decisions for major financial initiatives.) About four hundred large German firms had representatives of banks (not just the Big Three) sitting on their supervisory boards in the early 1990s. This enormous financial influence in the manufacturing sector has brought a high degree of financial security and stability to German firms for long-term planning, and it has protected them from the hostile takeovers so common in the English-speaking world.

In sharp contrast to the close linkages between banks and industry, so important in Germany and Japan, is the practice in the United States, the United Kingdom and Canada where relationships between banks and firms in other sectors are much less continuous and direct. In the United States, the system of local banking has often promoted relationships between banks and industry (although not equity bank holdings in industrial enterprises), but in Canada and Britain, the tradition has been for a much more distant relationship. Canadian and British banks have kept their eye on the short-term return on the capital they lend. Historically, Canada's major domestically owned banks have been eager to lend capital to foreign-owned (usually American) firms, often in preference to making loans to smaller, Canadian-owned firms. The effect, as vividly illustrated in this 1972 report in *Fortune* magazine, has been to reduce Canadian manufacturing and to deprive Canadians of potential jobs:

> When Kimberly-Clark built a US$23 million paper mill in Hunts-ville, Ontario, to serve the Canadian market, it purchased enough equipment in the U.S. to supply 51-man years of employment. Had Kimberly-Clark not built the mill, a Canadian competitor would have captured the market and bought less equipment in the U.S. (resulting in only 16 man-years of employment). As for the balance of payments, the investment resulted in no net outflow of capital, and as soon as Kimberly-Clark pays off a Canadian bank loan, the subsidiary expects to pay US$2.8 million a year in dividends to the parent company in the U.S.[16]

Similarly, British banks have had a short-term, play-it-safe profit horizon, which has been detrimental to domestic industry. Four major banks—Barclays, Lloyds, Midland and National Westminster (Nat-West)—dominate British banking. The Big Four operate a network of branches in every part of the country (just as Canadian banks do), thus serving businesses by making and receiving payments throughout the U.K. Unlike their German counterparts with their long-term links to non-financial businesses, British banks, according to Collin Randle-some, a scholar in European management techniques, customarily "borrow short and lend short."[17] The big British banks have been reproached for having no real commitment to the well-being of British industry, in contrast to their German and Japanese counterparts, and have often been held responsible for the sharp decline in British manu-facturing. Unlike Germany and Japan, both countries with formidable export surpluses in manufacturing, Britain, once the world's greatest industrial power, has seen its industries shrink in recent decades, so that the country now has a perennial deficit in its manufacturing trade.

If the major British banks, with their City of London outlook (like that of Bay Street or Wall Street), have seen the whole world as their oyster, to the detriment of industrial Britain, this ethos was strongly reinforced when Thatcher's Conservatives came to power in 1979. The anti-inflationary monetarist policies of the Tories struck a body blow against British manufacturing. The index of industrial production plunged from 107.1 in 1979 to 96.6 in 1981, as two million jobs were lost. One widely reported quip by a delegate to a business conference was that "Mrs Thatcher prefers people who make money to people who make things."[18] Manufacturing output did not exceed its 1979 level until 1987, and it was not until 1989 that fixed investment in manufacturing reached its pre-1979 level in real terms.[19] Above all, the Thatcher revolution worked to the advantage of the City of London, the great beneficiaries being bankers and brokers.

One effect of the globalization of financial markets was that the flow of capital between countries vastly exceeded the trade in commodities. Capital flow increased to the extent that the ability of central banks to intervene to counter currency speculation was seriously compromised. In addition to undermining the decision-making scope of national governments, the interlinked global financial market greatly reinforced the power of capital to move from anywhere to anywhere at a moment's notice, which gives it the whip hand in its dealings with labour.

So far, I have stressed how the deregulation of capital markets has transformed the financial services industry, the movement of capital and the power of capital over labour, and that the technological revolution has played an indispensable role in these developments. In the globalized financial setting of the 1990s, computer technology has also improved opportunities for certain popular investment instruments. Such is the case with derivatives.

Over the past decade, investment in derivatives has expanded tremendously (derivatives are financial products deriving their value from other financial instruments). By purchasing derivatives, investors seek to hedge against risks caused by fluctuations in currency exchange rates, interest rates and commodity prices as well as to protect themselves against portfolio risks. Derivatives are also used as speculative investments that allow investors to "bet" the market to seek a higher profit than would usually be available, particularly when interest rates are low.[20] Futures contracts are a common form of derivative, through which an investor speculates on the price of a particular commodity or on the exchange rate of a foreign currency on a given date to come. Similarly, investors can purchase stock options, another type of derivative, through which they speculatively agree to buy a stock at a particular price on a set date in the future. Banks have engaged in so-called forward transactions, yet another kind of derivative, through which the bank agrees to allow an importer to pay for a purchase at a known rate of exchange in advance of the receipt of the order. And banks have also done swaps with other banks, exchanging, for example, dollars for yen, in advance of the time a customer needs the foreign currency to complete a deal. Through swaps, the banks acquire the foreign currency at a rate somewhat better than the one they offer their customers.[21]

Playing with derivatives can be a very high-stakes gamble. Investments are regularly made on margin, which means that investors only put up a small fraction of funds at the outset. If they win, they can make large amounts on a small sum of initial capital. But if they lose, they have to cover the positions they have staked out in the futures contract, stock option, forward transaction or swap. Losses can be so huge that they drag down major institutions. The misuse of derivatives played a central part in bankrupting Orange County, California, in 1994 and in breaking Britain's Baring Bank in 1995, as a consequence of the speculative activities of Nicholas Leeson, a junior trader based in the bank's Singapore branch.

If computers have played an important part in the huge expansion of the market for derivatives, they have generally caused the investment process to acquire new layers of abstraction, making it ever more remote from the production of goods and services. Investors, who are distant from productive enterprises, can move in and out of participation in their financing in a matter of minutes or hours. Partly as a consequence of such abstraction, there has arisen to a greater extent than ever before in history a confusion between the "money economy" and the "real economy." The forms taken by the "money economy" have proliferated in wondrous ways over the past fifteen years, whether through the creation of new types of investments, such as derivatives, or through new forms of credit, encountered in daily life in new types of credit cards. Such creations result from the marriage of new technology and a bright idea of someone who has figured out a potential niche, big or small, that the new technology has made possible.

One consequence of the development of computers and ever more elaborate software is to make possible the investment of funds for very short periods of time. An investment can now be made for a few hours, or even mere minutes. The telescoping of turnover times for transactions allows capital to be deployed and redeployed in ever-briefer cycles, giving ingenious entrepreneurs opportunities to make fortunes. New forms of credit play havoc with calculations of the amount of money in circulation because new forms of credit actually create new kinds of money. Central bankers must now worry about such fluidity when they decide how to adjust interest rates and control the money supply. On the happier side, there are doubtless Ph.D.s and possibly the odd Nobel prize awaiting those who come up with snappy definitions of the new forms of money that are created as a consequence of the establishment of new forms of credit.

Meanwhile, back in the real economy . . . people need and want food, clothing, housing, transportation, health care, books, movies, videos, restaurants and vacation destinations. None of the items on such a list are produced in any way, shape or form by the new kinds of money, credit or investments that have proliferated in recent years. The old problem of how to ensure that people can get what they need and want has not been affected by financial-technological wizardry. Some clever people have merely figured out how to amass some real wealth for themselves from the air—or cyberspace. And some of these alchemists have even joined the ranks of the super-rich.

One of the cleverest players of the new techno-financial games is Joseph Lewis, the British financier who reaps megaprofits by playing foreign exchange markets. Born in the East End of London, Lewis started out working in his father's profitable catering business. He then sold luxury goods to Japanese tourists and figured out that the real money was to be made not in the goods they bought but by profiting from selling foreign exchange to travellers for their trips abroad. In the late 1970s, Lewis left Britain for what is fashionably called "tax exile" in the Bahamas, where he mastered computerized foreign exchange dealing. He purchased a mansion worth £15 million (us$24 million) on exclusive Lyford Cay. Its computerized dealing room is the hub of his empire in a tax-free paradise. Here he plays the world's currency markets with a deft touch, often pacing the floor at 4 A.M., checking the computer screens.

In the *Sunday Times* Rich List for 1997, Joseph Lewis was ranked the wealthiest Briton, worth £3 billion (nearly us$5 billion). A Dutch shipyard is currently building a £40-million (us$6.5-million), 250-foot yacht for him.[22] Trumpeted in the *Times* Rich List as the new kind of superrich person who did not inherit his wealth from an old moneyed family, Lewis personifies the new techno-wizard billionaire. He has invented no useful product that makes life better for anyone. He has developed no service that enhances human well-being or enjoyment. He doesn't sing, dance or play football to delight millions. His sole qualification for helping himself to real wealth created by others is a knack for playing foreign exchange markets. Not bad, when you don't even have to pay taxes to the societies from which you extract the wealth.

But the newly made fortunes of financiers like Joseph Lewis, generated by deregulation, new technology and a global financial market, have also opened a door for some of the old and the established to cash in on the novel opportunities presented by a world awash in money.

In the year 1297, Francesco Grimaldi, an ambitious Italian nobleman, requested hospitality at the gates of the fortress of Monaco, a huge rocky outcropping jutting into the Mediterranean Sea on the French coastline, near the Italian border. Foolishly, the guard opened the gates, whereupon Grimaldi and his comrades-in-arms stormed inside and seized control. In this unlikely way, the Grimaldi family, forebears of the present Prince Rainier III, came to power. For seven centuries, through ups and downs, the Grimaldis have clung to their perch on the rock of

Monaco, and they have shown themselves adaptable to changing times. Holding on to power meant playing adept diplomatic games with Italian states, the pope, the Holy Roman Empire and the French monarchy. In the mid-nineteenth century, when the regime was short of cash, the Grimaldis hit on the idea of opening a casino at Monte Carlo, a move that drew the wealthy to the tiny Mediterranean enclave and made Monaco flush once again. Following slow times in the 1930s, Monaco profited hugely from the German Nazi and Italian Fascist wartime occupation of France. The casino drew Nazi and Fascist bigwigs in droves during the war, and Nazi money was invested in banks and real estate projects in Monaco.[23]

Today, the Grimaldis are making another adjustment—this time to the capitalism at the dawn of the twenty-first century. As capitalism has been going global, the tiny principality of Monaco—home of Western Europe's most undemocratic regime, where a monarchy exercises real power and an elected assembly has little—is on the cutting edge. The Monaco micro-state, which levies no income tax, attracts rich people. Tax avoidance and wealth have always been soulmates—for the rich as a whole, the goal has been to reduce their personal and corporate taxes. And for some of the truly privileged, that goal is achieved by relocating to a state that operates as a tax haven.

The world's micro-states, like Monaco, or other locales that serve as tax shelters such as Guernsey, Jersey, the Isle of Man and the Cayman Islands, have been hurled into financial importance by the vagaries of history. But it is no accident that various venues use their leading "resource"—a lack of substantial population—to entice big spenders by providing a tax haven. Even states that are not micro but merely small, like Luxembourg, now specialize in offering tax havens to rich individuals and corporations from larger countries. The most common practice among wealthy Germans who want to avoid taxation is to ship their money across the border to tax-free accounts in neighbouring Luxembourg.[24] Tax evasion by rich Germans has become a major problem for government tax collectors.

In Canada, the super-rich shelter tens of millions of dollars from

Revenue Canada in places like the Cayman Islands. The law requires the Canadian beneficiaries of foreign trusts to pay Canadian taxes, but the rich have found a way around that. Wealthy Canadians can direct millions of dollars to an entity in the Caymans that is like a trust but is not exactly a trust: a letter of intent is sent to the trustees in the Caymans stipulating whom a fund is to benefit. Strictly speaking, however, the beneficiaries have no legal, enforceable claim, which means they aren't obliged to pay Canadian tax. An investment instrument that behaves like a trust but technically is not one is thus custom-made for tax evasion.

Tax havens are an extreme form of the wealthy using their advantageous position to avoid sharing social responsibility by paying taxes at a level commensurate with their wealth. If any national government levies taxes that the rich regard as too high, they can simply relocate to a tax haven. Such an option keeps taxes generally low for the wealthy everywhere else in the world.

The tax flight of the rich has been intimately connected to the globalization of the economy. As markets and capital movements have become worldwide, the ability of the state to tax the rich has declined significantly. While the rich have always rationalized that they deserve tax advantages because they are the source of productive investments, and on the unstated grounds that they are the source of campaign funds for political parties, globalization has added a new and compelling argument for the skimpy taxation of the wealthy. The rich, like Joseph Lewis, are now in a position to pick up their marbles and go elsewhere if they don't like the taxes they pay. For both individuals and corporations, taking their marbles elsewhere has resulted in some very obscure places rising to global financial prominence. With a population of only thirty thousand, the Cayman Islands has become the fifth-largest source of bank loans in the world.[25]

New technology and deregulation have also facilitated the development of nebulous financial realms beyond state control or even awareness. One example is the so-called Eurodollar market, which originated as a consequence of the pre-eminent post-war position of the United States in the global economy and American government spending abroad. At the end of the Second World War, half of the goods and services in the world were produced in the United States. The Bretton Woods global economic system (designed by the U.S. and its allies at a conference at Bretton Woods, New Hampshire, in the summer of 1944) revived international commerce by creating the means to pump American dollars into Europe and Japan. After the war, Washington spent billions helping rebuild Europe under the Marshall Plan and billions more on the establishment of American military bases around the world, the largest concentration being in Western Europe. In addition, artificially low exchange rates were set for the West German deutschmark and the Japanese yen against the U.S. dollar, and this contributed to perennial trade surpluses for the Germans and the Japanese against the United States.

Because the U.S. was so dominant economically, with the dollar as the world's reserve currency as established at Bretton Woods, America's merchandise trade and current account (balance-of-payments) deficits were allowed to pile up year after year (as they still do). Taken together, foreign aid, military spending and ongoing U.S. trade deficits sent billions of dollars abroad. To deal with the rising American current account deficit, the Kennedy administration imposed an interest equalization tax in 1963. Its purpose was to discourage excessive borrowing of dollars by foreigners by making them pay more for their dollars than domestic borrowers had to pay.[26]

As the financial services analyst Martin Mayer points out in his book *The Bankers*, the consequence was that soon "there was a large and busy 'Eurodollar' market where lenders and borrowers did business at interest rates higher than those where the dollar made its home."[27] In the Eurodollar market, business is carried on by parties not necessarily connected to the U.S. or American companies. In other words, a very substantial amount of American currency is now in circulation outside the U.S. and well beyond the regulatory authority of the American government or the Federal Reserve System, the U.S. central bank. An odd feature of the Eurodollar market is that it allows huge sums of U.S. dollars to be borrowed by Americans at home, with the interest rate benchmark being the London Interbank Offered Rate (Libor) rather than the domestic U.S. prime rate. By borrowing in the Eurodollar market, American companies are able to evade the efforts of the Fed to control the size of the U.S. money supply. In effect, these companies do an end run around the Fed and increase the available money supply when that suits them. In 1969, the Eurodollar market totalled us$15 billion, then thought to be a large amount of unregulated money. Now that sum looks tiny. In 1994, the Eurodollar contract, which gives its purchaser an obligation to borrow us$1 million at the Libor rate in London in three months (and the seller the obligation to sell), was more heavily traded than any other financial instrument in the world. Its 105 million contracts, traded over the period of a year, had a notional value of us$105 quadrillion.[28]

Beyond the Eurodollar market, there are other instances of U.S. dollars circulating outside the ambit of American authorities. Panama and Liberia have long used U.S. dollars as their local currencies. And in Russia and other republics of the former Soviet Union, people and companies have hoarded many billions of U.S. dollars. (Ironically, this hoarding of U.S. dollars by Russians is the economic equivalent of a free loan by these Russians to the United States.) In cases like these where local currencies are not trusted, U.S. dollars are also used extensively in domestic transactions.

And since a significant sector of capitalism exists outside the law, much American money is employed in criminal activities, particularly drug smuggling and illegal arms transactions. Efforts by U.S. authorities to limit such use of dollars by requiring banks to report deposits or withdrawals of more than $3,000 are easily circumvented. Martin Mayer points out that "mules can easily be hired to take out one dollar less than the reporting total and spirit the money out to, say, St. Martin in the Caribbean, where there is a casino that uses and thus can launder a lot of cash."[29]

If criminals prefer cash and look for their banking facilities in places where few questions are asked, at the other end of the spectrum is a bank whose capital is raised entirely from taxpayers and whose loans go mainly to governments. The World Bank has been around for over half a century. Its ostensible goal is to promote long-term economic development, particularly in the Third World.

The International Bank for Reconstruction and Development—the World Bank's formal name—was a creation of the Bretton Woods international economic system. The World Bank, which came into existence in December 1945, had a role that was to be distinct from the International Monetary Fund, the other financial organization planned at Bretton Woods. The principal task of the IMF was to lend money to states experiencing short- to middle-term balance-of-payments problems. For its part, the World Bank was in the business of long-term economic development. The idea was that the World Bank's loans were to help countries move to a higher stage of economic development, which it was expected would improve the well-being of the people of poor countries.

Theory and practice have turned out to be very different, however. From its headquarters in Washington and under the direction of its president—every president of the World Bank has been an American—the World Bank has dispensed much more than loans to the Third World. It has promulgated an intensely ideological view of how Asian, African and Latin American nations ought to behave if they are to achieve economic development. To an overwhelming extent, loans have been made to countries to assist them in making the structural changes so that a private enterprise economy can thrive. World Bank loans have been a tool through which the rich nations pry open the economies of poor nations for their own benefit.

Throughout its history, the World Bank has shown a very strong inclination to favour capital-intensive megaprojects that have frequently turned out to be technologically inappropriate for the countries receiving loans. Far too often the people in the affected areas have been completely ignored when decisions are made to undertake projects drastically affecting their way of life. In some cases the construction of huge dams—dams have been a magnet for World Bank loans—has meant that tens of thousands of people living in an area about to be flooded as a consequence of the dam have not been told what is to happen until the last possible moment. In a 1994 internal report for the World Bank, it was revealed that between 1986 and 1993 the bank had backed close to two hundred projects whose consequence was to force people to leave their homes and property. As the California-based author Catherine Caufield put it in her recent book on the World Bank, "When they are completed, these projects—dams, roads, pipelines, canals, and urban renewal—will have dislocated 2.5 million people."[30]

Caufield paints a damning picture of the World Bank as an institution permitting well-heeled bureaucrats to impose their preconceptions on countries about whose societies they know little. The vast sums lent over the past half century have bolstered the elites in the countries affected, while the mass of the population has often suffered. Caufield concludes that the World Bank, financed as it is by taxes mostly raised in the advanced countries, has largely been "a matter of poor people in rich countries giving money to rich people in poor countries."[31]

It would be wrong to suggest that bankers and other financiers run contemporary capitalism all by themselves. The great industrialists retain immense power. There is no doubt, however, that globalization and deregulation have given financial capital, as opposed to industrial capital, new leverage that is being used with telling effect vis-à-vis the state, other capitalists and wage and salary earners. To grasp just how the financial capitalists wield power against these others, it is necessary to see the extent to which this is the age of money, as I claimed at the beginning of this chapter. More precisely, it is the age of the money lender.

It is banks and bondholders whose concerns have been reflected in the policies of virtually all the governments in the advanced countries. As William Greider notes, "The values of finance capital have won precedence over all others."[32] For bankers and bondholders, as we have seen, the overriding issue is inflation. Avoiding its resumption has become the leading goal of governments and central bankers. The war against inflation has dominated economic life in North America and Europe since the victory of the monetarists over the Keynesians in the early 1980s. The result has been an international economy whose chief characteristics are slow growth and high real interest rates. For money lenders, the

1970s was a terrible decade—the era of stagflation, when high inflation coexisted with a low rate of economic growth. During the period of stagflation, soaring inflation cut into the profit margins of bankers and the bond market, reducing real interest rates to very low levels. At times, real interest rates even became negative—the ultimate nightmare of lenders. (The real interest rate is calculated by subtracting the rate of inflation from the nominal rate of interest. If, for instance, inflation is running at an annual rate of 12 percent—a realistic rate for much of the 1970s—and the nominal interest rate is 10 percent, this results in a real interest rate that is negative—minus 2 percent.)

What ended the woeful era of runaway inflation in the 1970s, which was so devastating for money lenders, were the highly restrictive monetary policies of Paul C. Volcker, chairman of the U.S. Federal Reserve Board in the U.S. and similar policies instituted by the Thatcher government in Britain. The monetarist takeover of policy making at the beginning of the Thatcher–Reagan era broke the back of inflation and put the bond market and the bankers at the controls. Ever since then, central banks have sided with the bond market by making the achievement of zero inflation the highest priority, despite the severely negative consequences this has had for economic growth and employment. Even when there has been virtually no sign of a resumption of inflation, central banks have ceded to the bond market wide authority in the setting of interest rates, thus ensuring a very high rate of return for bondholders. Under this regime, the real return on bonds—which includes the appreciating market value of the bonds in addition to real interest rates—has been extremely high in the 1990s compared with other periods in the twentieth century. For instance, the real profit on holding American bonds has averaged 8.2 percent in the 1990s, compared with 6.7 percent in the 1980s. This compares with an average rate of return for the whole of the twentieth century on long-term U.S. bonds of merely 1.6 percent. Only in the 1920s, a previous era of restrictive monetary policies, was the real return on U.S. bonds higher, at 8.8 percent.[33]

In Canada, real interest rates have also been extremely high in the

1980s and 1990s in comparison with earlier historical periods. During the 1960s, the real interest rate in Canada averaged 3.2 percent, while in the 1970s, during the era of stagflation, it dropped to 1.2 percent. In the 1980s, average real interest rates in Canada shot up to 6.6 percent, and during the period of the Bank of Canada's extreme tightening of monetary policy, from 1990 to 1992, they reached an astronomical 8 percent.[34] In Britain, France and Italy, there has also been a very high real return for bondholders.

High real interest rates have tremendously worsened the conditions under which the governments in the advanced countries must wage their battle against deficits and accumulated public sector debts. Not only have governments had to pay crippling amounts in interest to those financing their debts, but because high interest rates have restricted economic growth, governments have been denied the additional tax revenues that would have been a consequence of an expanding economy. Moreover, slow growth, which has kept unemployment and underemployment high in most countries, has also saddled the state with an extremely high bill for social assistance and unemployment insurance.

For businesses producing goods and services, high real interest rates have also had negative effects. The cost of borrowing money has been exorbitant, and in the face of slow economic growth, which is in part a consequence of high interest rates, the opportunity to make productive investments has been seriously diminished. Why put money into long-term productive investments when the short-term returns on bonds and the speculative returns on stock market investments have been so attractive? The economic regime of the post-war decades was much more favourable to industrialists than the regime that began with the Volcker–Thatcher revolution of 1979–80.

Even when interest rates came down in the late 1990s, the returns to bondholders remained very attractive. In Canada, in the autumn of 1997, the real rate of interest for the lowest-priced loans was running at close to 4 percent, much lower than the punitive rates of the early 1990s, but still no bargain compared with earlier periods in the twentieth century.

In the United States at the same time, the real rate of interest for the lowest-priced loans ran at about 6 percent. Moreover, the Bank of Canada and the U.S. Fed stood at the ready, poised to raise interest rates at the slightest hint of a resumption of inflation.

Throughout the industrialized world, the biggest losers as a consequence of the bondholders' regime have been wage and salary earners. The antagonism between the interests of the bond market and those of wage and salary earners can be seen in the way the bond market falls in response to government reports that announce that a large number of jobs have been created. And as we have seen, when the bond market falls, interest rates are automatically pushed up. This has the direct effect of slowing economic growth, which reduces the potential for future job creation. Government and central bank policies that support the zero inflation and high real interest rate aspirations of the bond market necessarily negatively affect wage and salary earners.

In the globalized capitalism at the dawn of the new millennium, the financial sector has become so powerful that it requires its own government. On the model of the German Bundesbank, central banks, now largely insulated from the interference of elected governments, see their special mandate as safeguarding the holdings of the world's individual creditors. To protect bankers and bondholders, central bankers are ever watchful for any hint of the resumption of inflation. Better a slow-growth economy in which money retains its value than one with higher growth and higher inflation, they believe.

The war against inflation has been class politics with a vengeance. Through their restrictive monetary policies, central banks have ensured high real interest rates, exactly what bankers and bondholders most desire. They have also ensured the perpetuation of high unemployment and underemployment, and with that they have prevented wage and salary earners from gaining any effective leverage to force a redistribution of income and social power in their favour. In an incisive column in the *New York Times*, James K. Galbraith, an economist at the Johnson School of Public Affairs at the University of Texas, identified the priorities of the current chairman of the Federal Reserve Board, Alan

Greenspan, when it raised U.S. interest rates by a quarter of a percent in March 1997. Galbraith wrote:

> The only risks Mr. Greenspan sees are these: First, a continued tight labour market. Second, the rising minimum wage later this year. And third, the possibility that "larger increases in fringe benefits could put upward pressure on overall compensation."
>
> The gentleman could not have been more clear. He is not concerned about inflation. He is concerned about the possibility, remote and uncertain though it is, that the American worker might start to demand, and receive, a slightly bigger share of the economic growth than has occurred in the past seven years.[35]

Bankers and other financiers have not had a smooth ride over the past quarter century. While their power within the system has been rising, their fortunes have followed a chaotic course. When we look back over the past twenty-five years, what is clear is that the world has been moving from one kind of speculative or "bubble" economy to another.

In the 1970s, it was the petroleum economy. Then, the wisdom of the day was that the price of oil and natural gas would go on rising to dizzying heights and that no amount of investment, private or public, in petroleum megaprojects could be too much. But in the early 1980s, oil prices did what they were not supposed to do—they crashed. Instead of advancing to US$60 a barrel as petro-bugs had anticipated, the price of oil slumped to the range of US$10 a barrel, where it stayed for years. The legacy, as with the bursting of any bubble economy, was a proliferation of bankruptcies and a spate of bad debts on the books of major financial institutions.

The next bubble economy was the product of the seething real estate market of the 1980s. Those in the know put out the word that the age of the great cities was at hand and that investments in real estate were the new road to riches. The property bubble economy was global in scope, with its epicentre in Tokyo. In the most desirable commercial districts of Tokyo, land values quadrupled from the mid-1980s to the peak in 1990. Then came the crash in 1991, when those same desirable properties lost 80 percent of their value, leaving Japanese banks mired in a sea of bad debts. But Tokyo was only the most extreme case. New York, London, Paris and Toronto all had their own versions of the same phenomenon. For Canadians, the symbol of those years of real estate excess were the Reichmanns, whose Olympia & York seemed destined in the mid-1980s to stride from triumph to triumph. In France in 1987, I met one of the principal architects of the Reichmanns' most ambitious venture, the Canary Wharf project in London's East End. He was full of optimism about the mammoth scheme, which was to reclaim a huge area of the depressed London docklands and transform it into a new city within the city featuring corporate offices, shopping facilities and residences. The multibillion-dollar venture was premised on property values continuing to soar and on the willingness, as a direct consequence of this, of financial institutions based in the City of London to acquire new offices and corporate headquarters in Canary Wharf. When the land bubble burst, however, and property values fell, the house of cards came crashing down. For Canadian banks, it was a megadisaster. When Olympia & York filed for bankruptcy protection, the banks were left with such a huge debt that there was talk for a time that one major Canadian bank could be close to failure.

In the United States, the real estate boom and subsequent bust left behind the catastrophic collapse of the savings and loan (S&L) industry in the late 1980s and early 1990s. (S&Ls were created to finance building.) When the land bust came, construction projects in the great American cities ground to a halt. The vastly overextended S&Ls were deluged by tens of thousands of panic-stricken people who often tussled with police in their hopeless efforts to get money out of their savings accounts. The government bailout of the S&Ls ended up costing American taxpayers at least $300 billion.[36]

The real estate explosion attracted millions of ordinary people in the advanced countries who saw rising property values as their access to what one Toronto man described to me as his "own pile." I can recall middle-class Torontonians standing in front of their houses in the late

1980s fondly calculating how much money their houses had made for them that week. Those were the days when Toronto real estate promoters liked to describe their city as Manhattan North.

In all bubble economies, plenty of people become so caught up in the frenzied upward trend that they convince themselves it will go on forever, that unlike all the previous bubble economies over the past 250 years this one will never burst. And many people, in Toronto and other places throughout the industrialized world, mortgaged themselves to the hilt and bought at the very peak of the market at the end of the 1980s, only to take the personal plunge when real estate prices fell. For many such people, who did not have the celebrity of the Reichmanns, financial ruin was the consequence.

The 1990s' version of the bubble economy has been the fantastic rise in prices on the stock and bond markets. There is a very clear connection between the burst bubble of the 1980s and its successor in the 1990s. As William Greider has argued, the U.S. Federal Reserve Board for several years in the early 1990s expanded the availability of credit beyond the capacity of the real economy to absorb it at a time when the United States was experiencing recession. Greider makes the connection with the collapse of land prices in the 1980s: ". . . the Federal Reserve was actually supplying easy credit as an indirect way to bail out the troubled commercial banks."[37] By holding interest rates down, the Fed was helping put the banks back on their feet. As Greider explains, "The easy credit conditions enabled the banks to profitably borrow short and buy long—borrowing at 3 percent to acquire huge volumes of long-term bonds that yielded 6 or 7 percent and replenishing their balance sheets by capturing the spread between the two."[38]

Global stock and bond market rallies were fuelled by the liquidity so generously provided by the Fed. With real economies flat, and therefore with opportunities for capital investment in plant renewal and expansion very limited, the new liquidity bloated financial instruments, stocks and bonds. The bubble of the early 1990s in the bond market continued until fears of inflation and a return to higher interest rates caused its sudden collapse.

But that was not the end of the speculative economy of the 1990s. By 1995, when it had become clear that the U.S. economy was growing at a moderate pace, with little sign of inflation, the bond and particularly the stock market took off. With opportunities for investments still limited in the real economy, stocks became the outlet of choice for investors. And as the market soared from high to high, investors came to expect the large returns from rising stock values as a given. In the autumn of 1997, the price-to-earnings ratio for the average stock traded on U.S. exchanges was about 20 to 1, compared with a historic average of about 14 to 1. That means investors were paying about 50 percent more for dividends than they normally have been willing to pay. They were driven on not by the prospect of the dividend but by the lust for yet higher stock prices.

Like the land boom of the 1980s, the stock bubble of the 1990s has been a self-sustaining phenomenon. There has been plenty of liquidity around seeking an outlet. The outlet has been stock prices, which have kept rising despite an ever more tenuous connection with what was happening in the real economy. But that's the way with all bubbles.

The money lenders of the world have redesigned the way the global economy works to give themselves the security they crave—above all, security against inflation. Ironically, in their very drive for security, they have made the economy more fragile. They have weakened states, undermined industries and threatened wage and salary earners with unemployment, underemployment and incomes that will not grow. And in the feverish bubble economies of our age, the one thing the money lenders have not found is security.

## Chapter 6

# The New Working Class/Middle Class

I can still remember the shrill whistles and horns sounding from the factories at noon to announce that it was lunchtime. In the early 1950s, in the downtown Toronto neighbourhood where I grew up, the men went to work first thing in the morning. Because there were a lot of plants and workshops nearby—our deadend street terminated at a large Union Carbide plant—many of the men came home for lunch when the whistles blew, but others took their lunch pails with them. The women looked after babies and toddlers and sent the older kids off to school—there were a lot of kids in those baby boom days—and then they shopped for household necessities, cleaned house and cooked.

During the post-war decades in Canada, most wage and salary earners were men. The typical family was supported by a single male income earner. The men on our street—sheet-metal workers, truck drivers, printers, carpenters, assembly-line workers—earned a living wage. They were paying down their mortgages—a three-storey house on our street cost C$8,800 in 1946. They were buying cars, an amazing collection of almost exclusively secondhand vehicles, and they spent hours on weekends lying on their backs under these cars covered with grease as they tried to coax more life out of them. Those were the days when car owners were often looking for kids, adults and other drivers to push their cars down the street to get them to start.

Men's wages also financed the purchase of the first television sets—often bought "on time." One difference between that era and the present is that people on average work longer hours now than they did then. (In the late 1990s, as a consequence of working longer hours, both unpaid and paid, the average American worked the equivalent of four more weeks a year than in the 1960s.)[1] Some of the younger women on our street also went off to work in plants and offices first thing in the morning. I can remember them coming home as it was getting dark with their kerchiefs tied around their heads.

The family home was the centre of life in a way that is hard to imagine today. It was almost unheard of for the people I knew to go to restaurants. McDonald's, Harvey's, Wendy's and Burger King didn't exist. There were lunch counters where you could have a coffee and there were takeout and sit-in fish-and-chip places, but overwhelmingly you ate at home. Grocery stores, drugstores, dairies, bakeries and ice companies delivered their wares to the door. Deliveries were made by deliverymen with horses and wagons or by kids after school on their bicycles. Over the course of the decade, as the number of cars increased, supermarkets gradually replaced most of the neighbourhood grocery stores. The shopping pattern changed as the daily outings and deliveries decreased in favour of weekly trips in the car on Friday evenings to the supermarket.

Some of my neighbours were better off than others. The skilled printer across the street certainly made a lot more money than the sixteen-year-old high school dropout next door who worked in a butcher's shop until he cut off his right hand in the bacon-slicing machine one day. What social class did these people belong to? If you had asked them, they would probably have described themselves as "working people." Despite their differences, all these people were a part of the working class.

My neighbourhood was comparatively homogeneous. There were Protestants and Catholics and a few Jewish families, but almost everyone was Anglo Canadian. That began to change dramatically, however, in the mid-1950s as the first Italian families moved to our street. To me and the other kids, this was something new. Suddenly there were neighbours who couldn't speak English and who broke the pattern of our established friendships and enmities. Within two or three years, most of the people on our street sold their houses to Italian families and moved out, many of them to the suburbs. We moved to middle-class North Toronto when I was fifteen, a world very different from the old downtown neighbourhood.

The post-war Canada I grew up in represented the zenith of a particular kind of capitalism, a capitalism different in important respects from the one we know today. The Second World War was a time of intense industrialization in Canada, so that by the 1950s the country was far more urban and industrial than it had been a couple of decades earlier. During the 1950s, the industrial working class constituted a higher percentage of the labour force than previously, or since. By 1960, farmers, once the largest occupational group in the country, had declined to a mere 13.2 percent of the labour force; by 1994, they made up only 4.1 percent of the labour force.[2] In terms of numbers, the post-war decades were the day of the industrial worker. Industrial workers constituted 32.7 percent of the employed labour force in 1960, less than in the United States at 35.3 percent or Britain at 47.7 percent.[3] Workers in manufacturing were the large majority of those classified as industrial employees (others worked in construction and transportation). In 1960, 24.6 percent of Canadians in the employed labour force worked in manufacturing (in the U.S. the percentage was 26.5 percent, in Britain 38.4 percent).[4]

A smaller proportion of Canadians were employed in industry and in manufacturing than in the United States and Britain because Canada still had a very large resource sector and continued to import far more manufactured goods per capita than any other advanced country. Despite this, the mostly male workers in Canada's domestically owned factories and in the branch plants—over 50 percent of manufacturing in the 1950s was carried out in American-owned subsidiaries—constituted a very powerful phalanx within the labour force. They laboured in factories that deployed the technology and the system of work organization that was characteristic of what we can call the second industrial revolution.

Beginning in the late-nineteenth century, the second industrial revolution involved the rise of new industries, principally steel, chemicals and electrical products. Later came automobiles, airplanes and related industries such as glass, rubber and advanced types of machinery. Although the first industrial revolution, with its origins in the mid-eighteenth century, had featured simple applications of mechanical energy—water power and steam—the second industrial revolution depended on much more advanced science and technology. The so-called Fordist system of the second industrial revolution deployed workers in ever-larger factories, where every aspect of the production process was broken down into simple, repetitive steps designed to maximize output. Henry Ford's assembly line was the ultimate expression of the system, reducing as it did each worker's contribution to endlessly repeated simple motions. According to the formula developed in the early twentieth century by Frederick Taylor—his "scientific management" was the gospel of the second industrial revolution—the entire work process was set out by management and executed on the plant floor exactly as planned. Time-motion studies were used to make further refinements. Workers did what machines could not yet do. There was a high degree of division of labour, with a large number of formally separated job designations, using what was for the most part a semi-skilled workforce. It was a form of mass production in which efficiency was realized through the application of Taylor's methods, but also through the achievement of economies of scale. Fordism, at its peak in the 1950s and 1960s, excelled in the production of standarized products for a mass market.

The human consequences of this system of production were paradoxical: workers gained considerable bargaining power and solidarity through it in times of full employment; but they were deeply alienated by a method of production that denied them any sense of ownership and creativity over what they were producing.

In the era of full employment that followed the war, the North American industrial working class used its strategic position in the productive system to insist on higher real wages. The great industrial unions—the Steelworkers, Autoworkers, Rubber Workers, Chemical Workers and

Machinists—were organized in the 1930s during the Depression, but their heyday was in the years following the war, when they did not hesitate to use the strike weapon to force their employers to give them a larger share of the huge productivity gains of the second industrial revolution. In sharp contrast to the failure of real industrial wages to rise over the past two decades, industrial workers and their families made regular, real gains to their incomes during the post-war era. Between 1951 and 1973, the average annual income of a Canadian family more than doubled from C$5,356 to C$11,279 (in constant 1971 dollars).[5]

North American trade unionists set the winning of higher wages and benefits for their members as their top priority. Their goals did not extend to overcoming the alienation experienced by workers in the factories of the Fordist age; the assumption was that management took over once a worker was inside the factory gate. The union saw its job as making sure that the reward for the dull, repetitive, stressful work increased as rapidly as possible. There was, to be sure, a difference in political strategy between American and Canadian trade unionists. The leaders of American industrial unions did not believe in directly affiliating with a political party, while their Canadian counterparts, most of whom were organized into Canadian sections of the same American unions, had a social democratic leadership that played a critical role in the creation of the New Democratic Party in 1961.

In the Fordist age, industrial workers were the key political constituency in favour of the welfare state. In North America and Western Europe, the working class had learned crucial lessons from the Depression and the war. The Depression had taught that capitalism left on its own was no guarantee of full employment, that the system was prone to terrible periods of collapse that made factories and workers destitute. And workers had learned from the war and its immediate aftermath that government could do a great deal to set things right. During the Depression, much in the manner of their descendants in the 1990s, business leaders and orthodox economists had repeatedly warned against the government spending money to increase economic demand. This would bring ruin and delay recovery, they said. But during the war, workers saw governments doing exactly what the voices of capitalist orthodoxy had inveighed against. In both the United States and Canada, it was wartime spending by governments that was decisive in ending the mass unemployment of the Depression, as everyone could plainly observe.

Workers, who fought in the armies that defeated the Nazis and the Fascists, developed the conviction that they had a right to a better deal. They had helped save their countries and now they should share in the post-war prosperity. Workers would not stand for long periods of high unemployment in the post-war years, and they had the unity and political muscle to make their sentiments count. Political suicide awaited parties and governments that failed to commit themselves to policies of full employment. The experience of the war created a sense of collectivity—a feeling that we were all in it together. It took decades before capitalist individualism was once again able to prevail over this war-taught collective consciousness. The defeat of the Nazis and Fascists relegated the hardline political right to the margin on economic and social issues. While American McCarthyites could fulminate against the red menace, no one of any political consequence was prepared to argue that government didn't have a key role to play in ensuring that everyone had a job.

With the right wing isolated and the working class a force to be reckoned with, the way was opened for the Great Social Compromise of the post-war era. This crucial social understanding was the fruit of the very wide political coalition that had won the war. For the first time in history, the working class gained a share of power, although it was a limited share, to be sure. The Great Social Compromise was based on the notion that while the economy was mainly to be an affair of the market, with the capitalists making the profits, workers were to have jobs and an ever-higher standard of living.

Central to the Great Social Compromise were Keynesian economics and the welfare state. The socioeconomic strategy of John Maynard Keynes, the renowned British economist, was developed to prevent a resumption of the Depression. The key lesson learned by the Keynesians was that governments could and must intervene to ensure full employment, that capitalism left to its own devices provided no guarantee of economic growth and jobs for all who wanted work. The Keynesian prescription was that when economic growth stalled, governments should increase spending, cut taxes and decrease interest rates. Alternatively, when the economy was overheating, governments were to apply the brakes by raising taxes, cutting spending and raising interest rates.

These full-employment policies were conceptually linked to the creation of the post-war welfare state. Although the welfare state had important antecedents that predated the Second World War—Bismarck's social security system in late-nineteenth-century Germany, or Roosevelt's New Deal social security in the 1930s—it was in the decades following the war that the North American and Western European welfare states experienced their prodigious development. The welfare state was a direct outcome of full-employment economics. That was because spending on social programs by government ensured a basic level of demand during periods of economic downturn. Such spending amounted to economic ballast. Indeed, social spending was ideally countercyclical in its conception. Outlays increased during slow times, and decreased when the economy was once again strong, in both cases exactly in accordance with Keynesian prescription.

The Great Social Compromise differed in its details and scope from country to country. In the United States, it was an informal affair, with the emphasis placed on growth through the market economy. There, the new industrial unions fought very fierce battles in a wave of strikes in the major industries to win substantial wage increases. American working-class militancy was high in the post-war era in comparison with other advanced countries, not least because the Great Social Compromise was less extensive in America than elsewhere. In other countries, the Great Social Compromise was more clearly spelled out. In West Germany, the phrase *social market* economy was written into the country's basic law (constitution) in 1949. Ever since then, Germany has been constitutionally committed to achieving a synthesis between a market economy and social well-being. In the early 1950s, West German "co-determination" legislation gave workers the right to elect their own representatives to the boards of directors of many large corporations. Throughout Western Europe and North America, the Great Social Compromise involved a partial release of wage and salary earners from the strictures of the market economy.

For a century before the rise of the welfare state, wage and salary earners, except in those rare cases where they enjoyed substantial inherited wealth, had their fortunes relentlessly tied to the ups and downs of the economy. When jobs were plentiful, they could find work, and with luck and marketable skills, a living wage. But when the economy turned down, they often faced unemployment. Job loss meant ruin for workers, most of whom didn't (and still don't) have substantial savings.

Without a job, workers lost their homes to bank foreclosures. Their families often broke up under the strain. If they were lucky, they could fall back on extended family and move in with parents or brothers and sisters. But if they lived in recently established communities, such as those in the Canadian Prairies, they usually didn't have relatives to count on, and desperation was only a few missed pay packets away. When out of work, people rode the rails from one end of Canada or the United States to the other in search of employment. In the hard years of the 1930s, they turned to soup kitchens or the dole, where there was one, or they ended up in government labour camps, working in the forest or national parks for a pittance, submitting themselves to a harsh, authoritarian regime.

After the war, full employment became the essential, and feasible, answer to this working-class problem, but the welfare state was also crucial in providing a safety net that the jobless or those in ill health could rely on. In every country in Western Europe and North America, welfare states were constructed in the post-war decades. Their major features were unemployment insurance; universal public pension plans; social assistance for the long-term unemployed and the disabled; and, except for the United States, universal medicare of one kind or another. Closely associated with these measures was substantial public sector spending to broaden access to post-secondary educational institutions.

Social spending was much more comprehensive in Europe than in

North America. University education was free in France, while in the United States tuition fees remained extremely high for most first-rate post-secondary institutions. At its peak, the welfare state absorbed about 25 percent of the GDP in France, West Germany and other Western European countries, while in the U.S. it accounted for only about 14 percent of GDP, and in Canada 18 percent.

As early as the late 1950s, when the post-war mixed economy was at its height, the beginning of the transition to the new economy of our own era was already under way. Among other things, the transition changed the working class. Over the past four decades, the social class that in the post-war era predominantly comprised industrial workers has undergone a basic transformation as a consequence of new technology, the relative decline of manufacturing, the explosive rise of the service sector and the entry of a large number of women and ethnic minorities into the labour force.

There is nothing novel about a social class being transformed as a consequence of technological and societal changes. The process of what we can call the "de-composition" and "re-composition" of social classes has occurred a number of times in recent centuries. Unavoidably, the transformation of a social class raises the important question of what name we should use to identify the class. And just as unavoidably, old names linger from the past and blur our understanding of the transformation under way. In Canada, the term *working class* has colloquially referred to industrial workers, while *middle class* has described salaried white-collar and professional employees. An earlier generation might have thought of a skilled printer when they heard the word *worker*, and an even earlier generation could have pictured a blacksmith as the typical working man. In the early-twentieth century, there were thousands of blacksmiths in North America. But the demise of the trade when the automobile replaced the horse-drawn carriage did not mark the end of the working class, nor did the disappearance of the skilled printer a few decades later as a consequence of new technology.

Over the past four decades, the once predominantly male and industrial working class has been transformed into a social class much more equally divided between men and women, whose decisive majority is employed in the service sector of the economy. In 1994, women constituted 45.6 percent of the U.S. labour force and 44.7 percent of the Canadian labour force.[6] There is no need here to quarrel with everyday usage in identifying the class that has emerged from this process of change. I will call it the *working class/middle class* and I will show why industrial and service sector wage and salary earners actually belong to one distinct social class.

When I speak of the working class/middle class, I am including in it those people who work for a wage or a salary in a non-managerial position. Defined this way, the working class/middle class comprises about 70 percent of the labour force of the advanced industrial countries. The other 30 percent includes the wealthy, the managerial elite, and highly affluent professionals—many doctors, lawyers and accountants—at one end of the scale, and the working poor, underemployed and the non-working poor at the other end. Also included in the other 30 percent are small businesspeople, independent farmers and fishermen, and self-employed people like consultants and artisans.

Essential to the emergence of today's working class/middle class was the evolution of "thinking machines"—computers—which were to transform the productive process in industry as well as in the service sector. And it is clear that at the dawn of the new millennium, we are still in the early stages of the impact of this new technology on the productive process. Still more revolutionary changes await us in the decades ahead.

Contemporary technological developments are far more radical than anything that has occurred over the past several centuries. Formerly, technological advances in agriculture and in industry involved labour-saving practices, with novel forms of machinery powered by new sources of energy replacing human muscle and sweat, but the computer can process information, replacing human brainpower. And as the computer revolution proceeds, computers can take on increasingly complex tasks (just ask the world chess champion Gary Kasparov what he thinks of Deep Blue).

Like previous technological advances, the development of computerized production systems has not occurred in a societal vacuum. As we have seen, during the post-war decades, corporations were obliged to concede real wage increases to employees, and this motivated business to find ways to replace labour with machines. Higher productivity has not been an end in itself; technological solutions were sought precisely because of the relationship between capital and labour.

The first computers in the post-war era were mammoth affairs, the size of a house, equipped with vacuum tubes similar to those used in radios. These early computer monsters cost many millions of dollars to construct, and just about the only entity that could afford one was the U.S. Strategic Air Command (SAC)—whose giant computer helped survey the skies of North America to warn of the approach of Soviet bombers. By the 1960s, transistor-based computers were developed. These computers, the size of a refrigerator and costing only a few hundred thousand dollars, were used by corporations to assist their storage and processing of information and to improve production planning. The next advance, from transistors to silicon microchips, established the basis for the computers of our age.

The microchip lies at the heart of the contemporary transformation of the production process, resolving the problems of the earlier vacuum-tube and transistor-based computers. It made computers much cheaper and smaller and opened the way for the processing of vast amounts of information. The laptop I am using to write this book can process more information more rapidly than a computer that cost several hundred million dollars in the 1950s. The computer revolution has had huge consequences for both industry and the service sector. Computer-driven production systems have supplanted Fordist techniques. The lean production methods typical of cyber capitalism mean that parts, machinery and sub-assemblies can be ordered when needed and delivered by suppliers "just in time" (JIT). Through computerized production, customization replaces standardization.

For example, when General Motors assembles cars at its plant in Oshawa, Ontario, orders for parts are sent to suppliers only ninety minutes before they are required on the production line. As the car-in-progress proceeds through the plant—the assembly line has been replaced so that computer-driven vehicles deliver the car from one work station to the next, where groups of workers do their jobs—a computer orders the parts needed for this particular car. Each car differs from the one in front of it and the one behind it, according to the specifications ordered by a customer. Long gone are the days when Ford manufactured huge numbers of identical Model Ts for a mass market—Henry Ford used to say of them, "You can have any colour you like as long as it's black."

One consequence of this finely tuned, customized system of production is that it increases still further the motivation of industrial corporations to reduce their permanent workforce to the lowest possible level. Since corporations know they can produce exactly what is needed when it is needed, they strongly prefer to hold down the size of their workforce and to demand overtime from their employees as necessary. Thus the character of the technology itself has contributed to downsizing in many highly profitable corporations like General Motors of Canada, whose management in 1995 elected to shed 2,500 employees in the same year as its profits were up 36 percent.

Technology alone does not fully explain such layoffs. Also at work is a management mindset that insists that profitable, even highly profitable, companies have a right to shed workers to make still more money. In a world dominated by finance capital, the managers of large corporations now set their profit goals by drawing lines in the sand. If our company is making only 11 or 12 percent a year in its return on equity while other companies are making 16 or 17 percent, then it is our duty to move toward greater profitably, top managers claim. We can't ask our shareholders to accept a little less than other companies in order to preserve jobs, they assert. If we do that, our shareholders will abandon us. Therefore, we have the right to lay workers off even when we are highly profitable. (In return for a commitment not to name the specific companies, I have been shown internal memos written by Canadian corporate managers that argue precisely this case.)

If the consequences of the contemporary technological revolution have already been spectacular in manufacturing, and have led to the shedding of millions of jobs in the industrialized countries, the consequences in the service sector are scarcely less awesome. Computers have already transformed work in offices, banks, insurance companies, newspapers, universities and telephone companies where increased technological productivity has also reduced the workforce. In offices, secretarial functions have changed so dramatically that in countless workplaces not only have many secretaries lost their jobs but those who remain are often organized into a factory-style setting. At York University in Toronto, where I have taught for over twenty-five years, many departmental secretaries who once had their own offices now work in large open areas in groups of three or four. Less control over the pace of their work and the environment inevitably increases stress. Similarly, the computerized system used by telephone companies means fewer operators are needed and ensures that those with jobs are fed calls by the computer at a relentless speed so they never have the informal breaks that the old technology occasionally permitted.

Bank machines have replaced huge numbers of tellers. By the early 1990s, there were about 120,000 automated teller machines (ATMs) installed in the U.S., from which customers were making nine billion withdrawals a year.7 And that is the most visible of the changes. As we saw in the last chapter, the computer revolution has been indispensable to the entire revolution in financial services and to the onset of a global financial market.

Journalists now file their material to newspapers via computers, whether they are working in the newsroom or sending it by modem from across the world. This means they are doing their own inputting, so most of those formerly needed to key in the texts have been let go. In universities, students are now given a specific time slot to register for courses by phone. At the other end of the line is a voice-mail system hooked up to a computer that admits students to courses and eliminates the need for workers who formerly handled registration. This short list of changes could be endlessly extended to cover other service sector operations.

In his book *The End of Work*, the American economist Jeremy Rifkin showed how earlier advances in technology led to the displacement of millions of workers. He presents a powerful case that the contemporary computer-based transformation is more revolutionary in its implications than all the preceding labour-saving advances. "The Third Industrial Revolution is forcing a worldwide economic crisis of monumental proportions as millions lose their jobs to technological innovation . . ." Rifkin writes.[8] He is surely right that the proportion of people employed in industry will continue to decline, as it has for the past four decades. And his forecast that many millions of white-collar jobs will be also eliminated as a result of the further introduction of computer technology seems unassailable. The implication of his argument is that unless the productivity gains that have accrued as a consequence of the contemporary technological revolution are widely shared by the whole of the working population, through a shorter work week and higher pay, we are likely to face an unprecedented unemployment crisis in the industrialized world. One of the major causes of the Great Depression was the failure to share the productivity gains of that era widely enough. And one of the reasons for the vast economic success of the post-war decades was that at long last, after a decade of Depression and a world war, the productivity gains of the second industrial revolution were finally shared, to a degree at least, with the working class.

If technology has played a big part in spawning the contemporary crisis of unemployment and underemployment in the industrialized world, other causes include the shifting of jobs in labour-intensive industries to low-wage countries; the collapse of the Keynesian economic system in favour of more classical and conservative doctrines such as monetarism (tight money and high interest rates); and the shift in the balance of power within capitalism away from the industrialists to bankers and the bond market.

Post-war economic policies in the advanced countries made full employment a primary objective. Keynesian countercyclical fiscal and monetary policies were used to achieve that objective. By the 1970s, however, under a variety of pressures from the new inflation generated by the American prosecution of the Vietnam War and the oil price shocks of 1973–74 and 1979, to the demise of the post-war Bretton Woods economic regime with its fixed exchange rates for currencies, the Keynesian system collapsed. In the era of slower growth that ensued, fiscal crises emerged in most of the major industrialized countries, pointing the way to the huge government deficits and debts of the 1980s and 1990s. The debt crisis was used by those promoting the new capitalist orthodoxy (neoconservatism) as a reason for reducing the outlays of the welfare state and for withdrawing the state from ambitious undertakings to promote job creation. Ironically, the monetarist policies initiated by conservatives such as Margaret Thatcher in Britain and the monetarist Reaganites in the U.S. plunged their economies into deep recessions, which worsened the public sector debt crisis, for which they had blamed the Keynesians.

The transition from the old industrial economy of the post-war decades to the new globalized, finance-centred economy has radically transformed the wage and salary earning class. Two characteristics of the new class stand out. First, women make up a much larger proportion of wage and salary earners than in the past. Second, the non-goods-producing service sector has become the undisputed centre both of the new economy and of its wage and salary earning class.

The increase in the proportion of women in the labour force has been the consequence of two simultaneous processes: the number of women aged fifteen to sixty-four in the labour force has expanded, and the number of men aged fifteen to sixty-four in the labour force has been declining (in some countries this decline has been substantial). In Canada, tens of thousands of women went to work during the Second World War to produce munitions when a million Canadian men were in the armed forces. In the immediate post-war years, these women left the workforce, under active pressure from government, employers and unions. But in the 1950s, women began returning to the labour force in increasing numbers. In 1960, women still constituted only 26.6 percent of the

Canadian labour force. By 1994, this proportion had shot up to 44.7 percent. Among the countries that were to form the G-7 in the 1970s, Canada had the lowest level of female participation in the workforce in 1960. But after that date, the presence of Canadian women in the labour force was extremely high. In the United States, women made up 32.5 percent of the labour force in 1960, and by 1994, their proportion had increased to 45.6 percent.[9] Between 1960 and 1994, there were also marked increases in the proportion of women in the labour force in the Federal Republic of Germany (37.3 percent to 42.4 percent), France (33.3 percent to 43.8 percent), Britain (32.7 percent to 43.7 percent), and Italy (30.7 percent to 36.4 percent).[10]

The significant difference between North America and Western Europe is that European living standards were much lower than in Canada and the United States in 1960, so with the exception of Italy, female participation in the labour force was already higher in Western Europe than in North America by that date. To support a family, a single working-class wage often sufficed in North America in the 1950s and 1960s, while it typically did not in Europe. The family model with the husband employed and the wife at home was a feature of North American life in the 1950s to a greater extent than in Western Europe. (Since 1960, French and German living standards, and living standards in other northern European countries, have caught up with those in North America.)

The country with the experience least like the others in the G-7 was Japan, where 40.7 percent of the labour force was already made up of women as long ago as 1960. To support a family in Japan in 1960, female labour was much more often needed than in North America. For the next third of a century, that proportion remained virtually stable, rising a little at times, falling at others, so that by 1994, the proportion of women in the Japanese labour force was 40.5 percent.[11] Japan began the period with the lowest per capita income in the G-7 and ended it with the highest.

Another factor in the transformation of the old working class into the new working class/middle class has been the decline in male participation in the labour force. To make sense of this decline, we need to see what has been happening to participation in the labour force across the whole of the adult population. Here, there have been significant differences within the G-7, between the U.S., Britain and Canada on the one hand, and the Continental European countries and Japan on the other. Between 1960 and 1994, the proportion of the total adult population—aged fifteen to sixty-four—that was in the labour force increased significantly in the U.S. (from 66.2 percent to 77.9 percent), in Britain (from 72 percent to 74.5 percent), and in Canada (from 62.8 percent to 75.2 percent).[12] Meanwhile, in the Federal Republic of Germany (West Germany before 1990, when it became unified Germany), the proportion of the adult population that was in the labour force edged up only slightly, from 70.3 percent to 71.5 percent between 1960 and 1994. In both France and Italy, the proportion of the adult population in the labour force actually declined over the third of a century in question, in France from 70.4 percent to 67.5 percent, and in Italy from 66.6 percent to 60 percent. (In the French and Italian cases, there is good reason to conclude that the size of the so-called black market economy has played a role in the extent of the decline of the labour force reported in official figures. In Italy, the number of people who are earning an income without reporting it is especially high. It is not unusual for Italians to work in an office during the day, and then to turn to a second job in the evenings or on weekends, perhaps as a waiter in a restaurant.) In Japan, there was only a slight increase in the proportion of the adult population in the labour force between 1960 and 1994—from 75.8 percent to 76.4 percent.[13]

In all the G-7 countries, the proportion of men aged fifteen to sixty-four who were in the labour force declined between 1960 and 1994. In the U.S., 90.5 percent of adult males were in the labour force in 1960, while only 85.3 percent of them were by 1994. In Canada, over the period we are examining, the proportion of adult males in the labour force declined from 91.1 percent to 82.6 percent. In Britain, the decline was from an extraordinary high of 99.1 percent in 1960 to 83.3 percent in 1994. In Japan, the decline was the least significant, from 92.2 percent to 90.6 percent. In Germany, France and Italy, the decline was pronounced: Germany, from 94.4 percent to 80.8 percent; France, from 94.6 percent to 75.9 percent (the lowest in the G-7); and Italy, from 95.3 percent to 76.9 percent.[14]

The decrease in the proportion of men in the labour force had three main causes: the much greater number of younger men pursuing post-secondary education; the large increase in the number of men taking early retirement (particularly important in France); and a marked increase in the number of men driven out of the labour force and marginalized, a part of the important trend that has led to the rise of the new urban poor.

The labour force has also become much more ethnically diverse. As a consequence of immigration from Asia, the Caribbean, Latin America, Africa, the Middle East and South Asia, the contemporary working class/middle class in both North America and Western Europe is substantially different in its composition from the largely white working class of the post-war era.

The rise of the service sector is the other major factor in the transformation of the labour force. The service sector is a massive category that includes wholesaling, retailing, banking and other financial services, advertising, education, health care, law and judiciary, other professionals and most of those employed by government. In some ways, it is easier to think of the service sector as including all those in civilian employment with the exception of manufacturing, transportation, construction and the primary sector (mining, agriculture, fishery and forestry).

As early as 1960, 54.1 percent of the Canadian workforce was employed in the service sector (in the U.S. the percentage was 56.2 percent, in West Germany 39.1 percent, in Britain 47.6 percent).[15] In Canada by 1994, 73.3 percent of the labour force was employed in the service sector, the highest percentage in any G-7 country. Meanwhile, the percentage of the labour force employed in manufacturing had plunged to 14.4 percent, the lowest in the G-7.[16] The plunge in the proportion of Canadians employed in manufacturing meant that while the employed workforce doubled in size between 1962 and 1990, the number employed in manufacturing increased by only 18 percent.[17] It is worth noting that by 1994 the proportion of Canadians employed in manufacturing was only fractionally higher than the proportion who had been farmers in 1960 (14.4 percent compared with 13.2 percent).[18]

What has been happening to manufacturing employment in the late twentieth century is very similar to what happened to the agricultural workforce a century ago. Farmers, once the largest occupation group in Canada, constituted a mere 4.1 percent of the labour force by 1994.[19] It is reasonable to project that the proportion of the labour force employed in manufacturing will continue to decline in decades to come, so that several decades into the twenty-first century it will not be much different from the proportion now working in the agricultural sector.

Despite some minor differences, the marked shift toward employment in the service sector has occurred in all G-7 countries. In the U.S., the proportion of the labour force in the service sector jumped from 56.2 percent to 73.1 percent between 1960 and 1994, while that employed in manufacturing dropped to 16 percent. In the Federal Republic of Germany, the trend was the same. However, in the German case, the proportion employed in the service sector was significantly lower than in North America: 39.1 percent of the labour force in 1960 and 59.1 percent in 1994. Meanwhile in Germany, the proportion employed in manufacturing, while declining, was still much higher than in North America, at 25.6 percent in 1994.

Again Japan followed a somewhat different course from the others. The proportion of Japan's labour force in the service sector increased from 41.3 percent to 60.2 percent between 1960 and 1994. But unlike the other G-7 countries, the proportion of Japan's workforce that was in the manufacturing sector continued to increase during the 1960s and early 1970s. In 1960 that proportion was 21.3 percent, and by 1974 it had increased to 27.2 percent. Only then did it begin to decline to 23.2 percent in 1994. (Japan reached its zenith as a manufacturing nation later than any of the other G-7 countries.)[20]

The forest of numbers on the past few pages shows us the outlines of a revolution in the makeup of the wage and salary workforce in the advanced industrialized countries. Although some observers have seen this era as the end of the working class—at times Jeremy Rifkin comes close to taking this position, as suggested in his chapter titled "Requiem for the Working Class"—the trends actually reveal not the disappearance of the working class but rather its transformation into a new class of wage and salary earners.[21] The evidence suggests that wage and salary earners are fated to be with us for a long time to come, despite technological revolution. Those who work for a salary or a wage in non-managerial positions form the large majority of the adult population in all the advanced countries.

Why do I conclude that this large and diverse section of the population constitutes a single social class? I have already made the case that there are two kinds of social classes: dominant and dominated, and that dominant and dominated social classes are inexorably linked in unequal relationship with each other.

The key to understanding the relationship between social classes is the role each social class plays in the productive process. Throughout the history of capitalism, the most significant fault line has been between those who own the means of production and the sources of wealth on the one hand, and those who sell their labour power for a wage or a salary on the other. Capitalists from the super-rich to the not so rich exercise power over others because they decide whose labour will be purchased and whose will not. And wage and salary earners in non-managerial positions—those I suggest make up the new working class/middle class—are the sellers of labour power. Capitalists' considerable community of interest, despite their intense struggles for dominance over one another, is precisely the fact that they are the purchasers of labour. There is little they will not do to protect this privileged societal relationship from which their power flows.

And it is the obverse of this condition of power that creates a commonality among those who sell their labour. Whether they are a part of the minority of this segment of the population working in manufacturing or in the majority, working in the service sector, whether they work in the private or public sector, the position of wage and salary earners in contemporary society has strikingly common features. Over the past two decades, the sellers of labour in the industrialized countries have faced two realities: their real incomes have hardly increased while those of their bosses have soared; and they confront more or less permanent job insecurity. These circumstances have linked the fates of this very large and diverse group of people. To be sure, the intensity of these threats has differed from country to country, from one specific job sector to another, and it has affected the young more harshly than those who have been in the labour force for a decade or more. But there have been broad similarities in the experience of wage and salary earners in the industrialized world from the mid-1970s to the mid-1990s, and it is those similarities that place them in a single, if admittedly diverse, social class.

The fact that those who make up the working class/middle class have faced broadly similar economic and social pressures does not mean that they understand the world in the same way. Indeed, the individual men and women who form this class do not normally regard their status as wage or salary earners as the most important feature of their personal identities. Whether one is a woman or a man, a member of a visible minority group or of the white majority, gay or straight, these facts of one's existence stand on their own, and are unrelated to belonging to a social class. There is much truth in the notion that today's powerful systems of communication make it more possible than ever before for individuals to fashion their own identities. There is nothing implausible about individuals adopting an outlook and even a culture that links them with others who may reside on the other side of their country or even the other side of the globe.

But while being a wage or salary earner may not be the determinant of an individual's identity, it is nonetheless important. At crucial times, it can become the most vital aspect of a person's life. When a man or woman needs full-time instead of part-time work, or is in danger of losing a job after a corporate merger has occurred, or belongs to a union deciding whether to go on strike, nothing matters more than being a wage or salary earner. As individuals with mortgages to pay and families to support, autoworkers at the Canadian plants of General Motors made the difficult decision to strike one of the world's most powerful corporations in September 1996. The teachers of Ontario did the same when they concluded that to protect the educational system and their jobs they had to embark on a political strike against the Ontario government in October 1997. The fifty-five thousand Ontario civil servants who went on strike (the first in their history) in the winter of 1996 against the Ontario government had to decide as individuals, each and every day, whether to stay on the picket line or to cross it and return to work. Over 80 percent of them stayed out during the five-week strike. It is easy to look from afar at such wage and salary earners in a time of crisis and assume that they are members of a group following their leaders. But that is a very incomplete view. They are also individuals making personal decisions, discovering at a moment of crisis just who they are and where they belong.

Particular groups—women, ethnic minorities—may address these questions in their own way, conditioned by their own experience, but just as the problems that have arisen as a consequence of discrimination against women will not be resolved by addressing class questions, it is also true that addressing gender or racial discrimination will not resolve the question of the inequality of social classes.

In the final analysis, wage and salary earners occupy a single social class because their experiences in relation to the dominant social class are more convergent than divergent. Today's wage and salary earners are face to face with a capitalism that is more monolithic in character than the system that prevailed during the post-war decades. The contemporary experience of teachers, nurses, academics, bank employees and other employees in the service sector has become ever more like the experience of industrial workers. Whether this means that those who make up the working class/middle class will identify with one another and make common cause is a different matter.

## Chapter 7

# Divine Right

In the autumn of 1995, a Gallup Poll asked respondents in Britain whether they believed that there was a "class struggle" taking place in British society. Eighty-one percent of those polled replied in the affirmative to the question. The poll result provided insight into the attitude of the British after sixteen years of the neoconservative governments of Margaret Thatcher and John Major. A year and a half later, the British electorate decisively rejected the Conservatives, replacing them with Tony Blair and the Labour Party. The mid-1990s was a time when the super-rich were expanding their wealth at a colossal pace, while ordinary Britons were merely holding the line or experiencing falling real incomes. When the same question had been asked by a Gallup Poll in Britain in 1961, at the height of the post-war Great Social Compromise, just 56 percent of respondents said there was a class struggle taking place in Britain.

In some places at some times, a huge number of people have exhibited a strong consciousness of class and have been motivated in their societal and political behaviour by class awareness. German, British, French and Italian workers waged nationally distinct but broadly similar class-wide campaigns for higher wages and improved social programs in the early post-war years. The point must be made, however, that when we say that social classes exist, that is not the same thing as saying that those who belong to a social class are conscious of that fact, or that belonging to a particular social class is the most important thing in the world to them. Indeed, just because people belong to the same social class does not mean that they will share a sense of solidarity. There have been plenty of instances of fratricidal conflicts within social classes, as people compete viciously for a slice of what may be an all-too-crowded social space. In Canada and the U.S., craft unions, which control access to highly paid trades (electricians, carpenters and bricklayers, for example), have often been run to protect present members and to keep at bay non-members who want access to these trades.

The point has been made that social classes never exist in isolation. As their unequal relationships are played out, the members of social classes become self-aware. The evolution of class consciousness involves, in varying degrees, the perception of self and the discovery of the "other." The experience of class, though it is often shocked into being by immediate experience, is also strongly conditioned by national cultures. French workers, with their revolutionary tradition stretching back two centuries, often engage in political strikes aimed at pressuring governments on issues such as the minimum wage, early retirement and protection of social programs. In 1968, a political strike that involved ten million people came close to toppling the government of Charles de Gaulle. In Britain, where political strikes are much less common, the working-class tradition has involved hard-fought battles in particular industries, such as steel and coal.

While French and British workers have very different traditions, the idea of social class has been and remains much closer to the surface of British culture than of the cultures of other advanced countries like the United States and Canada. In Britain, as soon as someone opens his or her mouth and speaks, he or she is identifiable as a member of a particular social class. And not a few people in Britain have taken great pains to alter their accents—à la Lizzie in *Pygmalion*—to ostensibly improve their status. I have known Labour Party politicians who play it both ways—speaking in plummy tones in conversations with the political elite and sliding into Cockney back home in the constituency.

Canadians and Americans like to think that they have put all that British nonsense about class behind them. But every culture has its techniques for quickly determining who is who and who belongs where. Shortly after meeting someone for the first time, a Canadian or American asks what the new acquaintance does, a question regarded as highly rude in Europe. The answer to the question—I am a fund manager, I teach political science, I am a child care worker, I work in the GM plant in Oshawa, I am a corporate lawyer—tells the story. It slots a person into a social class just as surely as a Yorkshire or Cambridge accent does. North American parents know what it means when their son or daughter marries the bus driver instead of the head of the firm.

On not a few occasions, it has been ruefully noted by observers on the political left that if the workers possessed a clear class consciousness, the struggle with the bosses would have been over long ago. Alas, it must be noted that in most historical periods, the consciousness of dominant classes is clearer and more cohesive than that of dominated classes. Indeed, that is not so surprising. The self-awareness of the dominant is a crucial aspect of their ability to remain dominant.

For those inclined to scoff at the very idea that members of social classes can have cohesive opinions, let me cite an example. In June 1997, Lionel Jospin, the newly elected Socialist prime minister of France, was enjoying a honeymoon with voters—63 percent expressed confidence in him, according to a poll taken at that time by *Le Figaro* and the polling organization Sofrès. At the same time, the heads of French businesses were even more negative: a poll taken by the magazine *Challenges* and Sofrès revealed that 73 percent of them had no confidence in Jospin.[1] Electoral honeymoons can have very clearly defined class boundaries, as Jospin's certainly did. What the heads of businesses hated most about Jospin, not surprisingly, was the Socialist Party's popular proposal to reduce the work week from thirty-nine to thirty-five hours a week without a reduction in pay. Eighty-three percent of heads of businesses opposed this idea, which had been strongly featured in Jospin's victorious electoral campaign.[2]

The members of dominant classes do not normally proclaim baldly that they control society and have no intention of giving up their power. They rarely admit that for them the continued sway of the few over the many is an end in itself. Over the long term, ruling classes do best when they legitimize their rule by presenting it in a universalist guise, justifying their dominance as the only way to achieve some lofty and worthy purpose. That purpose may be to fulfil God's will, as when, in centuries past, kings and aristocrats justified their rule as an expression of divine right. Or it may be to ensure that the best traditions of the past are sustained and preserved for the future, as when Tories, in the manner of Edmund Burke, the late-eighteenth-century British Conservative politician and thinker, argued for the benefits of a hereditary class system. Or, it might be—in a case familiar to us all—to ensure that the economy expands as rapidly and productively as possible, as when present-day free market advocates argue for deregulation and the dismantling of the welfare state so that business can be allowed to do its thing.

These days the divine right argument for the rule of kings and aristocrats over all the rest seems a little threadbare. We shuffle uneasily in our seats when presented with it. In its day, however—and its day endured for centuries—divine right made a formidable case for the legitimacy of a ruling class. Church, state and ruling class were united in defence of the notion that their system was ordained by God, and that any thought of challenging it was absurd. The beauty of this assertion was that it did not seek legitimization through any promise to ameliorate the material condition of society as a whole. This was a social order with no meritocratic pretensions, a great advantage for a ruling class. (One of the greatest disadvantages for today's capitalists is that they are stuck with the idea of progress and cannot abandon it even if they wanted to. Proponents of capitalism regularly claim that their system is the best there is at delivering the goods to the largest number of people, a claim advocates of earlier social systems did not make.)

In 1381, when the commoner Wat Tyler led a successful peasants' revolt in England, his movement's demand was for an end to servitude, a concrete aim being to abolish the crushing burden of heavy tax on the peasantry. Tyler's movement did not actually seek power for itself but rather hoped for a reform of royal power, whereby the king would give consideration to the peasants' grievances. The peasants and their leaders could not conceive of the possibility of overthrowing the ruling class. Naturally, when royal authority was reestablished, participants in the peasant movement and its leaders were summarily slaughtered. (Ruling-class fury against the revolt of the masses has customarily involved colossal repression.)

In Shakespeare's plays, written at the end of the sixteenth century and the beginning of the seventeenth, every emotion of the human heart—greed, jealousy, nobility, sacrifice, cowardice—is explored. And the social classes of Elizabethan England are vividly brought to life. Shakespearean kings and aristocrats are venal, human and heroic. But the divine right of kings and aristocrats is never challenged.

By the time we move to the Toryism of Edmund Burke, the divine right paradigm had been undermined by the development of the natural sciences and new notions of psychology that situated humanity in a material world remote from the divinely ordered firmament of the past. When Burke came on the scene, Hobbes, Locke and Rousseau had firmly planted human society on this earth, so that the carefully nurtured idea of a wall separating kings and aristocrats from the rest of the population, so essential to the divine right paradigm, was no longer tenable. Kings and aristocrats were blood-and-guts denizens of the planet earth the same as everyone else. In the era of the French Revolution, a more up-to-date defence for the ruling class was needed. (Burke detested the French Revolution because it involved class war, while he had supported the American Revolution as a struggle to preserve the traditional rights of Englishmen.)

What emerged was what we now regard as traditional British (and in a more watered-down form, Canadian) Toryism. British Toryism of the Burkean variety betrays its modernity by situating human beings and society within the natural order. The defence of the ruling class—then dominated by the great landowners—was that this class of men, as a consequence of its breeding and societal position, was best able to preserve the values handed down from the past and to preserve order, stability,

justice and liberty for the future. As Roger Scruton, the British conservative theorist put it, society in Burke's eyes "is not a contract among the
living, but a partnership between the dead and the living and the
unborn. . . . We, the living members of society, are its trustees, bound by
the duties of our tenancy."3 Note the difference between Burkean Toryism and that of Margaret Thatcher, who summarized her philosophy
faithfully when she said: "There is no such thing as society."4

Who better, in Burkean conception, to oversee our preservation of
the traditions of the past than a ruling class constituted of the men who
had been bred to do just this? Here, we assuredly do not have the idea
of the recruitment of ambitious souls from below—Burke would have
been appalled by Horatio Alger's belief that a poor man could advance
himself to a lofty rank. Instead the notion prevailed that the members
of all social classes are bred to their roles and ought to find fulfilment
within the class into which each is born. Divinity had retreated, at least
a little, with this concept, but the walls between the classes were kept
safely high. Henry Fielding's eighteenth-century novel *Tom Jones* is the
rollicking, ribald story of a young man of noble birth who by mischance
grows up among those of a much lower social station. The tale has a
happy ending—he finds his way back to the aristocracy. *Tom Jones* is a
Tory (non-Thatcherite) tale.

In our era, legitimization of the rule of the capitalists is rooted in a
realist guise. It is claimed that the free market is the most efficient means
yet devised to satisfy the needs and appetites of the human race. The
claim goes beyond the efficacy of the private market to a concept of
human nature and motivation. Contemporary orthodoxy holds that
human beings are rational economic actors, constantly driven to achieve
the marginal utility that goes with getting the biggest bang for a buck.
(While I have certainly met some people who would rather be at a sale
than anywhere else, I've met others who'd rather be sailing.) This quest
for marginal utility allegedly promotes constant progress and the greater
good within capitalism. Those who effectively pursue the free market
will be rewarded, while those who fail in its pursuit will perish.

Rule by the capitalists in our age is thereby vindicated in social

Darwinist terms. Thirty years ago, the harsh edges of capitalism were blunted by the Great Social Compromise with labour, but the singular outcome of neoconservatism has been to return capitalism to the stark terms of survival of the fittest. The world, it seems, is divided between those who have the drive, the guts, the entrepreneurial verve to make it and those who do not. And the second group is much the larger of the two. The drones are the vast majority of the human population, and they must not be allowed to get in the way of the much smaller but indispensable group who make things happen. They are the agents of material progress, conceiving and marketing new goods and services. They are the ones who benefit all of humankind by opening markets everywhere, by bringing people of diverse cultures together in a common global system of production and consumption. These are the true exemplars of our age, taking risks with their own assets, in the quest to achieve more. No reward is too great for people such as these, for in the process of seeking more for themselves, they create more for all of us. In this way, contemporary orthodoxy justifies inequality.

The idea that the working class/middle class is populated by the overindulged and slothful is so commonplace today that examples are available in virtually any issue of a daily newspaper. In a front-page news story on why German firms are moving jobs to Eastern Europe, the *International Herald Tribune* recently said this of Germany: "Europe's economic powerhouse became pampered by some of the world's highest wages and shortest working hours."[5] Remember, this is a news story, not an interpretative remark by a columnist. The mainstream press endlessly repeats the axiom that workers in Western Europe must give up much of what they have gained so that their countries can be successful in the great age of restructuring that is under way.

While any call for higher wages and salaries for the working class/middle class or for more generous social programs is treated with disdain in the mainstream press, its laudatory attitude to profit and wealth is marked. We live in an age of conspicuous wealth—if you've got it, flaunt it. When the *Sunday Times* published its Rich List for 1997, the tone was unmistakably celebratory: "The enterprise culture is here at last. Soaring asset values have brought a vast increase in wealth for Britain's millionaire class . . ." Indeed, in just one year, the average wealth of those in the top five hundred in Britain skyrocketed from £140 million to £173.7 million, an increase of £33.7 million (about US$54 million).[6]

According to today's rationale for rule by the capitalists, it makes perfect sense to argue that the super-rich, the self-made leaders, are finally accumulating what is rightfully due them in their pursuit of the collective greater good, while workers have had more than they deserve. The sharply contrasting attitude to the supposedly superior motivations and objectives of the rich and the super-rich as opposed to the petty special interests of the working class/middle class tells us a great deal about capitalist consciousness. The mainstream media (a very good guidepost to the standard values of contemporary capitalism) are complicit in asserting that the most important and creative actors in our socio-economic order are the capitalists.

The fact that proponents of present-day capitalism conceive of people as divided into two orders of humanity—one for capitalist super-achievers, and an inferior one for all the rest—is demonstrated by their advocacy of diametrically opposed reward systems for the two groups. For capitalists, the wisdom goes, the higher the potential for profit, the greater the creative effort expended, but workers who are paid too much and enjoy too many benefits grow lazy. While capitalists respond wonderfully to the carrot, workers do better when the stick is applied to them. Threaten workers with a loss in pay, fire a large number as an object lessen to those who remain, warn them that the whole operation can be shifted to a low-wage country and positive results are assured.

Nothing illustrates the notion of two humanities better than the orthodox capitalist view of why public sector entities should be privatized. The issue is worth examining in some detail because, as will be seen, it is an instance of almost pure capitalist ideology—of capitalist consciousness—at work.

According to this orthodox view (again, check your daily newspaper), privatization is a good idea because it increases productivity. Read these accounts closely and you will find that no real evidence is ever presented to support this proposition. It is simply axiomatic that private sector companies are more efficient, less wasteful, than public sector companies. Why are they assumed to be more efficient? Because when private owners run a company, merely the drive to maximize profit is bound to increase productivity. The profit motive and profit makers are the prime movers in human economic advance. It is just that plain. In a short book urging support for John Major's Tories in their doomed election campaign of 1997, David Willetts, a British Conservative Member of Parliament, put the truism this way: "The free market is the most dynamic, inventive and liberating economic principle known to man. It is now triumphant across the world. They are privatizing in Peru, cutting taxes in Poland, deregulating in Namibia. It was Ronald Reagan and Margaret Thatcher who showed the way: their influence will be felt around the world for decades to come."7

There you have it—the case for privatization. Who needs empirical evidence?

Throughout the industrialized world, a large number of public sector companies have been or are being privatized. Indeed, one of the key aspects of the transition from the mixed economy capitalism of the postwar decades to the market-centred global capitalism of the present has been privatization. The pioneer privatizing government was that of Thatcher's Conservatives. From the time her government first came to power in 1979 until 1990, 42 percent of British industries that were in the public sector were sold off to the private sector. This amounted to a transfer of about 6 percent of GDP from public sector to private sector ownership.

Among the largest sell-offs were 50.2 percent of British Telecom, for £3.9 billion (US$6.3 billion) in November 1984; British Gas for £5.6 billion (US$9.1 billion) in December 1986; 31.5 percent of British Petroleum for £7.2 billion (US$11.7 billion) in October 1987; British Steel for £2.5 billion (US$4.1 billion) in December 1988; and the public water distribution systems for £5.2 billion (US$8.5 billion) in December 1989. These sell-offs were followed in the 1990s by the privatization of the twelve electricity distribution companies in England and Wales in

December 1990 and the two electric power generation companies in March 1991, and then the Scottish power companies in June 1991. The rest of British Telecom was sold in December 1991.[8]

(The largest single venture in privatization in Europe actually was in the former East Germany, following German unification in 1990. By February 1992, 5,584 former state-owned companies, from very small to very large ones, had been sold off.[9] In the case of East Germany, though, sell-offs took place within an economy whose productivity was much lower than the West's, so this experience in no way compares with privatization in the advanced economies.) In the advanced industrialized world, British privatization has led all others in sheer scale.

Has Britain's extensive privatization actually increased productivity? Only in a limited way and in the short term: while firms were being prepared for privatization but remained in the public sector, they often shed a significant number of employees while maintaining their output, and thus achieved a one-shot increase in productivity. Following their privatization, however, no evidence exists of further productivity gains. (It is a doleful fact that job shedding in the public or private sphere can result in one-time productivity gains, at least in the short term. Over the longer term, as the smaller workforce grows weary from overwork, the productivity gains tend to decline.)

It is of course possible to demonstrate that some organizations are more productive than others, and to point to cases where productivity has been increased through the introduction of new technology, as a consequence of redesigned production processes and by shedding labour while simultaneously increasing the workload of the remaining labour force. Both privately owned and publicly owned firms have increased productivity in these ways. What has never been demonstrated is that privatization in itself leads to higher productivity.

The British drive for privatization has been duplicated, although on a smaller scale, in other European countries. In France, the massive nationalization of the early days of the Socialist government of François Mitterrand in 1981 has largely been reversed through privatization later undertaken by the Socialists, and especially by the Gaullists who controlled the national assembly from 1986 to 1988 and then from 1993 until the reelection of a Socialist government in 1997 (neo-Gaullist Jacques Chirac, elected in 1995, continues as France's president). Even companies like Renault, nationalized immediately after the Second World War, have been partially privatized. Once 100 percent state owned, Renault is now 46 percent owned by the French government.

In Italy, the country with the largest level of public ownership in Western Europe, there has been much talk of privatization, but privatization has proceeded at a relatively slow pace. Most Italian public enterprises are organized into two enormous holding companies: the Istituto per la Ricostruzione Industriale (IRI) in the industrial sector, and the Ente Nazionale Idrocarburi (ENI) in the energy sector. In 1986, the luxury automaker Alfa Romeo was sold to Fiat for 1,050 billion lire, but payment was deferred to be made in five annual payments beginning in 1993 (the deferral in real-cost terms cut the price in half).[10] Since 1992, shares in more than thirty state-owned companies have been sold, with Telecom Italia, the giant phone company, fully privatized in October 1997. In the Italian case, productivity of state-owned companies improved during the period of preparation for privatization, but there is little evidence of improvement continuing once the firms were sold off to the private sector.[11]

Ironically, in light of current orthodoxy, during the post-war decades, both France and Italy made use of public ownership as a means to boost productivity so that the two countries could catch up with industrial leaders like the United States and West Germany. On average, public sector industrial companies enjoyed higher productivity than their private sector counterparts in France and Italy. (I make no claim here that this higher productivity was a consequence of public ownership.) The 1960s were the glory years of the French and Italian economic "miracles," when the two countries achieved rates of economic growth ahead of the other major industrial economies, with the exception of Japan. With public sector companies helping set the pace, France and Italy grew much more rapidly than the United States, Britain and West Germany, where public sector industry was much less prevalent.

In the United States, the urge to privatize has been limited, for the simple reason that the United States had fewer entities in the public sector in the first place. There have been privatizations of some state-owned power utilities and even of prison administration. But in Canada, where the public sector, both federal and provincial, has been much larger than its American counterpart, there has been a major privatization movement. The federal government has privatized Petro Canada, Canadian National Railways and Air Canada, and various provincial and municipal governments have privatized such services as the retailing of alcoholic beverages, garbage collection and road maintenance.

In the Canadian cases, as in the British or other European cases, no systematic evidence has ever been presented to substantiate the claim that major productivity gains have accrued from privatization. Proselytizers for privatization just assert that private sector companies simply are, because they must be, more efficient than public sector companies. No one has ever shown that during the decades when Renault was owned 100 percent by the French government, it was a less efficient automaker than its private sector rival Peugeot-Citroën. Nor was there ever evidence during the decades when the Canadian National Railway was publicly owned that it was less efficient than the privately owned Canadian Pacific Railway. Similarly, those who currently advocate the privatization of Ontario Hydro, the giant electric power utility that has been in the public sector for nine decades, cannot point to greater efficiencies in large private sector power utilities either in North America or in Europe.

In August 1997, an internal report commissioned by Ontario Hydro revealed alarming mismanagement of its nuclear plants. Although privatizers welcomed the news of poor management in a public sector utility, they were also faced with the news that privately owned utilities operating nuclear reactors were in similar trouble in many parts of the United States, some close to bankruptcy. A December 1995 report by New York–based Moody's Investors Service Inc. estimated that U.S. utilities were stuck with deteriorating facilities, most of them nuclear reactors, whose investment value totalled US$135 billion.[12] As managers of aging and uncompetitive nuclear plants, neither the public nor the private sector was looking good.

The argument for privatization is an unvarnished expression of capitalist class consciousness arising from capitalism's basic tenet that the free market is superior. That is not to say, of course, that the motivation for particular privatizations is mainly ideological as very powerful vested interests stand to profit in concrete terms. Privatization in Britain was regarded by many as disadvantaging taxpayers by selling important assets for less than their true value. Indeed, the late Lord Stockton (Harold Macmillan), a former Conservative prime minister, derided Thatcher's privatizations as "selling the family silver."[13]

Brokerage houses and corporate law firms have also made a killing on the privatization of state-owned firms. And among the most vociferous advocates of privatization have been the top managers of public sector companies hoping to become much more highly paid CEOs of the privatized successor companies. The dreams of huge pay packets came true for managers of the privatized British electric power utilities and water distribution systems. For example, the CEO of privatized North West Water has an annual salary of £2.4 million (about US$3.7 million), immensely higher than the salary of a public sector chief executive.

As for the wider societal benefits that have supposedly flowed from privatization, what have they been? Few in Britain have noticed any improvement in the telephone, electrical, or water distribution services they have received since privatization. Although some private water management companies have done a better job than others, in general they have earned a reputation for profiteering and failing to make sufficient reinvestments to maintain high-quality systems.

One example of the failure to reinvest that led to negative consequences for the public occurred in Yorkshire, England. The tale of Yorkshire Water, a private company operating in northern England, is worth recounting in some detail. In the summer of 1995, a severe drought hit western Yorkshire, and few residents of the region will ever forget their encounter with Yorkshire Water. From the middle of the summer until the end of the year, the water supply used by 600,000 residents and local industries dwindled disastrously.

The shortage was exacerbated because Yorkshire Water had failed to reinvest enough money to upgrade the system or provide sufficient service in case of a serious drought. In 1995, 26 percent of the water collected by the company—eighty million gallons a day—was lost owing to leakage. The onset of the shortage coincided with an announcement that the company had made an annual profit of £160 million (us$256 million). As the drought continued for months, Yorkshire Water's public relations man went on television to urge restraint in water use. He claimed he had not taken a shower in three months and demonstrated how a person could wash with only a few cups of water in the sink. This attempt to rally the public backfired, however, when local media caught the PR man sneaking out of the district to have a shower at his mother-in-law's house.

Eventually the water shortage grew so serious that Yorkshire Water was impelled to rent every available tanker truck in the country to ferry water into the district twenty-four hours a day. It was the largest peacetime tanker operation in history. The public was angered when one executive of Yorkshire Water suggested that local companies should move their operations elsewhere to cut down on the demand for water. In November, public fury mounted when the company announced a 50 percent rise in profits and a 10 percent increase in dividends to shareholders. Even the Tory government at Westminster grew critical of the performance of Yorkshire Water when health authorities warned of the risk of water-shortage-related outbreaks of dysentery and gastrointestinal illnesses. Since privatization, there have been 250 successful prosecutions of water companies for causing environmental damage, but fines have been too low to influence the behaviour of the companies. Water prices have skyrocketed since privatization in many parts of the country. In Devon and Cornwall, for instance, rates have shot up by 450 percent since 1989. And water meters have been introduced for residential customers in many areas, giving rise to concerns that poor families are rationing water use and thus creating an overall health risk.

Citizens have even fewer ways of bringing effective pressure to bear on those running the private utilities than was the case with their public sector predecessors. At least the public companies were under the jurisdiction of politicians who would want to satisfy constituents and be returned to office. The owners and directors of large private companies, as we know all too well, are not elected by the people.

And so we have the remarkable spectacle of a huge transfer of assets from the public to the private sector over the past two decades in many countries. And this whole experiment has been undertaken without convincing empirical evidence that the public is better served. The enterprise has been launched solely for the benefit of particular capitalists, their singular interests shrouded in the truistic superiority of the market system. The drive for privatization is an especially vivid example of capitalist class consciousness at work in our time.

When all the rhetoric about private sector efficiency and money wasting in the public sector is stripped away, the rationale for privatization is exposed as the idea of two orders of human beings—the entrepreneurial and the non-entrepreneurial. No rewards can be too great for the entrepreneurial, who must be allowed to lead, if necessary by depriving others—closing down plants, slashing jobs and moving production facilities from one part of the world to another. If the non-entrepreneurs are brutally affected by such things, that is the price of progress.

In the final analysis, the dominance of the capitalist class today is justified, as was the rule of dominant classes in other historic periods, on the premise that lesser beings from lower social classes do not have the capacity to be in charge. Sigmund Freud once expressed such a view, writing about the human mind and comparing it to society as a whole: "Our mind . . . is no peacefully self-contained unity. It is rather to be compared with a modern State in which a mob, eager for enjoyment and destruction, has to be held down forcibly by a prudent superior class."[14]

This position is typical of today's elites, whose self-interest requires that they restrain the demands of their inferiors. They warn that disorder would follow if "the people," unequipped as they are to appreciate the big picture, were allowed to have an influence. Their accomplices in the media and academe issue dire predictions of economic disaster if wages and salaries are not held in check and if the cost of social programs is not reduced. At the same time, and with no apparent self-consciousness, the media support the further enrichment of the super-rich.

Dominant social classes have often been vengeful in the way they strike out at rebelliousness on the part of those in the dominated classes. Indeed, the secret fear of all ruling classes is that those below them will cast off their lassitude and overturn the existing social order.

A crucial example of hatred directed toward a dominated social class can be seen in the European Fascist movements of the twentieth century. Fascism emerged in the 1920s and 1930s as an expression of middle-class fear that the working class, enduring hardship and mindful of the success of Bolshevism in the Soviet Union, were on the brink of attaining power. One of the primary reasons that middle-class people were radicalized in support of the extreme right was the concern that their societies faced proletarianization.

The hyperinflation of 1923 in Germany ruined a large proportion of the middle class, which predisposed them to see Hitler as their bulwark against what they perceived as the ultimate catastrophe—being pushed down into the working class. Big-business support for Hitler came only later, in the early 1930s, when the Great Depression reached Germany: in the eyes of many, the unemployment of millions presaged a Soviet-style revolution. Without middle-class and big-business antipathy to the working class, Hitler could never have come to power.

On a subject about which generalizations need to be made with caution, one stands out. When they are threatened from below, the fury of dominant social classes knows few bounds.

## Chapter 8

# The Outlook of Wage
# and Salary Earners

On an October evening in 1997, over 20,000 teachers jammed into Maple Leaf Gardens in Toronto. The huge rally was a show of strength in the struggle between Ontario's primary and secondary school teachers and the Conservative provincial government. The Mike Harris Tories were committed to a forced-march transformation of the provincial education system, which involved deep cuts to the education budget. The government's proposed Bill 160 would remove such items as teacher preparation time, class size and the use of non-teachers in the classroom from the realm of collective bargaining between teachers and school boards. Instead, these matters would be decided by the cabinet at Queen's Park. Seldom had the province's 126,000 primary and secondary teachers, in both the public and Catholic school systems, been so united in their outlook. Never had they been so prepared to stage a province-wide strike, an act much more in the tradition of France's political strikes than that of labour protest in the English-speaking countries.

In his enthusiastically received address to the rally, the Canadian Labour Congress president, Bob White, described the teachers as working-class people. It was a symbolic moment of real importance. Earlier generations of teachers would have recoiled at the suggestion that they belonged to the working class. The teachers at Maple Leaf Gardens were not offended. A student of mine, who is an electrician and a union activist, said she thought it was time to welcome salaried employees like teachers into the working class. To her it seemed that such employees had been away on a long journey and now they were returning home.

Under the pressures of the 1990s, the consciousness of wage and salary earners has been changing. It is no longer incongruous for someone like Bob White, the former leader of the autoworkers' union, to speak for the unionized section of a social class that now includes teachers as well as industrial workers. The teachers' rally at Maple Leaf Gardens reminds us that social classes are constantly evolving.

We can easily make the mistake of assuming that the members of a social class share more of a common outlook than they actually do. But we must also guard against the mistake, when we are analyzing class consciousness, of expecting to find the stereotypical characteristics of a social class of several decades ago in a contemporary social class. It would be odd indeed if the outlook of the working class/middle class of today was not significantly different from that of the industrial working class of the post-war decades.

In the two post-war decades, the working class exhibited a pronounced consciousness of their common interests as a social class, and this solidarity was manifested in two immensely important developments: the popular support for the trade union movement in its struggles to improve living standards and working conditions; and the crucial political backing given by the working class to the creation and amelioration of social programs and public education.

While both of these developments occurred across the industrialized world at the time, the differences from country to country were also significant. In the 1950s in the United States, industrial unions staged a series of important strikes, but these events did not produce a socialist or social democratic political party linked to labour like those in Western European countries and in Canada. In France during the same years, there was widespread support for a socialist transformation of society among members of the working class. In West Germany, the idea of workers' participation in the management of industry resonated so deeply with workers that the Christian Democratic government felt pressured to pass legislation establishing worker representation on the boards of many large companies. In Britain, the first post-war political act of the working class was to throw Winston Churchill and the Conservatives out of power and to deliver a majority to the Labour Party in the 1945 general election. In Canada, a 1943 Gallup Poll that put the social democratic Cooperative Commonwealth Federation (CCF) ahead of the governing Liberals motivated the Mackenzie King government to espouse full-employment policies and to begin the construction of the welfare state. Such manifestations of working-class political action and consciousness—many more could be cited—could quite mistakenly be thought to have been characteristic of the industrial working class throughout the decades of its existence as a distinct social class. But nothing could be further from the truth.

As we have seen, the industrial working class developed gradually as a consequence of the second industrial revolution, beginning in the last decades of the nineteenth century. But in the late nineteenth and early twentieth centuries, industrial workers, those who worked in the new factories, were on the margins of working-class political action. When Samuel Gompers founded the American Federation of Labour (AFL) in the late nineteenth century, he had little interest in the ordinary industrial worker. His organization was intended for an aristocracy of labour, the skilled tradesmen of the era—printers, railway engineers, carpenters, bricklayers, plumbers and electricians. In those early days, the institutional centre of trade unionism were the "craft unions." It was only decades later in the 1930s and 1940s, during the explosive drive to organize industrial workers in the great factories of North America, that large-scale "industrial" unionism was born.

In the 1930s, wage earners in the factories of the second industrial revolution were faced with the catastrophe of the Great Depression. Millions lost their jobs. Out of that turmoil came the movement to protect and organize industrial workers in a way that broke with the craft-unionist notions of Gompers and the AFL. The new unions, in auto, steel, chemical, rubber and other types of industrial plants, gathered beneath the umbrella of the Congress of Industrial Organizations (CIO) under the leadership of John L. Lewis. In these new unions, everyone working in the plant who was not a part of management was in the same bargaining unit. Included were skilled tradesmen, semi-skilled workers on the assembly line and unskilled general labourers. With the formation of the new industrial unions, the working class was transforming itself. Its leadership was new, the principles around which it was organizing were different, and the centre of the working class itself had shifted.

So deep was the division between the new CIO unions and the old AFL unions that they split into two separate labour organizations in the United States. In Canada, where workers were mainly in unions with head offices in the U.S., the same split existed. The Canadian sections of the old AFL craft unions were mostly grouped together in the Trades and Labour Congress (TLC), while the Canadian sections of the new CIO industrial unions formed the Canadian Congress of Labour (CCL). The split endured until 1954 in the U.S., when the AFL and CIO once again reunited to form the AFL-CIO. Two years later, the split also ended in Canada when the TLC and CCL merged to form the Canadian Labour Congress (CLC).

The shift within the trade union movement from craft to industrial unions reflected, as we have seen, a change in the nature of the working class itself. It took more than half a century for the full effect of the transformation to be completely reflected in the character of the most important working-class organizations, the trade unions. Only in the 1950s, when the split in the labour movement was resolved, did the new industrial working class with its industrial unions come into its own.

As this potent example demonstrates, social classes evolve over long periods of time. Changes in technology and in working methods can occur long before they modify a social class's self-concept and mode of expression to correspond to the new realities. From our vantage point in the 1990s, we see the working class of the 1950s as the old working class, almost as though its character had existed from time immemorial. This fails to recognize that the working class of the 1950s was a new form. After decades of struggle within its own ranks, the working class had reinvented itself.

A similar process has been under way in recent decades in the formation of the contemporary working class/middle class. Today's wage and salary earners are certainly diverse in character, but it should not simply be assumed that those within this broad social class are so disparate in terms of income, skills, gender, ethnicity and race that they have no common perception of their relationship to the dominant capitalist class. On the contrary, there is plenty of evidence that a very large proportion of wage and salary earners do harbour common societal attitudes that differentiate their outlook from that of the members of the capitalist class.

Public opinion surveys reveal that the majority of people in most industrialized countries now see life prospects for themselves and their children much more negatively than they did a decade or two ago. In France in the mid-1990s, for example, opinion polls showed that 80 percent of the population feared unemployment or a reduced standard of living. This was in sharp contrast to the view of 80 percent of the French in the mid-1980s that their lot in life would improve.[1]

(In reporting the findings of public opinion polls in the industrialized countries, I am making the reasonable assumption that their results broadly reflect the views of the working class/middle class that comprises about 70 percent of adults. In such surveys, the presence of a sizeable number of respondents who are not wage and salary earners blurs the results as expressions of class consciousness to a certain extent. If wage and salary earners alone were surveyed, the contrast between their views and those of the economic elite would be even sharper.)

In Canada more people thought the domestic standard of living would decrease rather than increase in the next twenty years. Polled in December 1996 by Gallup, 46 percent of respondents made this gloomy forecast, compared with 25 percent who thought Canadian living standards would increase. Significantly, among those aged thirty to fifty, over half of the respondents predicted a fall in living standards, while only 19 percent expected an increase.[2] These were the shell-shocked survivors of an era when wage and salary earners had been devastated by corporate downsizing and when their incomes had failed to increase. Respondents to these polls were projecting their own experience into the future.

In a poll from March 1997, 45 percent of Canadians said they were worse off than four years earlier, while 32 percent reckoned they were better off. This negative perception held for every region and for all age groups, with the exception of those aged eighteen to twenty-nine, 53 percent of whom thought they were better off than four years earlier.[3] And like the French, Canadians looked back on a past when things had seemed to be improving. Fifty percent of respondents to a Gallup Poll question said they figured their standard of living was higher than that of their parents, compared with 26 percent who thought their living standard was lower. Significantly, this perception grew ever stronger from younger to older respondents. Only 23 percent of those aged eighteen to twenty-nine thought themselves better off than their parents. Among the other age groups, the responses were as follows: 30–39, 45 percent; 40–49, 54 percent; 50–64, 69 percent; and over 65, 75 percent.[4] The older the age group, the more its members had experienced and could remember the era of the Great Social Compromise when the real incomes of wage and salary earners were increasing. Younger Canadians, with their experience restricted to a time when incomes remained flat, and for many actually declined, have a notably less rosy view of their living standards.

In May 1997, when asked what they thought was the most important question facing the country, Canadians put unemployment far ahead of all other concerns. Forty-four percent of those polled picked unemployment as Canada's most serious problem, far ahead of the 14 percent who chose government deficit and debt.[5]

Like the French and Canadians, Americans also expressed broad dissatisfaction with the state of affairs in their society. In November 1995, one year after the election of a Republican-controlled Congress, 64 percent of Americans said they were dissatisfied, compared with 33 percent who expressed satisfaction. A majority of Americans polled opposed measures proposed by the Republicans to slash social and educational spending whose main beneficiaries were the poor, the elderly and the young. Fifty-three percent of those polled were opposed to cutting the tax credit for the poor; 66 percent were against cuts to Medicaid spending (assistance to the poor); 75 percent opposed cuts to Medicare spending (assistance to the elderly poor); and 74 percent were against cuts to student loans.[6]

Perhaps surprisingly for the world's most staunchly free enterprise country, 58 percent of Americans surveyed told the Gallup Poll that they believed that large corporations had too much power. To put that in perspective, a majority of Americans also displayed their characteristic suspicion of government, with 63 percent of them opining that the Internal Revenue Service (IRS) had too much power. Sixty percent thought the federal government in Washington was too powerful, while only 36 percent had that view of labour unions.[7]

These public opinion polls from France, Canada and the United States indicate a common outlook among wage and salary earners even in societies as different as France and the United States. In all three cases, jobs are high on the list of concerns, ahead of government deficits and public sector debt. This sharply reverses the priorities of business and of economic orthodoxy, which regard public sector deficit and debt reduction as paramount in importance. And unlike business, wage and salary earners remain strong supporters of social programs and public education and are insistently opposed to cuts in these areas.

Common experience naturally underlies a common outlook. Wage and salary earners are under great pressure today in every industrialized country. As we have seen, the real incomes of many wage and salary earners have declined. Moreover, wage and salary earners, whether they work in the private or public sector, have been through repeated rounds of downsizing. Survivors are left looking over their shoulders, ever wary that another assault could begin at any time.

While there is unmistakable evidence of a common outlook among the majority of wage and salary earners, it is also clear that highly diverse expressions of political allegiance are found among members of the working class/middle class. The fact that a sizeable minority of wage and salary earners vote for parties of the right, and in some cases, the extreme right, has an important impact on the outcome of elections. In recent decades in many industrialized countries, a portion of the working class/middle class has attached itself to the political projects of the extreme right. In the late 1960s, a sizeable number of American industrial workers supported backlash anti-black candidates like George Wallace, the former Alabama governor who ran for the presidency in 1968. A significant minority of American blue-collar voters, the so-called Reagan Democrats, supported Ronald Reagan in the presidential elections of 1980 and 1984. In the 1994 U.S. Congressional elections, angry white voters, both men and women, particularly those with only a high school education or less, those whose real incomes had fallen sharply, deserted the Democrats and helped the Republicans win control of the Senate and the House of Representatives.[8] More recently, Patrick J. Buchanan, who sought the Republican presidential nomination in 1996 on a xenophobic America First program, drew a considerable blue-collar following. In Britain in the 1960s, a large number of working-class voters saw themselves as followers of Enoch Powell, the extreme-right-wing Conservative whose stock in trade was to denounce immigration to Britain from the Caribbean and South Asia. In the 1980s, a substantial minority of wage and salary earners voted for Margaret Thatcher. In Canada, the populist right-wing Reform Party led by Preston Manning has attracted blue-collar supporters in promulgating policies that involve immigrant- and Quebec-bashing. In 1995, when the people of Ontario elected a harsh right-wing Conservative government led by Mike Harris, large numbers of wage and salary earners were drawn to the political right's argument that they were overtaxed and that a main reason for their overtaxation was too many people on welfare.

A similar extreme-right tendency developed in Western Europe, most notably seen in the rise of the Front National in France under the leadership of Jean-Marie Le Pen, a former paratrooper. Since the early 1980s, the Front National has built its political support around the link it makes between the issues of unemployment and immigration. Le Pen promises to expel three million foreigners from France, most of them from North Africa, and thereby to provide jobs for the French. The Front National, which won 15 percent of the vote in the first of two rounds of legislative elections in the spring of 1997, is supported by a considerable working-class constituency, concentrated in places like the suburbs of Paris, Marseille and the auto manufacturing city of Mulhouse in Alsace. On the other hand, when France elected a Socialist government in 1997, wage and salary earners responded to the case made by the political left that they were the victims of a punitive economic order under which the public health care and educational systems that they value were withering.

From such behaviour, it could be assumed that the wage and salary earners of the working class/middle class have flipped and flopped from one end of the political spectrum to the other. There will, of course, always be some support among wage and salary earners for all major political parties. There are certainly differences in political affiliation between male and female wage and salary earners. And there are differences having to do with particular occupational groups, ethnicity and race. A sizeable number of wage and salary earners in all industrialized countries display fiercely illiberal ideas on the subjects of race, gender and immigration.

None of these political tendencies or parties of the populist and extreme right has developed primarily as a vehicle for the views of wage and salary earners. In each case, the primary constituencies to offer significant backing to these xenophobic movements have been small business owners and shopkeepers, the constituencies that supported Fascism in the 1920s and 1930s. But as was the case with classical Fascism, these movements have also succeeded in winning support from alienated blue-collar workers, who find in the radical assault on established political parties and the government of the day a vehicle for their own dissatisfactions. While none of these movements has attracted the support of anything close to a majority of wage and salary earners, permanent long-term unemployment and the message linking immigration to joblessness have had their effect in winning the allegiance of a working-class constituency.

Despite the contradictory behaviour, can it nonetheless be said that there are attitudes common to most wage and salary earners that distinguish them from members of the capitalist class? The answer to this question is yes, though that answer may be surprising. In North America and Western Europe, in the way they vote in general elections and in the things they tell pollsters, wage and salary earners do display a more or less consistent set of attitudes, which are indeed clearly distinguishable from those of capitalists.

As the French, Canadian and American poll results clearly illustrate, wage and salary earners are much more concerned about job creation and reducing unemployment than about cutting government spending and tackling government deficits. Wage and salary earners strongly support social programs and public education systems from which they feel that they or members of their families benefit. In opinion surveys in various industrialized countries, wage and salary earners have favoured increased government spending on social and educational programs even if this necessitates an increase in taxes. These core values have been under repeated assault in recent years from free market proselytizers. Indeed, in the late 1990s, there is strong evidence of a renewal of commitment to the core values among wage and salary earners, weary of downsizing and cuts to social programs and increasingly hostile to the rhetoric about globalization's benefits.

In stark contrast, members of the capitalist class display a very different set of core attitudes. They approve cuts to social spending and tax reductions, regarding the achievement of low inflation and the reduction of government deficits as more important than job creation. With minor variations, these attitudes are expressed throughout North America and Europe by business lobby organizations and conservative political parties. In Canada, these views are promulgated by the Business Council on National Issues (BCNI) and the Reform and Progressive Conservative parties. In the United States, they are advanced by the Business Roundtable and the Republican Party. British Conservatives, the overwhelming party of choice for British capitalists, hold strongly to these views, while German Christian Democrats, the main party of the right in Germany, adhere to a more centrist version of these ideas.

While making the point that wage and salary earners have societal values that differ substantially from those of capitalists, we must not push this too far. The disagreement is considerable but far from absolute. Many wage and salary earners accept the idea of a market-centred economy in which most firms are privately owned. While they want quite different outcomes in the economy and society than the capitalists do, they accept the basic paradigm of capitalist society and its economic system. Even though a majority of wage and salary earners will not vote for parties of the right, all major parties, even the Communist parties of Western Europe, operate within the broad assumptions of the capitalist system. Elections, therefore, contest only a relatively limited terrain of disagreement.

We regularly see the differing core attitudes of wage and salary earners on the one hand and capitalists on the other in the mainstream media, which, as we have noted, overwhelmingly favours the outlook of the capitalists. The media like to contrast these two sets of views as representing a struggle between realism and delusional thinking. In June 1997, when the people of France revealed that they espoused the attitudes of the working class/middle class when they threw out a right-of-centre government, which had been clearly committed to the viewpoint of the capitalists, the Anglo-American media were caustic in their response. Were the French out of their minds? The *Washington Post*'s editorial was headlined "Wishful France,"[9] and that of the *Economist* was titled "Poor France." The *Economist* reiterated capitalist orthodoxy when it refuted the newly elected government's employment strategy, stating that "jobs could not be created without cutting public spending."[10] The idea that the priorities of the working class/middle class could serve as the basis for viable government policies was derisively dismissed. The *Washington Post* and the *Economist* were fully in accord with the outlook of the heads of French private companies, 91 percent of whom expressed the view, when polled, that the French Socialist government had little chance of success in its battle to create jobs and reduce unemployment.[11]

If I am right that there is a distinction between the core attitudes of wage and salary earners and those of capitalists, why do the more numerous wage and salary earners not simply elect governments in tune with their views?

I have little doubt that if a referendum were to give the peoples of the industrialized world a straightforward choice between the two sets of attitudes summarized here, those of the working class/middle class would prevail in every single industrialized country, even in the United States. But political choices are not made in an abstract realm. Real political choices are made in a setting where many questions are on the table simultaneously, so that few elections come down to a choice between clearly differentiated sets of fundamental options. And real political choices are made in an environment where the capitalist class enjoys far greater power than wage and salary earners. To ignore capitalist hegemony in the way political choices are made is to ignore reality.

The working class/middle class does not vote as a single bloc in any industrialized country. To be sure, across Western Europe, many more wage and salary earners vote for Socialist and social democratic parties than for parties of the right. And in the United States, many more wage and salary earners vote for the Democrats than for the Republicans. In Canada, the centrist Liberal Party wins more votes of wage and salary earners at the federal level than does any other party. In elections in major Western European countries, a majority of wage and salary earners never vote for parties of the right, even when those parties win power. In Britain, during the era of Thatcher and Major when Conservatives won elections in 1979, 1983, 1987 and 1992, the Tories never won anything close to a majority of the votes of wage and salary earners. In the United States, since the Great Depression of the 1930s, a majority of the votes cast by wage and salary earners has gone to the Democrats in every presidential and Congressional election. In the unusual Canadian case, where a centrist Liberal Party has retained major party status between parties of the right and left, a majority of votes cast by wage and salary earners has never gone to a party of the right since the Great Depression, even in the Conservative landslides of 1958 and 1984. When parties of the right take elections, they certainly manage to win more of the votes of wage and salary earners than usual, but never a majority of those votes. The basic pattern of class voting remains intact even in those cases.

Not surprisingly, capitalists vote more single-mindedly than do wage and salary earners. No matter how much praise a social democratic leader like François Mitterrand, Tony Blair or Bob Rae may receive from business leaders, only a tiny proportion of executives ever vote for parties of the left. In 1988, when Mitterrand was reelected to the French presidency, he won the votes of only 3 percent of business executives, more of whom voted for Le Pen of the Front National. In the autumn of 1995, 87 percent of top American chief executive officers told *Business Week* pollsters that they opposed President Bill Clinton, while only 9 percent said they supported him.[12]

In addition, voter turnout varies markedly according to social class, with voting rates higher among affluent voters than among the less affluent. This is crucial in the United States, which has a uniquely low rate of voter turnout among advanced countries. In U.S. presidential elections, about half the eligible voters participate, and in non-presidential-year Congressional elections, the turnout is much lower—it was 39 percent in 1994. When Newt Gingrich led the Republicans to victory in both houses of Congress in 1994, only one adult in five actually voted for the Republicans. To interpret such a mandate as reflective of the views of the American population as a whole, when 80 percent of Americans did not vote for the Republicans, is to indulge in fantasy. Moreover, societal power influences the way elections work and how governments behave. In our society, because the capitalist class is the hiring and firing class, its decisions have a determining effect on the course of the economy, which explains why everyone pays more attention to what business and business lobbies have to say during elections than to statements from any other so-called pressure group.

In a society with one social class dominant over another, the dominant class's hegemony is most visible in the way the economy runs. This is true whether the right or the left is in power. But the hegemony of the dominant class extends well beyond such direct and obvious economic decision making to the entire structure of society to societal values and culture in the widest sense of the term.

On February 27, 1997, the management of the French auto manufacturer Renault issued a brief statement in Paris announcing that it would close its plant in Vilvorde, Belgium, in the coming summer. The decision came as a brutal blow to 3,100 Belgian autoworkers whose jobs were to vanish. Personal plans for the future—mortgage payments, retirement hopes—were suddenly thrown into terrible doubt. The action was unexpected because the Vilvorde factory had been completely overhauled at considerable cost over the previous two years, and the workers in the plant had accepted a restructuring regimen so that they would keep their jobs. The plant was as productive as others in the Renault system.

In the post-war decades, Renault became synonymous with French industry. Nationalized at the end of the war because its management had collaborated with the occupying Germans, Renault also became a symbol of working-class strength in France. The militant Congrès Général du Travail (CGT), entrenched in the plants of the automaker, won gains in wages and working conditions that set the standards in France. In the early 1990s, Renault was partially privatized and has been fighting for survival in the increasingly volatile European auto market. The company bounced back from difficult years in the mid-1980s with successful new models, the Clio, Twingo and Megane, to sustain a ten-year run of profits. In 1996, though, Renault was back in the red to the tune of 5 billion French francs (about US$864 million).[13]

For Belgian and other European autoworkers, the announced closure of the Vilvorde plant was ominous. In recent years, tens of thousands of jobs have been lost in Europe as the European automakers adapt to competition by the Japanese and the Americans. Currently, the Japanese sell just over 10 percent of the cars in Western Europe, supplying them from their European plants as well as from those in Japan.[14] But as the European Union eases restrictions on the sale of Japanese autos, the pressure on Europe's manufacturers is certain to grow. For their part, the American auto producers Ford and GM have supplied their European markets from plants in Europe that are almost entirely separate from their North American production system.

For Belgium, the stakes in the Vilvorde closing were enormous because the Belgians were per capita the biggest auto producers in the world. In 1996, the country's thirty-four thousand autoworkers produced 1.2 million vehicles annually. All five car-production plants in Belgium were owned by foreigners: Vilvorde by Renault and the other four by Ford, Volkswagen, General Motors and Volvo.[15] The Belgians feared that as European automakers strove to increase productivity to meet the Japanese challenge, they might close other Belgian plants, since it was easier politically for them to shut down operations in Belgium than in the countries where they were based. Naturally enough, the sentiment was widespread in Belgium in the aftermath of the Renault announcement that a French company had sacrificed Belgian jobs to save jobs in France. Would the reaction pit Belgian workers against French workers?

From the moment the shutdown announcement was made, the European trade union movement strove to avoid just that result, its goal being to create a Europe-wide working-class alliance in support of the Belgian employees. In the days that followed, the Renault workers at Vilvorde occupied their plant. Thousands of them and additional contingents of Renault workers from France and Spain marched through the streets of Brussels, and demonstrations were held in the French cities where Renaults were made. In an unprecedented show of solidarity, all Renault's plants in Europe, principally in France and Spain, conducted a simultaneous one-hour strike in opposition to the shutdown. As one Belgian unionist, in an angry open letter to Renault's chairman, Louis Schweitzer, put it: "I am not going to speak to you of the social drama you have created at Vilvorde. . . . I do not have the impression that that would interest you or that you would think about it for a second . . . but

I must thank you for having created a unique opportunity for the first European trade union struggle."[16]

These initial demonstrations by Renault workers were soon followed by a much wider working-class political mobilization. Three weeks after the closure announcement, seventy thousand workers, mainly from Belgium, France, Italy and the Netherlands, marched through the streets of Brussels to bring the issue squarely before the political leadership of the European Union. This demonstration was significant, not just because of the numbers involved but conceptually as well; the banner under which they marched was "l'Europe sociale."[17] The concept of "social Europe"—the idea that the European Union had to commit to social programs, to full employment and the rights of wage and salary earners—was one with immense potential. For the first time the phrase "social Europe" was more than a rhetorical device used by politicians: it was becoming an actual expression of the aspirations of a very large number of workers. The importance of the Brussels demonstration was underlined by the participation of the French Socialist leader, Lionel Jospin. Ten weeks later he was to lead the Socialists and their allies to victory in legislative elections and to be sworn in as prime minister of France.

Since the launch of the single European market in the mid-1980s, bankers and industrialists have spearheaded the move to a European economy in place of national economies. Although Socialist and social democratic political parties in Europe always supported the idea of European union, working-class militants were deeply suspicious of it, and with good reason. Throughout the transition to the single market, working-class movements fought for social protection against the new market freedoms being won by the corporations. But with the announced closing of the Vilvorde plant, the question of European union took a sudden turn. The seventy thousand who marched in Brussels were not theoreticians speculating about the potential for a European social union to complement the economic union. There had been plenty of that before. Those who marched were working-class activists taking the first step out from behind the barricades of their separate nations to embrace the idea of a common European struggle against the logic of globalization.

The massive turnout in Brussels of autoworkers from across Europe, employed by all the major auto companies, showed that they knew they were involved in a common struggle. Jerry Hicks, who worked at the Rolls-Royce plant in Bristol, England, made the trip to Brussels because, as he said, "My community is that of the workers." He couldn't see much difference between Rolls-Royce and Renault: "Perhaps the trademark's prestigious," he said of Rolls-Royce, "but the methods are the same." When Cataldo Ballistreri, who has worked for Fiat in Turin, Italy, for twenty years, heard about the demonstration, he booked his plane ticket the same night and went to Brussels with a dozen other militants from Rome and Milan. "Today the practice of the owners is to fire the workers in one country and to say to the others, 'This could be you,'" he remarked. He would like to see a "social Europe" one day, "but how can we think that Europe exists for the people, with eighteen million unemployed in the countries of the European Community?" Sylvie Foster, a Belgian who has worked at the Volkswagen plant at Forest, near Brussels, for ten years, had a brother-in-law who worked for Renault at Vilvorde. "When we heard the news of the shutdown, we didn't believe it," she said. "The first reaction was to tell ourselves that tomorrow the Germans could do the same thing and close our plant."[18]

Vilvorde mattered because it raised the question whether workers were capable of defending themselves on a European or an international scale against the effects of the corporate globalization agenda. William Greider, author of *One World, Ready or Not: The Manic Logic of Global Capitalism*, has written about the way successful multinationals, in their effort to thrive, end up creating a vast capacity for overproduction. By the year 2000, he estimates, the world auto industry will be able to manufacture about seventy-nine million vehicles for a global market that will total about fifty-eight million buyers.[19] To stay abreast of the competition, auto manufacturers continue to open new plants in various parts of the world. The inexorable effect will be the closing of already existing plants, and in addition the laying-off of tens of thousands of autoworkers in plants that manage to stay open.

But the battle fought by European workers against plant shutdowns and corporate downsizing has not been limited to the auto industry. At the same time as workers were mobilizing against the Renault shutdown at Vilvorde and German coalminers were marching to protest the loss of government support for the coal industry, 300,000 Italian workers demonstrated to put pressure on their supposedly left-wing government, and German steelworkers took to the streets of Frankfurt, their country's financial capital, in a battle to keep their jobs.[20]

In the past, workers' struggles were largely confined to confrontations against corporate managers and state authorities within the boundaries of a single country. Most production was for the national market, and workers could appeal to their local communities and their fellow citizens in battles for their jobs. When those who produce goods and services live in the same community or country as those who consume the products, everyone understands that they share a common interest. If those who consume insist on bringing in the products of outside competitors, they may gain the advantage of a lower price, but they also cut off their nose to spite their face by depriving members of their own community of their jobs. In this case, a lower price may end up meaning higher outlays for unemployment benefits.

But when production and consumption are internationalized, the sense of community disappears. Those who consume are far away from those who produce. Cost cutting and bargain hunting might deprive someone somewhere of a job, but it would not be your job or the job of someone you knew. It is not accidental that neoconservative globalization promoters have launched an assault on the idea that people are both consumers and producers and therefore must look out for their interests as both. They want a world in which people think of themselves only as consumers.

In an age when those who consume goods and services are remote from those who produce them, workers have lost one of the crucial advantages of the shared "citizenship" of the past. In the attempt of European autoworkers to mount a Europe-wide struggle to save their jobs, there was a concrete effort to resolve this problem and once again to integrate the community of interests between consumers and producers. The battle over Vilvorde was a harbinger of battles to come.

But the immediate goal of the Vilvorde movement was to keep the Renault plant open, and that battle was ultimately lost. The final chapter in the closing of the plant was intimately caught up in the drama of French politics. When he participated in the Brussels demonstration in mid-March 1997, Lionel Jospin would have scoffed at the suggestion that he was to become prime minister of France on June 2. But one week after the Brussels demonstration, France's president, Jacques Chirac, in a gigantic political miscalculation, called elections to the National Assembly one year sooner than was necessary. During his victorious electoral campaign, Jospin expressed hope that the Renault plant at Vilvorde could be saved in the event of a Socialist victory. He never formally promised to keep the plant open, but he said he would take another look at the Renault decision to close the plant. At the very end of the campaign, Jospin appeared at an election rally in Lille with workers from Vilvorde.

Shortly after he was elected prime minister, Jospin appointed an independent expert to review the Vilvorde situation. A month later, the expert's report confirmed Renault management's decision to shut down the plant. In response to angry accusations from the Vilvorde workers that he had betrayed them, Jospin insisted that he had kept his word. In the end, the Vilvorde workers won a much more generous benefits package than they would have if the conservatives had won the French election. In addition, the Vilvorde plant was to be refurbished as the site of a future industrial plant where several hundred jobs would be located. Still, the European movement to save the Vilvorde plant had failed to achieve its goal. In the battle, lessons had been learned that would be valuable for the future, but they were bitter lessons.

## Chapter 9

# Poverty and Backlash

I t may be true, as the old saying goes, that the poor are always with us. But the face of poverty is being redrawn as the world is transformed by the new capitalism. What has stiffened the spine of the poor in ways that the affluent find highly disconcerting is the rise of a new and rapidly expanding cohort of city dwellers living in poverty. Although poverty is a more serious problem in some countries than in others—it is more severe in the United States, Britain and Canada than it is in France or Sweden—there has been a general increase in the number of poor throughout the industrialized countries. And even if the number of poor in rural areas has remained fairly stable, their number in the cities has skyrocketed.

Although rural poverty has a lower profile than urban, it has actually been intensifying in significant ways over the past couple of decades. In the United States, despite the celebrated and heroic efforts of such union leaders as Cesar Chavez, the incomes of farm labourers have been declining dramatically. Real wages for the more than two million American farm workers have fallen, on average, by 20 to 25 percent over the past twenty years, making it very difficult for those affected to afford housing and other basic necessities. Even without taking inflation into account, wages are lower than they used to be. In Watsonville, California, for example, the average wage for picking strawberries declined from us$6.55 an hour in 1985 to us$6.25 an hour in 1997. In nearby Salinas, the piece rate for picking broccoli was 20 percent lower in 1997 than in the mid-1980s. California farm workers complain that their incomes have fallen over the past few years from about us$9,000 a year to about us$8,000. One reason for their worsening wages is the plentiful supply of immigrant workers, most of them Mexican, which allows the farm owners to hire those willing to work for the lowest wages.[1] In Florida, where immigrant farm labour is also plentiful, there have been cases of employers paying workers as little as us$2 or us$3 an hour and cheating them out of overtime and Social Security.[2]

While rural poverty remains serious, most of the new poverty in the advanced countries is urban. As the nation-state has receded as the locus of economic activity, a new economic model has emerged in which the proportion of the workforce that earns a living wage employed in full-time work—the primary workforce—has receded and a greatly expanded secondary workforce has grown up. Those in the secondary workforce move in and out of it as jobs are created and lost, and often subsist on part-time incomes when they would prefer full-time work. Over the past several decades, the proportion of the population unable to earn a living has steadily increased. Taken together, these developments have pushed a very large number of people into marginalization and, in many cases, outright poverty.

The explosive growth of the new urban poor provides a classic illustration of the political economy of underdevelopment. In an inner-city neighbourhood, as manufacturing jobs are lost as a consequence of recession or globalization, a large part of the population is marginalized. Workers who formerly had full-time jobs are pushed into periods of unemployment with spells of part-time, low-paying work. Such workers and their families are frequently driven into debt as their incomes fall. They are also forced into the invidious position of becoming clients of the welfare system.

As a part of the population is reduced to an ever more marginal position, those with the assets to leave the inner city often do so. The departure of those who still have full-time work and disposable income further depresses the community, lowering property values and sharply reducing the demand for the goods and services of local businesses. The downward spiral continues as some of those businesses shut down, while others cut the number of their employees and still others move out of the community. The consequence of this vicious cycle is the creation of regions of cities occupied by the new poor or sub-proletariat.

In *Inside the Inner City*, a penetrating study of how one community in Britain, the London borough of Hackney, experienced just such a vicious cycle of underdevelopment in the 1980s, Paul Harrison concludes that the process at work in Hackney parallels that in other such communities in Europe and North America: "A sub-proletariat has been produced and is growing in numbers: under-educated, unskilled or de-skilled, unemployed and increasingly unemployable, and dangerously concentrated in poor regions and inner cities."[3]

In 1985, I visited one community in south Chicago that had been devastated by the shutdown of the local steel mill. On the day the plant closed, as I was told by the unemployed members of the United Steelworkers local, their world came to an end. Many of them lost their homes, others drifted away from the community and marriages broke apart. A few militants stayed on to fight for decent severance packages for the workers. The fate of those workers was similar to that of others across south Chicago: the destruction of local communities generated the growth of the new urban poor. And at the same time as industrial jobs were being lost, those who could leave—the people who represented stability and accomplishment—moved away. In their place, all too often, drug dealers and petty criminals became the new status symbols of "success."

On the day I drove across south Chicago, looking at one derelict plant after another, with steel fences rotting and windows smashed, I had the impression that some terrible physical calamity had struck. And it went on for mile after mile. South Chicago had been home to the world's largest concentration of heavy industry. And even south Chicago, huge as it was, was a microcosm of the whole North East and Midwest United States.

The term *underclass* has often been used in the United States to depict those left behind as a consequence of gigantic socioeconomic upheavals like the one in south Chicago. (In my opinion, underclass is a pejorative term because it negatively labels the victims of a social catastrophe, stripping them of dignity and hope and any capacity for self-determination. Instead, I use the term *urban poor*. I acknowledge that some analysts in the United States who use the term underclass do so simply because it is the word in everyday use. Such writers use underclass in a way that carries no pejorative tone.) Ronald B. Mincy and Susan J. Weiner of the Urban Institute in Washington, D.C., in their useful study of the urban poor, have defined those in the underclass as "people who have trouble entering and remaining in the labour force, and [who] derive much of their income from informal, illegal or irregular employment or from public assistance."[4] According to data from their study and using the above definition, the U.S. urban poor population grew from 700,000 in 1970 to nearly 2.5 million by 1980. Since then, this segment of the population has continued to expand.[5] By 1993, more than five million black children—45.9 percent of all black children—were living below the poverty line in the United States. In 1970, 41.5 percent of black children in the United States lived below the poverty line.[6] Many of these children inhabited southern states, the traditional centre of black poverty in the past, but the majority did not. Poverty suffered by black children was on the rise in the inner cities across the United States.

If young men without a completed high school education who would formerly have worked in industry form a large part of the new poor, so too do single mothers and their children. The number of lone-parent families, especially those headed by women, has been growing in every advanced industrialized country. To be sure, there are very considerable differences in the extent of this phenomenon from country to country. At the very low end are countries like Japan and Ireland. In Japan in 1973, lone-parent families constituted 3.6 percent of families with dependent children. By 1983, this proportion had increased to 4.1 percent. In Ireland between 1975 and 1981, the percentage of families with dependent children headed by a lone parent increased from 5.6 to 7.1 percent. In the middle range of incidence of lone-parent families are countries such as France and Switzerland. In France between 1968 and 1982, the percentage of families with dependent children headed by a lone parent increased from 9.5 to 10.2 percent. In Switzerland between 1960 and 1980, the proportion of such families increased from 11.6 to 12.0 percent. At the higher end are countries like Sweden and Britain. From 1960 to 1980, the proportion of families with dependent children headed by a lone parent increased significantly from 9.0 to 14.2 percent in Sweden. In Britain between 1971 and 1984, the percentage increased sharply from 8.0 to 13.0.

Among the industrialized countries, the United States is in a class by itself when it comes to lone-parent families. In 1960, 11.0 percent of families with dependent children were headed by a single parent. By 1984, this proportion had more than doubled to 26.0 percent. To put it in real numbers, between 1960 and 1984, the number of families with dependent children headed by a lone parent in the United States increased from nearly 2.8 million to just over 8.5 million.[7] By 1993, the number of families in the U.S. headed by a lone female had skyrocketed to 12.4 million. And most alarming of all, 28.6 percent of such households had annual incomes of less than US$10,000.[8]

Lone-parent families, overwhelmingly headed by women, clearly do not all face the same circumstances. Some are considerably better off than others. However, it is generally true that single mothers confront an array of significant social barriers that tend to push them and their children into poverty. In the U.S. in 1993, families with children headed by a lone female were 3.98 times as likely as the average family to have incomes in the bottom 10 percent of families.[9] This is partly due to the general trend toward a reduction in the real incomes of wage and salary earners over the past two decades. It is also due to the fact that incomes of women in the labour force remain significantly lower than the incomes of men. And the conditions of families with one income earner have diverged from those with two income earners, particularly since the former has become increasingly common during the past twenty years.

Single mothers with dependent children are the group among the new poor whose numbers are increasing most rapidly. One reason for this is that there are obstacles to single women with children remaining in the labour force at all. In countries such as Sweden and France, where excellent, publicly funded, early-childhood education and child-care programs are available, the child-care problem can often be overcome. In the United States, Britain and Canada, though, where universal early-childhood education and child-care programs are not available, the cost of child care is often prohibitive for single working women with low incomes.

In the United States, not only families headed by a single parent have been sinking into poverty. Young families with children, particularly those headed by parents without university degrees, have experienced an economic freefall. Between 1973 and 1994, the median income of families headed by parents under thirty years of age dropped by 33 percent after adjusting for inflation. A 1997 study of the plight of young American families pointed out that this loss of income was "greater than the 27 percent drop in per capita personal income that occurred during the Great Depression from 1929 to 1933."[10] To combat the downward spiral that has been the fate of their families, many young American women have been increasing the time they spend in the paid labour force and many others have been postponing childbearing until after age thirty. But the adoption of such strategies for coping has not halted a fall in incomes that has dragged down young families of all races and in every region. Real median incomes for families headed by whites under thirty fell 22 percent between 1973 and 1994; those headed by young Hispanics dropped 28 percent; and those headed by young blacks declined by a precipitous 46 percent. Although young families headed by single parents were even worse off, those headed by married couples experienced, on average, a 12 percent decline in their real incomes.[11] The consequence, according to the 1997 study cited above, is that in "every region of the country, nearly one-third (30 percent) to one-half of children in young families are now poor."[12]

Among young families, the major group able to escape the downward income trend was families headed by a university graduate. On average, young families with children headed by a college graduate experienced a 14 percent increase in their real incomes between 1973 and 1992.[13] The problem was that higher education was growing ever more expensive, and was simply beyond the means of many average families. While in 1975, the average cost of tuition and room and board at a public college ate up 16 percent of the income of a moderate-income family, by 1994, these costs consumed 26 percent of such an income.[14]

Propelling the explosion of urban poverty throughout the industrialized world has been the introduction of new technology and the related decline in basic manufacturing jobs. These developments have combined to push an enormous number of unskilled and semi-skilled workers out of the primary workforce. Between 1974 and 1988, the number of jobs in the United States in standard steelmaking plunged from 480,000 to 260,000. In the auto sector, General Motors cut its American production employees by 150,000 during the 1980s.[15] In Canada, the recession of the early 1980s led to a steep decline in manufacturing employment, and many of the jobs lost were never regained when the economy recovered. A decade later, the severe recession of the early 1990s again led to massive job losses in the Canadian manufacturing sector. And it was during this same time that the first effects of the Canada–U.S. Free Trade Agreement (FTA), which came into effect in 1989, were felt in the permanent loss of many Canadian manufacturing jobs. American firms no longer needed to maintain Canadian production plants to gain duty-free access to the Canadian market, and many took the opportunity to shut down their Canadian operations. Canadian firms, as well, were free to move to the low-wage, non-unionized U.S. South and to supply their Canadian and U.S. markets from there. In Britain, the Thatcher government's policies led to a severe contraction in the manufacturing sector during the early 1980s. Across the Channel in France, the efforts of the Socialist government of François Mitterrand to revive the fortunes of traditional industries such as steel failed in the early 1980s. Tens of thousands of job losses followed in the steel industry and automaking in France, in regions such as Lorraine, in the industrial suburbs of Paris and in other traditional manufacturing centres.

Where eighty workers once had jobs on one section of the assembly line at the Chrysler plant in Windsor, Ontario, eight technicians now oversee robots on the same section of the line. And with globalization, many manufacturing jobs have been moved to developing countries. By the early 1990s, more than half a million workers were employed in the so-called Maquiladora factories, located in the Mexican towns along the U.S. border.[16] The output of these factories was aimed at the American market, but their location on the Mexican side of the Rio Grande allowed the mostly American-owned companies to hire much cheaper labour, to operate with reduced safety standards and to spew filth into the environment.

New technology has enabled companies to organize production on a truly global scale, so that, for example, key-punch operators in Southeast Asia can help make products assembled and sold in North America. Similarly, auto parts can be manufactured in Latin America or Asia for inclusion in vehicles assembled in North America or Western Europe. And in the new information processing industry, skilled but cheap labour is readily available for the production of computer software in India and other parts of the Third World.

In North America and Western Europe, the loss of millions of full-time industrial jobs has hit males the hardest, most often those without a secondary school diploma. In the U.S., the median wage for men declined by almost 9 percent between 1979 and 1996, a graphic illustration of the impact of the disappearance of the manufacturing jobs that so many men had relied on in the past. During the same period, women's median wages increased by 7.6 percent.[17] This still left men, on average, with higher incomes than women: men were being pushed into the low-wage environment that most working women had always endured.

In the United States, the decline in men's wages paralleled a steep drop in the number of workers who belonged to unions. In 1960, 35 percent of non-agricultural workers belonged to unions; in 1989 the proportion had dropped to about 17 percent. In the early 1950s, more than 40 percent of young men joined unions when they entered the labour force. By the late 1980s, the proportion was lower than 20 percent. The decline in union membership in the U.S. was most dramatic among young men coming into the labour force without a post-secondary education.[18] In Canada, the proportion of the workforce that is unionized has remained much higher than in the United States. In 1992, 35 percent of Canadian non-agricultural employees were members of unions, about 3.9 million people. But the composition of the trade union movement has undergone an enormous change. In 1992, 41 percent of union members in Canada were women and 37 percent were in the service sector, more than four times their share in 1966.[19] And over the past twenty years, the marked general increase in the level of joblessness may be seen across the industrialized world. Some countries have done better than others—the U.S. has much lower unemployment than France or Italy—but the broad pattern has been toward increasing unemployment. The chart below shows the average unemployment rates for the G-7 countries over the past three decades.

## Unemployment in G-7 Countries

|         | 1964–1973 | 1974–1979 | 1980–1989 | 1990–1994 |
|---------|-----------|-----------|-----------|-----------|
| U.S.    | 4.5%      | 6.7%      | 7.2%      | 6.6%      |
| Japan   | 1.2%      | 1.9%      | 2.5%      | 2.3%      |
| Germany | 0.8%      | 3.2%      | 5.9%      | 6.0%      |
| France  | 2.2%      | 4.5%      | 9.0%      | 10.5%     |
| Italy   | 5.5%      | 6.6%      | 9.5%      | 10.4%     |
| Britain | 3.0%      | 5.0%      | 10.0%     | 9.2%      |
| Canada  | 4.8%      | 7.2%      | 9.3%      | 10.2%     |

In the United States, poverty and race are intimately connected. Although millions of Americans of all races have been reduced to poverty by the gale-strength winds of change, African Americans have been hit by a hurricane. The rise of black urban poverty has been the trigger for backlash politics and the rise of the new right in the United States, so the story has significance for the whole of the industrialized world.

The number of African Americans living in poverty in the great American cities has skyrocketed over the past several decades as a consequence of two crucial developments. The first was the movement of hundreds of thousands of blacks from the rural South to the urban North and Midwest in the post-war era. Blacks came north, both because they were no longer needed in huge numbers to harvest cotton as a consequence of new technology, and because they were drawn to the job market in the great industrial cities like Chicago, Detroit, Cleveland, Buffalo, Pittsburgh, Philadelphia and New York, as well as countless smaller places. Despite fierce discrimination against them in the cities to which they migrated, an employed black working class developed during the 1950s and 1960s.

Then came the second critical development, the new technological revolution that was a major factor in the decline of the manufacturing industries of the North and Midwest where blacks had found jobs. Between 1967 and 1976, over a million jobs were lost in manufacturing, wholesale and retail—crucial sectors for blacks—in New York, Chicago, Philadelphia and Detroit.[20] In his excellent book on the failure of racial integration in the United States, *Tragic Failure*, the retired *New York Times* political columnist Tom Wicker pinpoints the vulnerability of working-class blacks at the historical moment when the number of blue-collar jobs declined sharply: "In 1970 more than 40 percent of all employed black males in the ten largest cities held blue-collar jobs, compared with only 22 percent of employed whites. That made African-Americans disproportionately vulnerable to blue-collar decline. Still, by 1974, 48 percent of black males aged twenty to twenty-four had hung on to skilled or semiskilled industrial and craft jobs that paid enough for them to support a family. By 1986, twelve years later, only 25 percent of black males in that age group had such jobs."[21]

At the same time as black males in the great American cities were being hit with a wave of job losses, an African-American middle class, mostly employed by government and in service sector jobs, was developing. Urban ghettos were transformed as a result of these developments. Industrial job holders, the previous backbone of these communities, were losing their jobs. And many of those in the new black middle class left the old neighbourhoods to move to the suburbs, where it was safer. Some job holders did stay in the ghettos, but the neighbourhoods that had offered hope to blacks in the years of the great migration from the South often became sinkholes of violence and despair. Many in the inner city who wanted work but could locate nothing permanent and certainly not at a living wage, as Wicker says, "found little else but idleness, anger, despair, nihilism, and crime, drug use and drug dealing."[22]

Crime and welfare have been the twin issues that have brought the urban poor glaringly to the attention of middle-class Americans, with enormous political consequences. Violent crime—murder, mugging, rape—is much more prevalent in the U.S. as a whole than in other industrialized countries but most prevalent in the inner cities. Crime subjects those living in poverty to physical torment and fear as well as to material deprivation. A study by the New York City Department of Health delved into the relationship between women who were murdered in New York City and their killers. The study revealed that from 1990 through 1994, nearly half were killed by current or former husbands or by boyfriends. More than half the victims in New York died in private homes, most often their own. Two-thirds of the victims were in the poorest of New York's boroughs, the Bronx and Brooklyn, and three-quarters of those killed by husbands and boyfriends were black or Hispanic.

The director of the Center for Violence Research and Prevention at Columbia University's School of Public Health, Dr. Jeff Fagan, said that the findings contradict the idea that "domestic violence knows no class or colour boundaries. The myth of the classlessness of domestic violence is one that has persisted since the 1960s." Dr. Fagan concluded that domestic violence "is a problem of poverty, associated with other characteristics like low marriage rates, high unemployment and social problems. Whatever we've done to prevent domestic violence has been more effective for white women and we have to figure out how to make it apply to poor women in poor areas."²³

Decades ago, fear of violent crime began driving the middle classes out of the inner cities. And this fear has fuelled the backlash against racial integration that has influenced American politics during the three decades since the presidential election of 1968. In that election, the renegade Democrat George Wallace made the blatant backlash case, but it was the Republican candidate, Richard Nixon, adept at presenting a coded backlash message, who was victorious.

The era when the politics of racial integration was actually in the ascendancy in the U.S. was remarkably brief. Propelled by the 1954 decision of the U.S. Supreme Court that ended segregation of public schools (at least in principle), the civil rights movement flourished in the 1960s. For a few years, the struggle to end segregation in the South won the support of most white Americans. When Police Commissioner Bull Connors directed his thugs wielding cattle prods to contain peaceful protesters in Birmingham, Alabama, the northern public reacted with indignation. The high point of governmental reforms that benefited African Americans occurred in Lyndon Johnson's legislative program in the mid-1960s: the Civil Rights Act of 1964, the Voting Rights Act of 1965 and the Open Housing Act of 1968.

Following these important advances, the anti-integration, anti-black backlash—so central to the conservative domination of American politics for the past thirty years—was not long in coming. The eruption of violence outside the South in the late 1960s in Detroit, Chicago, Newark, Los Angeles and in many other inner cities provoked fear and fury in the white suburbs. The success of the new right in the United States has rested, in large measure, on the willingness of a very sizeable number of wage and salary earning suburban whites to vote for politicians with two programs on offer: higher spending on police and prisons; and lower spending to aid the poor and to rebuild the inner cities.

New-right politicians—it is equally accurate to call them backlash politicians—have also served up a steady diet of attacks against affirmative action. Many whites who had supported an end to formal racial segregation never backed measures to ensure that blacks could get a fair share of jobs or university admissions. From the beginning, affirmative action programs were depicted by right-wing politicians as reverse discrimination. The new right specialized in horror stories of supposed cases of unqualified minorities, women and handicapped people depriving able-bodied white males of employment or admission to universities.

Backlash politics, fuel for the rise of the new right, helped create the conditions for the downward slide of the inner cities to their present condition of unemployment and social despair. And since the expansion of the new urban poor has coincided with the rise of the new right, not only in the United States but in other industrialized countries, the welfare state has become less generous, indeed more punitive, over the past two decades. In the United States, the federal government's guarantee of a minimum level of welfare for those with no other means of support, a provision established by the Roosevelt administration in the 1930s, was ended in 1996 with the passage of a historic welfare "reform" by a Republican Congress. Despite widespread criticism of a reform that experts said could leave a million more children living in destitution, President Bill Clinton, determined to deprive the Republicans of an election issue, signed the controversial bill.

In Ontario in 1995, one of the first measures of the right-wing government of Conservative Mike Harris was to cut welfare payments by 21.6 percent. Similarly in Britain, the Conservative governments of Margaret Thatcher and John Major presided over the tightening of regulations for the receipt of welfare and established an ever-more-punitive relationship between those receiving welfare and the department administering the benefits.


The Great Social Compromise of the post-war decades was predicated on what we can call a "one-nation" concept of society. "One nation" meant that everyone belonged within a single society, where the goal, even if it was a long-term one, was greater equality. Rather than being seen as acceptable, poverty was understood as a challenge to be over-come. Although the rhetoric of the era vastly outdistanced the achieve-ments, the rhetoric mattered, not least because it featured the poor as deserving empathy and assistance rather than condemnation. New social progams and improved education systems were advocated as ways to fur-ther the progress toward equality.

In many industrialized countries today—particularly in the English-speaking countries—the one-nation model has been replaced by a two-nation model. The two-nation model (the term was common parlance in Britain during the Thatcher years) assumes the truism of the poor always being with us. Furthermore, instead of seeing the existence of large numbers of poor as an indictment of society, the two-nation model involves a radical reversal of perspective, blaming the poor themselves for their plight. Favoured by the new right, the two-nation model con-demns the very measures that have been undertaken to deal with the problems of social inequality and poverty. Instead of understanding rising unemployment and underemployment as consequences of an eco-nomic model that puts the interests of bondholders first, the new right singles out welfare and the minimum wage as the causes of unemploy-ment. New-right politicians advocate reforms to welfare through mandatory workfare or time limits on the receipt of social assistance as the solutions to the problem. Rather than recognizing that an economy with slow growth and high real interest rates is the culprit in saddling governments with intractable debts, this belief system places the respon-sibility for public sector deficits and debts on the unemployed and underemployed and the social programs they rely on.

That reasoning helps construct one of the most effective weapons in the arsenal of the new right—the attack on high rates of taxation, one of the principal ways in which the populist right has attracted a work-ing-class following. The post-war welfare state saw full employment as the goal of economic policy. Indeed, in the 1950s and 1960s, that goal was within reach. Recessions occurred during these decades, but they were much milder than the deep downturns that followed. And with recovery, the return to very low rates of unemployment was quickly achieved. Conceived as it was in conjunction with full employment, the welfare state was designed to deal mainly with problems of relatively short duration. Long-term social assistance was necessary only in the small number of individual cases of catastrophic illness or permanent disability.

The rise of long-term unemployment and underemployment and the increase in poverty in urban areas has radically altered the operation of the welfare state. At the same time as long-term unemployment and underemployment have reduced the tax revenues available to the state to finance social programs, the outlays for programs designed as short-term assistance have had to be expanded to cope with what has become a long-term problem.

As we have seen, the globalized economy has enabled the rich to escape taxation through tax exile, the shifting of assets to tax havens, and as a result of the general lowering of marginal tax rates at the high end as states compete for capital investment. Wage and salary earners thereby end up footing the tax bill, both for the increased cost of social programs and for the ruinously high interest payments on the public sector debt. As we have also seen, wage and salary earners were the crucial political constituency that put its weight behind the creation of the welfare state in the post-war era. Now, however, the welfare state has become a double-edged sword for them. While they strongly support certain parts of it—health-care coverage, public pensions and the public education system—they have become ambivalent in their attitude to unemployment insurance and largely unsupportive of social assistance programs for the poor.

The tax issue has opened the door for the new right. By identifying the high taxes paid by wage and salary earners and by calling for a reduction in taxes, new-right politicians have been successful in driving a wedge between those who have jobs and those who do not. Their agenda has been furthered by right-wing social scientists who use their expertise to theorize that the poor are the authors of their own misfortune. Charles Murray, the right-wing American ideologue best known as co-author of the controversial book *The Bell Curve*, developed the theory of welfare dependence in the mid-1980s. In his earlier book titled

*Losing Ground*, Murray opined that social programs that had been designed to aid the poor ended up ensnaring them in a cycle of dependency from which they found it extremely difficult to escape.[24] It would be in the interests of the poor themselves, and the rest of society, he argued, to abolish social assistance. Such harsh medicine, he admitted, would have the effect of harming a few people who would be unable to cope. But, he maintained, many more would be saved by this form of tough love. The vast majority of those who had been on social assistance would make the rational decision, Murray asserted, to go out and find work once they realized that there would be no dole for them.

When I interviewed Murray at his home in Washington, D.C., in 1985, he was preoccupied with the issue of the rising number of children born to single mothers, particularly among inner-city African Americans. He told me that he had considered including in his book a proposal that teenage girls should receive a payment each year on their birthdays as a reward for avoiding pregnancy. Presumably this reward would offset the incentive to become pregnant that he believed welfare offered.

*Losing Ground* was a gift to the Republican Party in its unabashed assault on welfare recipients and in its quest for the support of working-class voters who longed for tax relief. It provided a supposedly academically respectable cover for replacing the liberal idea of a war on poverty with the new-right idea of a war against the poor.

Murray and the late R.J. Herrnstein took the case against the poor much further in 1994, when they published *The Bell Curve*.[25] In it, they argue that class divisions in American society are not the outcome of injustice and lack of equal opportunity. These divisions are to be explained instead by the distribution of innate intelligence within the population, from high to low, which is closely mirrored by the social-class positions in society from top to bottom. According to Herrnstein and Murray, those who have the top jobs and the highest incomes are demonstrably the people with the highest measurable intelligence. Meanwhile, they argue, the poor are those with sub-normal IQs. Here, then, is evidence of meritocracy in its purportedly academic guise.

The problem in American society according to Herrnstein and Murray is not that inequality is increasing as the nature of capitalism changes and an ever-larger number of people are marginalized but that poverty is brought on by the poor themselves as a result of their innate low intelligence. And their low intelligence also explains crime, violence and the rising number of children born out of wedlock. The danger in American society, Herrnstein and Murray say, is that those with low IQs have a much higher propensity to reproduce than do those with high IQs, so over time the mean American intelligence will drop, with woeful consequences for American society. Theirs is a Darwinist analysis in reverse: according to the authors of *The Bell Curve*, the dynamics of American society are promoting the survival of the unfittest at the expense of the fittest.

Even though Herrnstein and Murray claimed to be writing about social class rather than race, the disproportionately high number of African Americans among the poor made the book an inflammatory tract on the subject of race in the United States. Its conclusion is that efforts made through public policy to improve the circumstances of black Americans, to overcome the historic discrimination they have experienced, are misdirected. Herrnstein and Murray have produced a class analysis that depicts the wealthy as the deserving and the poor as a threat to the social order. Although they do not explicitly endorse this view, their book is clearly fodder for a would-be eugenics movement of the future whose goal would be to reengineer the American population to discourage the poor from having children. At a time of rising inequality in American society, *The Bell Curve* presents the case for a stockade society in which the privileged withdraw into their own separate realm and protect themselves from the poor. It is not that Herrnstein and Murray are advocates of a laissez-faire approach and are simply opposed to any forms of public policy. For them, the objective of public policy should be not the amelioration of the conditions of the poor but the protection of the rest of society *from* the poor.

A product of American new-right thinking, *The Bell Curve* is symptomatic of the way the issue of poverty has disturbed contemporary society. In every country in the industrialized world, those who constitute the new urban poor—the young and the unemployed—have become a symbol for violent crime. As unemployment and underemployment have worsened in comparison with the post-war decades, the number of marginalized young people who are rarely a part of the employed workforce has grown apace. The youthful urban poor commit a disproportionate number of the kinds of crimes—break-ins, muggings, car thefts and drug-pushing—that have become the plague of the cities in many industrialized countries. Crime, and even more, the fear of crime, have become potent political issues in North America and Western Europe. Fear of crime and of the youthful poor have been among the most important causes of the rise of the far right in many countries. And where racial minorities constitute a significant proportion of the new poor, these issues have been doubly powerful.

Poverty in American inner cities and the political response to it has had an important impact on the overall course of American politics. Indeed, they have also had a large effect on the politics of the Western world more generally. In the U.S., the backlash against the poor, particularly poor blacks, fuelled the rise of the new right. And the new right has spearheaded the assault on the welfare state. Racial backlash played a central role in breaking down the Great Social Compromise in the U.S. It was thus crucial to bringing to power the social forces that fostered globalization and the harsh new reality of today's class war in the industrialized world.

## Chapter 10

# The Life and Times
# of the "New Class"

W hen I attended the University of Toronto as a freshman in the autumn of 1960, I had a sense that I was studying at an institution that had a connection, however distant, with the original European universities founded in the Middle Ages. A mystique of the timelessness of the university prevailed. It seemed not excessively romantic to think of it in terms of the continuity of centuries. Naturally, I could not know that I was commencing my studies at the beginning of a decade when universities would be transformed.

Throughout the industrialized world, university enrolment grew in the 1960s and 1970s, as the offspring of families whose members had never before attended university sought to improve their circumstances. The systems of post-secondary education differed from country to country, but everywhere there was suddenly vastly greater accessibility for the sons and daughters of wage and salary earners. In the United States between 1965 and 1975, enrolment in public colleges went from 3.9 to 8.8 million students, while the numbers enrolled in private colleges grew from 2.0 to 2.4 million.[1] In Canada, enrolment rose from 128,600 in 1961–62 to 323,000 in 1971–72.[2]

Universities opened their doors wider because public and private sector bureaucracies, which were expanding exponentially during these years, needed their graduates. But there was more to it than that. The unique feature of post–Second World War society was that for the first time in history, the majority of the population in the industrialized world was not poor. Along with full employment, steadily rising real wages and newly established social programs, there was the idea that everyone should have a chance for an education, regardless of social background. This was one of the most important of the democratic ideas to be advanced following the Second World War.

Several thousand veterans enrolled in university at the end of the war. Across Canada, fifty-three thousand ex-soldiers entered universities between 1944 and 1951.[3] During my undergraduate days in the 1960s, student veterans were still famous for questioning the traditions and practices of a venerable institution and demanding relevance from the courses they took.

It was not until the huge wave of new students arrived in the 1960s, however, that the universities were inexorably changed. The buzzword relating to higher education was *accessibility*. Provincial governments, and the federal government, through its grants to the provinces for higher education, were committed to removing social and economic barriers to university attendance. The enrolments of existing universities quickly doubled, trebled and quadrupled. Whole new universities were created throughout the industrialized world. In Ontario, for instance, by the end of the decade half the universities were newly founded. Between 1960 and 1971, the number of teachers in Canadian universities shot up from 9,200 to 24,733.[4] The new universities were often launched by pedagogues of merit who expounded novel and experimental approaches to the study of the liberal arts and who were determined to break down barriers between the arts and sciences. Most of these worthy ideas, though, were swept aside by the sheer force of expansion that established institutions devoted to educating students on a mass basis. Nothing like this had ever been seen before. And in the expanding economy of the 1960s, there were jobs following university for most of the graduates, either in the private sector or, as was increasingly the case, in the public sector.

This vast new employment opportunity for university graduates

resulted from the shift away from manufacturing to the rapidly expanding service sector. During the decades following the Second World War,
the numbers of workers involved in "mental" as contrasted to "physical"
work grew exponentially. There had, of course, been doctors, accountants, engineers, nurses, teachers and lawyers before, but the sheer number of professionals in the post-war decades exceeded what had come
before. And the trend is far from over.

During the period from 1983 to 1994, the number of Americans
employed in civilian occupations increased from 100.8 million to 123 million.[5] The number of Americans employed in the manufacturing sector
remained constant during this time at 18.4 million.[6] By contrast, the number of lawyers in the U.S. grew from 612,000 to 821,000 between 1983
and 1994. The number of accountants and auditors grew from 1.1 million
to 1.5 million; the number of mathematical and computer scientists from
463,000 to 1.2 million; physicians, 519,000 to 628,000; registered nurses,
1.4 million to 2 million; and all types of teachers—pre-kindergarten and
kindergarten, elementary, secondary and post-secondary—from 3.5 million to 4.1 million.[7]

Together the members of these professions belonged to a group
rather grandly described as the "new class." Highly educated in relation
to the rest of the post-war labour force, they seemed not to fit easily
either in the ranks of the wage-earning industrial working class or the
capitalist class. And they were different from earlier middle strata—
small businesspeople or prosperous farmers—all of which led to speculation about what kind of societal role the new class would play. Would
they align themselves with wage and salary earners in their traditional
struggles for higher incomes and improved social programs? Would
they identify with the capitalist class, taking on the outlook of the
socially dominant and aspiring to the accumulation of wealth for themselves? Would they emerge as a class formation with their own values
and concerns quite distinct from those of the other two major social
classes? Would they shift societal concerns away from disputes over
incomes to questions of democratic control over their work environment? Some analysts believed that the new class would replace the

working class as the principal agent of social change. They speculated that the members of the new class would fight for a general democratization of society, and that they would champion the cause of decentralization of decision making in the workplace. Some hoped that the new class would reinvent work as a quest for fulfilment rather than as a mere means to an income.

As it turned out, the new class was not a class in the sense the working class and the capitalist class were. Those in the rapidly expanding professions shared the experience of higher education, but they earned their incomes in significantly different ways. In general, those in private practice, operating independent businesses, earned much more than those who were salaried employees. The independents were the conservative professionals, and they tended to be drawn toward the business model and the values of the market economy.

In the United States in 1995, the median net income for physicians in private practice was US$176,000 a year. The median net income for general surgeons was US$242,000, radiologists US$282,000, cardiologists US$295,000 and orthopedic surgeons US$304,000.[8] In the mid-1990s however, 417,000 of the 693,000 physicians in active service were salary earners, a direct consequence of the rise of Health Maintenance Organizations (HMOs). The median net income of salary-earning American physicians was US$59,280, but one-quarter of them were recent graduates who toiled as low-paid residents in hospitals, and this pulled the median income down significantly.[9] An increasing number of American doctors were salaried employees of health maintenance organizations— firms delivering health care to a large enrolled clientele. In 1995, the base salary of these doctors ranged between US$100,000 and US$150,000 a year.[10] The incomes of American doctors, on average, were considerably higher than those of other professionals whose ranks were almost exclusively made up of salary earners. For instance, in 1995, the median income for U.S. professors (all ranks) was US$43,800 a year, while that of full professors was US$65,400. And while 77 percent of physicians who were private practitioners had net incomes exceeding US$100,000 annually in 1995, this was the case for only 3 percent of professors.[11]

Also divided between an elite, high-income cohort and salaried ranks with lower rates of pay were lawyers, accountants and engineers. In these professions, as well as among physicians, the private practioners tended to assume leadership of the profession as a whole. The leaders of these professions jealously guarded their right to control entry into their ranks and protected themselves against attempts by uncredentialed interlopers to enter their domains. Doctors, for example, fought lengthy battles against midwives, chiropractors and those they considered to be quacks. When it came to staking out turf and maximizing income, these professionals followed in the footsteps of medieval and early modern craftsmen, guarding their monopolies in much the same way as the early craft unions that were predominant in the American Federation of Labour in the late nineteenth and early twentieth centuries. The elites within these professions wanted to be able to operate their own independent businesses. The leading physicians' organizations in North America fought against state-financed medicare systems in the very different environments of Canada and the United States.

In July 1962, when the social democratic Cooperative Commonwealth Federation (CCF) government of Saskatchewan implemented its medicare plan, the province's doctors promptly went on strike. The bitter strike, which lasted for three weeks, was backed by more than three-quarters of the physicians and was actively supported by the Canadian and American medical establishments as well as the North American insurance industry. The CCF won its fight in Saskatchewan, and medicare became a fact of life. A few years later, the system was duplicated across the country when the federal Liberal government established a plan by which it paid a large proportion of the bills for provincially implemented medicare schemes, provided that they were universal in character.

As it turned out, Canadian medicare did not threaten the position of doctors as operators of independent businesses. Medicare embodied a societal compromise that guaranteed Canadians access to a universal health-care system. But it did not end up turning most doctors into salaried employees, as the medical establishment had feared at the outset. Instead, doctors billed the public health-care plan for the services they dispensed. This fee-for-service system had the effect of allowing doctors to generate virtually as much business as they liked with a guarantee that they would be paid for it. (In the 1980s and 1990s, when provincial governments were grappling with deficits and debts and the federal government was cutting back on transfer payments to the provinces to finance medicare, caps were put on the amounts doctors were allowed to bill. The tap, which had been turned on with the fee-for-service system, was partially turned off.)

The consequence of Canadian fee-for-service medicare has been that the average income of doctors is high in comparison with that of other professionals. In 1992, the average net professional income of a Canadian physician was C$129,036, up from C$60,830 in 1980.[12] At the zenith of the profession are the top specialists whose after-expense incomes are in the range of several hundred thousand dollars a year. Many doctors are earning incomes that allow them to accumulate considerable amounts of capital. As they accumulate capital, a large number of them join the ranks of the capitalist class, which most of them already identify with socially and politically. As is the case in the United States, many Canadian doctors have become salaried employees. In 1990, the average salaried physician in Ontario earned C$112,066.[13]

In the United States, the medical profession and its allies in the insurance industry, supported by the powerful political right, were able to prevent the creation of a universal medicare system. To be sure, there were advocates of Canadian-style medicare. For example, during the 1970s Senator Edward Kennedy regularly presented evidence to Senate committees on the experience and advantages of the Canadian system. The most concerted attempt to extend the publicly funded health-care system in the U.S. beyond coverage for senior citizens and the poor was Bill Clinton's initiative during the first two years of his presidency. With the president's wife, Hillary Rodham Clinton, heading up the initiative, the Clinton administration unveiled a proposal to provide portable health-care coverage to all Americans. The plan would have maintained a major role for the private insurance industry and would not have resulted in a single universal system of the Canadian kind, but it represented an attempt to take a giant step in that direction.

From the outset, right-wing politicians took up the fight against the health-care plan, leading the struggle on behalf of conservative physicians and the insurance industry. What the right feared was that if Clinton won, he would thereby vastly extend support for the welfare state beyond the broad backing in American society for social security, the publicly funded retirement plan that was the only significant universal social program in existence in the United States. In his book on American progressives, *They Only Look Dead*, the *Washington Post* correspondent E.J. Dionne Jr. quoted a memo by the Republican strategist William Kristol that expressed the fears of the right, should Clinton be allowed to win on health care: "It will relegitimize middle-class dependence for 'security' on government spending and regulation. . . . It will revive the reputation of the party that spends and regulates, the Democrats, as the generous protector of middle-class interests. And it will at the same time strike a punishing blow against Republican claims to defend the middle class by restraining government." Dionne concluded that "the danger for the Republicans lay in the fact that once enacted, a universal health program would almost certainly prove to be widely popular, as it is in Canada, Great Britain, Germany and virtually every other industrial democracy."[14] Defeat on the health-care plan drove the Clinton administration to the right, where it remained during the days following the Republican capture of both Houses of Congress in the elections of November 1994, and even during Clinton's successful drive for reelection in 1996.

If North American physicians constitute the archetypical conservative professional group, lawyers are very similar in their social outlook and strategic conduct as a profession. Lawyers, like doctors, want the right to control access to the profession and to operate in the marketplace with as few restrictions as possible on the freedom to set rates as they see fit. In the United States, this strategy rewarded lawyers with incomes higher than those of most professionals. In 1995, the median income of an American lawyer was US$72,100, and that of law firm partners was US$135,000. Thirty-one percent of lawyers in the

United States earned more than US$100,000 annually.[15] In 1990, the average income of an Ontario lawyer was C$91,324.[16]

The fact that the careers of many lawyers are spent deal making on behalf of corporate clients—sometimes helping in the stripping of assets or the sacking of employees following corporate takeovers, and minimizing their clients' taxes while shielding them from prosecution for tax evasion—means that their social sympathies tend to lie overwhelmingly on the side of business and the market system. In contrast, there is a small minority of lawyers whose working lives are devoted to the interests of immigrants, the members of labour unions, those unable to afford counsel and the defence of civil liberties. But for lawyers, as for physicians, the professional ideal is to operate an independent practice, usually as a partner in a firm.

Broadly speaking, dentists, accountants, and engineers and architects have pursued a course similar to that of doctors and lawyers. In 1992, according to Revenue Canada's Statistics Division that year, the average taxable income of self-employed dentists in Ontario was C$109,128; self-employed Ontario accountants, C$60,868; and Ontario engineers and architects, C$40,457. Many dentists, accountants, and engineers and architects run their own independent businesses in the manner of physicians and lawyers, the quintessential conservative professionals.

When we turn our attention to teachers and nurses, we encounter professionals whose relationship to capitalism differs fundamentally from that of the generally conservative professionals just described. The overwhelming majority of teachers and nurses spend their working lives as salaried employees. And though a minority of teachers and nurses work in the private sector—for schools, hospitals or individual doctors, as the case may be—most are employed by public or quasi-public institutions.

Unlike the members of the conservative professions, teachers and nurses have seen their fortunes rise and fall since the Second World War. Their fate has closely mirrored that of the public sector within the capitalist economy. As post-war governments greatly increased expenditures on schools at all levels and on hospitals, there was a corresponding increase in the number of teachers and nurses. The baby boom generation put in its first appearance as primary school pupils in the early 1950s, and as the bulge worked its way through the system, the number of teachers at each successive level had to grow too. Meanwhile, the shift in the economy away from manufacturing to the service sector created a demand for those with secondary school and university diplomas.

The previously small, rather clubbish universities, with their well-bred teachers and students, were transformed in the 1960s into what were called multiversities. In the multiversities, a smorgasbord of learning was offered to the enlarged student populace. The emphasis was on processing numbers. As the concomittent number of teachers went up, so too did their salaries. Teachers improved their income vis-à-vis the workforce as a whole during the 1950s, but the great period of their income advance was the 1960s and the 1970s.

This golden age for teachers ended with the onset of the fiscal crisis of the state beginning in the mid-1970s, the rise of the politics of the new right and the effect of the lower birthrate after the mid-1960s. A lowered birthrate was bound to curtail the number of teachers hired at primary and secondary levels, though immigration provided new students in both Canada and the United States. And later there was to be the much touted "echo" generation, the children of the boomers, who represented a renewed, though smaller, wave of students, beginning in the mid-1970s. But the fiscal crisis soon changed the economic environment for teachers. The term "cutbacks" has typified the public sector educational environment ever since.

In 1971, I was hired at York University in Toronto, a burgeoning suburban university whose monstrous architecture testifies to its 1960s origins. Then twenty-nine, I was the youngest faculty member of a small political science department of seven. Very much in line with what was happening generally, I was still the department's youngest full-time member until the end of the 1980s. Some faculties did expand during those years, in disciplines such as administrative studies, environmental studies and business administration, but the rapid expansion of the universities, so evident in the 1960s and early 1970s, screeched to a halt in the mid-1970s.

At the primary and secondary school levels, a similar process was under way as the public sector budget crunch began to bite. Faced with tougher times, teachers in many provinces and states, particularly at the primary and secondary levels, but also at universities such as York, formed unions. On occasion teachers did what had been unthinkable in the past: they went on strike, sometimes for long periods, sometimes with considerable public support, sometimes without it. Indeed, teachers and nurses were two of the key groups of public sector employees to unionize during the 1970s. By the end of the decade, the Canadian trade union movement had been transformed. The Canadian Union of Public Employees (CUPE) had become the largest single union in the country, charging ahead of the Canadian section of the United Steel Workers of America (USWA), which had been the largest union in the post-war era.

Teachers have been under assault not only as a consequence of the budget crunch, but they have also become a favourite target for the abuse of the new right. In the English-speaking world, neoconservatives see in teachers the embodiment of the evils of post-war society. Teachers are, according to these critics, the underworked, self-interested purveyors of mediocre educational offerings, whose ethical centre is a rather weak-kneed humanism. Public schools, opponents charge, are no longer educating students in the basic skills of literacy and numeracy and are instead catering to a rampant egalitarianism, which results in everyone being promoted, regardless of merit, and in formal and unambiguous standards being abolished.

Particularly in Britain and the United States, where private schools are much more widespread than in Canada, new-right critics have advocated a number of reforms whose purpose is to weaken the role of central departments of education, teachers and teachers' unions. (When Bob Dole chose teachers' unions as the most malevolent institution to attack the night he accepted the Republican presidential nomination in August 1996, he was merely offering up the standard rhetoric of the new right.)

Ostensibly, conservatives want the public school system to be more decentralized so that control shifts to local communities. What they really want is to push schools out of the public sector, to transform them into quasi-market or market institutions. One conservative idea is to replace the general financing of public education with a system through which parents would use vouchers to send their children to the school of their choice. William Kristol—whose terror that Clinton's health-care reform might succeed we have noted—described vouchers as a way "to help young people at risk to escape from dreadful government schools."[17] Another conservative idea is to turn school principals into budget directors, who would be recipients of a set annual budget that they would then allocate according to priorities set by the school's management, which would include input from the local community.

Taken together, the new right is attempting to weaken the position of teachers as an educational and societal force, to limit their incomes and to undermine their professional standing and solidarity. It has become fashionable among conservatives to champion the hiring of unqualified personnel at lower rates of pay to do jobs formerly done only by teachers. Such right-wing notions initially had greater effect in Britain and the United States than in Canada. After the election of a right-wing Conservative government in Ontario in 1995, however, teachers in Ontario found themselves facing just this outlook. When 126,000 primary and secondary school teachers in Ontario took to the picket lines in a work stoppage on October 27, 1997, they were fighting to preserve the integrity of the public educational system against pressures to model it along the lines of conservative experiments in Britain and the U.S.

In 1995–96, the average teacher's salary in Canada, including primary and secondary school teachers, was C$50,119. Ontario had the highest average salary for teachers, C$54,416, and Prince Edward Island the lowest at C$41,059. In 1995–96, the average teacher's salary in the United States, when translated into Canadian dollars, was C$54,076.[18]

At the university level, the fate of teachers whose incomes, numbers and social standing rose during the 1960s and 1970s has been similar to that of primary and secondary school teachers. As university budgets have been cut by fiscally strapped and right-wing governments, they have been pressured to evolve into professional finishing schools and to forge an ever closer interface with the private sector. Programs that have a direct training benefit in the eyes of the private sector are favoured, while others once thought crucial to a serious centre of scholarship and study, particularly in the arts and humanities, have been allowed to wither. By the 1990s, hard-up universities were auctioning off programs, schools, benches—anything they could think of—to wealthy corporate and individual donors who wished to have their names linked with academe. In this unseemly process, universities were sometimes willing to give donors a considerable say in the content of programs. Increasingly, universities are run by bureaucrats indistinguishable from those in the private sector, whose claims to having been scholars of any sort are meagre.

If teachers at all levels are embattled in our era, they have often shown themselves to be formidable opponents of extreme forms of market ideology. Because of their communications skills and the seminal role they play in communities of every size, from the tiniest hamlets to megacities, teachers have become a significant political force in many countries. In France, for example, where the educational system is seen as having played a key role in the creation of the French nation and state, teachers have been especially powerful as defenders of non-market social values. No occupational group in France votes more massively for the Socialist Party than teachers. When teachers have reached out to other beleaguered wage and salary earners, as they often have in France, they have shown themselves to have a unique ability to pull together the diverse elements of the working class/middle class into an effective coalition.

Like other employees in the service sector, teachers have increasingly been drawn into trade union and political battles to defend themselves in an ever more hostile environment. In the spring of 1997, for example, the faculty at York University in Toronto waged the longest strike by a university faculty in the history of English-speaking Canada. The strike's immediate causes had to do with salary and retirement issues. For instance, the average faculty salary at York in 1995–96 was C$72,934, compared with an Ontario average of C$76,503 and an average of C$83,002 at the University of Toronto. As the strike went on, however—it lasted for more than a month—it became evident that broader issues were engaged. For one thing, the ferocity of the conflict between the union and university management could not be explained solely by the issues on the table. The strike crystallized the inchoate but rising faculty opposition to the university's corporate orientation.

For many years at York, and other universities in Canada and the United States, there has been a widening gulf between what almost amounts to two separate institutions. A large remnant of the original university still exists, with its faculty members who have had scant pay increases for years and who work out of offices that grow shabbier for lack of upkeep. They often teach in classrooms where windows won't shut, heating systems are unreliable and classrooms are cluttered with garbage, because no one has cleaned them after use by the previous class. This marooned part of the institution, experienced by most of the students, where two decades of cutbacks have taken their toll, is ever more isolated from the rest of the university where new construction is under way, where new mini-institutes are housed, where bureaucrats spend their time attending to the corporate interface.

In the end, the York faculty forced the university to improve its initial offer, although not by much. The York strike was a shot fired across the bow of university administrations right across Canada, warning them that there are limits to how far faculties will tolerate a corporate agenda at their institutions. The strike was reminiscent of the battle at Crédit Foncier in Paris in the winter of 1997, discussed in an earlier chapter, where office workers fought to prevent the closing of the institution. At Crédit Foncier and York University, educated salaried employees displayed a previously uncharacteristic militancy. The position of relative privilege they had occupied in society had been severely eroded. In ways they found culturally appropriate, they were fighting back. Battles such as those at York and Crédit Foncier point the way toward future battles in the service sector.

Nursing has become an embattled profession for many of the same reasons as teaching has. If the changing demographics of industrial countries are kinder to health-care workers than to educators, because of the aging of the population the fiscal crisis of the state has imperilled their position in the same way. The proportion of gross domestic product consumed by health care has soared in recent decades in all industrialized countries. That proportion is highest in the United States, the only country in the West in which a private health-care system predominates.

The number of nursing jobs grew rapidly as new hospitals were established between the late 1940s and the mid-1970s. In the post-war decades, nursing was a predominantly female profession operating within the strictures of a highly stratified, authoritarian medical hierarchy. As a ghettoized female occupation, nursing had been grossly underpaid during the post-war decades, a time when their professional leaders tended to see nurses as doctors' helpers. By the 1970s, though, the nursing profession had completely changed. The old leadership had been replaced by young, pro-union militants who were intent on staking out their professional turf vis-à-vis physicians. Nurses' associations were transformed into unions. They were determined to win salary increases that would reflect their professional training and hard labour. And they were often quite prepared to strike, if that was necessary, something utterly inconceivable for the nursing profession a couple of decades earlier. For nurses, the years of professional self-assertion and reorganization into unions were quickly followed by the effects of the public sector budget crunch. As health-care budgets have stopped expanding in places like Ontario, a wave of hospital closings and layoffs of nurses and other hospital personnel has followed.

An irony of the new capitalism at the dawn of the millennium is that its social arrangements make it more difficult to allocate the resources needed to fund health care than was the case in the age of the Great Social Compromise a quarter of a century ago. New high-tech medical procedures and the needs of an ageing population have driven costs up dramatically, but it is a measure of the failure of society as a whole to benefit from the productivity gains of new technology that health-care costs have become more of a societal strain in the late 1990s than they were in the early 1970s.

In Ontario, large numbers of nurses are being laid off, and those keeping their jobs have lived with a wage freeze that began in March 1993. (In 1990, the average salary of a registered nurse in Ontario was C\$33,319.)[19] Simultaneously, access to many types of medical procedures is subject to delays. Today nurses, like teachers, experience considerable stress from overwork and the ever-present threat of further job losses.

Since the 1960s, the number of professionals has grown hugely, but these people have taken two divergent paths. The conservative professions—physicians, dentists, lawyers, accountants and engineers—have mostly taken a path that has kept them close to the practices and outlook of business. The larger number who have taken the other path, predominantly teachers and nurses, share the general fate of non-managerial wage and salary earners. Under assault as a consequence of the public sector budgetary crises that abound in industrialized countries, they are experiencing attacks on their professional standing, job losses, overwork and frozen incomes.

Distinct from the conservative professions and from teachers and nurses is the rapidly expanding category of mathematical and computer scientists. Those who populate this wing of the professions experience a wide range of possible circumstances. Many are salaried employees, working for firms ranging in size from the global giants to the tiniest companies eking out a living on the edge of the new high-tech sector. Others are independent business operators and consultants who sell their services to firms. This highly varied occupational group certainly shares in the general optimism that comes from being a part of a thriving economic sector, but given the variety of their circumstances, its members can hardly be expected to share a common societal outlook. The "new nerds" include Bill Gates in their number, but for the tens of thousands of lowly hackers toiling for giants like Microsoft or in tiny companies or partnerships, the familiar division into dominant and dominated social classes is very much in evidence.

The highly educated, the members of the new class, certainly play a more important role in society than ever before. In today's class war, it is clear that some are being drawn into the ranks of the capitalists, while a greater proportion are being pulled in the direction of fellow wage and salary earners.

## Chapter 11

# The Third
# American Empire

O ne afternoon in the winter of 1997, I was sitting in a coffee bar
in San Sebastián, a Basque city on the northern coast of Spain.
The youngish women and men in the bar were sipping cappuccino and
sangria, watching the waves of the Atlantic pounding the shore. The
music played for their entertainment by a local radio station was the
sound of Nashville. I relate this not because it was novel, but rather
because it is commonplace. We are living in an American global empire.
Its ethos extends almost everywhere on the planet. Television ads in
France are ever more American in their imagery and in their use of
scraps of English to get their messages across. And on the billboards of
the world are displayed Calvin Klein's version of the empire's icon—the
pallid, wanton, vulnerable female.

The late 1990s has been an age of American triumphalism. The proponents of American-inspired globalization see victory everywhere, and
discount the idea that there could be alternatives to the world system
they are designing. What the world needs is the American model writ
large, they loudly proclaim. Proponents of the American system believe
that the U.S. national economy developed historically as a consequence
of three working principles: freedom for enterprise to do its thing,
unconstrained by too much state interference; free mobility of capital;
and freedom of commerce to operate anywhere within the emerging

international market. Believers in the American economic model want to see these principles enshrined as the conceptual basis of the new global economy. Thus transposed, the principles come out as follows: privatization of state-owned firms and deregulation of labour markets to allow for maximum freedom for private enterprise; the elimination of capital controls to permit the free mobility of capital internationally; and global free trade. Allow all this to happen, the proponents argue, and the world will grow more prosperous and peaceful. Some of them concede that there will be difficulties along the way to the brave new world of their dreams.

In the 1990s, for the third time in the twentieth century, the United States is remaking the world in its own image. The first time—we can call it the first American empire—came after the First World War when President Woodrow Wilson travelled to Paris in 1919 to join with the leaders of the other allied nations to impose peace terms on the defeated Germans and Austrians. American armies, which reinforced the British and French on the Western Front in 1917, were decisive in breaking the back of the Germans in the great allied offensive of September 1918. When Wilson arrived, the Europeans waited for this man of peace, and of unequalled power, to remake the world.

Wilson's short-lived global system rested on two pillars: the Treaty of Versailles, meant to keep defeated Germany down; and the League of Nations, meant to provide collective international security for the future. But having played a decisive role in the creation of the system, the United States then failed to use its power to sustain it. By a single vote in the Senate in 1920, the Wilson administration fell short of the two-thirds backing required to win ratification for U.S. membership in the league. Without the United States in the league, the muscle necessary to make the system work was lacking. In the 1930s, when Japan invaded Manchuria, and later when Italy invaded Ethiopia, the league was exposed as a paper tiger. If the Americans fatally undermined the collective security arrangements they had themselves designed, they also stood by and did nothing, along with the British and French, as Adolf Hitler's Third Reich established an air force, vastly expanded his army, remilitarized the Rhineland and annexed Austria—all in defiance of the provisions of the Treaty of Versailles.

In 1919, the United States emerged from the war as the world's leading creditor power, taking over that role from the faltering British Empire. At first, the Americans shouldered this responsibility when they helped the Germans finance the reparations payments they owed other nations under the Versailles Treaty. But they turned their back on the global economic system when they returned to economic protectionism at the end of the 1920s. One of the important causes of the Great Depression of the 1930s was the unwillingness of the United States to play the role of creditor of last resort when the stock market crashed in 1929. Pumping liquidity back into the global system when a crash occurs is an indispensable task for a hegemonic power.

The United States was powerful enough to remake the world at the end of the First World War, but unwilling to use the economic, military and political capacity it alone represented to sustain the system. Even though New York replaced London as the financial capital of the world, most of American business did not yet see its interests indissolubly linked to the survival of an American-centred global system. Especially in Chicago and other parts of the Midwest, isolationism reigned. The goal of the isolationists was to keep the United States out of any future involvement in European security. The first American empire came and went in a few short years.

The second American empire was much more substantial and enduring. Militarily it began even before Japan brought the United States into the Second World War with its attack on Pearl Harbor on December 7, 1941. In the months following the fall of France in June 1940, the Roosevelt administration established a very close alliance with beleaguered Britain, supplying the island nation with armaments in return for the lease of British bases. The economic system of the second American empire was inaugurated in the closing days of the war, in the summer of 1944, with the launch of the Bretton Woods scheme for the reconstruction of the post-war international economy.

The Bretton Woods system attempted to Americanize the post-war economy by fixing the American dollar at the centre of the global economy and by setting up institutions to promote international capital mobility and free trade. Over the objections of John Maynard Keynes, who represented Britain at Bretton Woods, the U.S. dollar was, as we have noted, designated as the reserve currency of the global economy. This meant that other currencies were to be convertible into U.S. dollars, to be pegged against the dollar at fixed rates of exchange. The U.S. dollar was linked to gold at a price of us$35 an ounce; in theory at least, foreign central banks could exchange their dollar holdings for the gold that backed them. Meanwhile, the International Monetary Fund, the World Bank (both created at Bretton Woods) and the General Agreement on Tariffs and Trade (GATT) (not set up until 1948) were to assist in the drive for free mobility for capital and for free trade.

The underlying, although unstated, assumption the second American empire rested on was that the United States would retain its huge economic lead over all other powers for the indefinite future. The architects of the post-war American system assumed that the United States could afford to run a balance-of-payments (current-account) deficit against its major trading partners over the long term. That deficit was built right into the logic of the system. To provide liquidity to restart international commerce after the war, the United States pumped funds into other countries in several ways: spending on U.S. military bases around the world; investment in the Marshall Plan for the rebuilding of Western Europe; and direct investment in many parts of the world, particularly Western Europe, by American corporations intent on increasing their productive capacity abroad. In addition, the undervalued deutschmark and yen lowered the price of German and Japanese labour with respect to American labour, and thus opened the door to a relaunch of export industries. First came the West German economic miracle of the 1950s and later the larger and even more important Japanese takeoff of the 1960s and subsequent decades.

By the 1960s, the limits of the empire forged at Bretton Woods were becoming apparent. Early in the decade, U.S. gold reserves were already insufficient to provide backing for all the dollars held abroad by foreign

central banks. At the time, this was regarded as little more than a theoretical problem, but it had ominous implications for the future. Then
came the Vietnam War and the simultaneous invasion of American markets by West German and Japanese industrial producers. By the beginning of the 1970s, the United States was running a deficit, not merely
on its current account, but on its trade in manufactured products as well.
For American manufacturers, who had led the world since the late nineteenth century, this was a historic turn of the wheel. The era when it
could be assumed as a matter of course that American industries were
the most productive was at an end.

Confronted by the problem of an overheated war economy and the
invasion of domestic and foreign markets by competitors, the U.S.
government fell prey to the temptation to monetize its rising debt:
instead of cutting spending and increasing taxes, the United States
increased its money supply, a fateful ploy, which played an important
part in generating the new inflation of the 1970s. The demise of the
Bretton Woods system commenced in 1971 when President Richard
Nixon announced in a live television address to the American people
that he was severing the link between the dollar and gold. Nixon's sudden initiative left foreign central banks holding about us$60 billion
from which he had unilaterally removed backing in gold. Nixon also
announced the imposition of a temporary 10 percent surcharge on
imports, thus hitting U.S. trading partners with an unanticipated
increase in the American tariff. Following these dramatic moves, the
Nixon administration pushed other nations to accept an upward reval-
uation of the rates of exchange for their currencies against the U.S.
dollar. In 1973, the Bretton Woods fixed exchange rate regime was
replaced by the non-system of floating exchange rates that has existed
ever since.

Nixon's stunning economic moves amounted to a simple recognition
of reality: in relation to the other major economic powers, the United
States was no longer the titan it had been. Over the next fifteen years,
American economic hegemony further dissolved as Europe and particularly Japan made major advances. The huge productivity gap that had

once yawned between American industry and that of Europe and Japan disappeared. In many sectors, this left the Europeans and Japanese setting the pace.

During the presidency of Ronald Reagan, the second American empire reached its nadir. By the mid-1980s, as a consequence of the massive American trade deficit with the rest of the world, especially Japan, the United States became a net debtor nation for the first time since 1919. (Since then, the U.S. net debt relative to the rest of the world has continued to grow. The United States now has the world's highest net debt. From US$145 billion in 1988, it soared to US$814 billion by 1995.)[1] While Americans held assets abroad in 1995 worth US$2.9 trillion, foreigners held assets in the U.S. worth US$3.7 trillion.[2] It was the underlying assumption of Bretton Woods—that the United States would retain its economic supremacy indefinitely—that proved to be the second American empire's ultimate undoing.

But rescue was at hand for the American global system at the end of the 1980s. It came in the form of the unanticipated, but highly welcome, self-immolation of the Soviet Union. The collapse of the Soviet Union and its Eastern European empire has given the U.S. a new lease on life as a global superpower. We can date the rise of the third American empire from November 9, 1989, the day the tottering East German regime opened the Berlin Wall. The opening of the Berlin Wall had dramatic effects for all the major global powers. It ushered in the final crisis in the existence of the Soviet Union and its empire, a crisis brought on by the societal contradictions within the Soviet system that had been deepening for several decades. It also facilitated the speedy unification of Germany, something no one had thought would occur for many years to come. And not only did Germany again become the predominant power in central Europe, but the European Community (now the European Union) could also dream of a future as a global power, no longer encumbered by Cold War rivalries.

For the United States, the effects were also epochal. For more than four decades, American global policy had centred on the containment of Soviet communism. Suddenly, and unexpectedly, the enemy fell on his face and expired. The United States had won the Cold War and had emerged as the world's only superpower.

The third American empire rests on four foundations: military superiority; the size of the American economy; the quest for globalization; and, at least as important as the first three, the present relative weakness of potential rivals. In the first and second empires, the vast industrial supremacy of the U.S. was crucial because it enabled the United States to assemble huge armed forces in a very short time, when the need arose. By contrast, the third American empire relies on the immense military superiority that has resulted from the collapse of the Soviet Union, the only rival that possessed a fighting force capable of posing a global threat to the United States. When we stand back from the present to survey the long sweep of history, the margin of American military superiority appears vast in comparison with that of other empires all the way back to the case of Rome. In the nineteenth century, at the height of British imperial power, British policy was to maintain a navy that was at least as mighty as the next two large navies combined. This was the military pillar on which the Pax Britannica rested. By comparison, present-day American military superiority is uncontestable. The current strategic view of the Pentagon is that the United States needs to spend enough on defence to be in a position to fight and win two major wars simultaneously in different parts of the world.

In 1993, the United States spent US$298 billion on defence. The next ten powers by expenditure on defence were Russia US$114 billion; China US$56 billion; France US$43 billion; Japan US$42 billion; Germany US$37 billion; the United Kingdom US$34 billion; Italy US$21 billion; Saudi Arabia US$20 billion; South Korea US$12 billion; and Taiwan US$10 billion—for a grand total of US$389 billion.[3] Incredibly, U.S. hard-liners have warned that this degree of American supremacy is insufficient. They want the United States to spend as much on defence as the next ten military powers combined.

At present no foreign power, or conceivable combination of foreign powers, is in a position to threaten the United States militarily. However, the long-term military power of a country depends on its economic potential. In 1945, at the dawn of the second American empire, not only did the United States enjoy a monopoly of atomic weapons, but it also produced an unprecedented 50 percent of the goods and services in the whole world. Its military hegemony depended on an economic supremacy that was much more unassailable in the post-war decades than is the case today. On the eve of the new millennium, the United States produces 20 percent of the goods and services in the world—still a huge proportion, but not enough to prevent the emergence of other military powers in the twenty-first century seeking to contest American supremacy. So while the second pillar of the present American empire is indeed the size of its economy, that economic foundation is far more meagre than it was during the second empire.

Moreover, the American domination of the post-war international economy was not merely quantitative, it was qualitative. American industries were much more productive than their foreign competitors in the post-war decades, and the Europeans and the Japanese had no doubt that American production and management techniques were the most advanced in the world. In addition, as the world's leading creditor nation, the United States was in a formidable position to invest abroad and to acquire control of industries based outside the United States. For example, American corporations dominated manufacturing and resource production in Canada by the late 1940s. During these same years, billions of dollars were being invested by American corporations in Britain, France, Germany and other parts of Europe, as well as in Japan. In France, intellectuals warned of the danger of American domination of their national economy. French Communists even fought, to no avail, to prevent Coca-Cola from becoming a major player in the French market. In Japan, the government adopted legislation to bar Americans from gaining a controlling interest in domestic corporations.

Despite the fact that the United States enjoyed immense advantages vis-à-vis its competitors at the start of the second American empire, the Europeans and the Japanese constructed economies that grew, on average, much more rapidly than the American economy during the post-war era. By the 1970s, as we have seen, they had in many cases surpassed American industrial productivity. American industries have not succeeded in regaining the productivity edge that they enjoyed in the post-war decades.

And in stark contrast to the post-war decades when the Americans were the leading foreign investors in the world, foreigners are now taking over industries in the United States at a much more rapid pace than Americans have been increasing their control of businesses abroad. Between 1980 and 1995, foreigners increased their direct investment (equity investment) in the United States more than fivefold, from us$126 billion to us$639 billion. During that same period, U.S. investors increased their direct investment abroad by a factor of 2.2 from us$396 billion to us$880 billion.[4]

This sea-change in investment patterns is exemplified by Canada's economic relationship to the U.S. Between 1980 and 1994, Canadian direct investment in the United States increased by more than 350 percent from us$12 billion to us$43 billion. During the same period, U.S. direct investment in Canada increased from us$45 billion to us$75 billion.[5] During this fourteen-year period, Canadian direct investment in the United States advanced from being just over a quarter as large as American investment in Canada to well over half as large. Moreover, Canadian investment in the United States was concentrated in the manufacturing sector, where it nearly doubled from us$9.7 billion to us$17 billion in the three years immediately following the 1989 Canada–U.S. Free Trade Agreement (FTA).[6] During the same period, American direct investment in Canada remained flat.[7]

Between 1980 and 1994, British direct investment in the United States skyrocketed from us$14 billion to us$114 billion, more than an 800 percent increase. During the same period, American direct investment in Britain nearly quadrupled form us$28 billion to us$111 billion.[8] By 1994 the total dollar value of British direct investment in the U.S. slightly exceeded American direct investment in the U.K., a dramatic change from 1980, when American direct investment in the U.K. had been double that of British direct investment in the U.S.

Most significant of all during the years from 1980 to 1994 was the rise of Japanese direct investment in the United States, which soared from

US$5 billion to US$103 billion, more than a twentyfold expansion. During the same years, American direct investment in Japan rose from US$6 billion to US$37 billion.9 While American direct investment in Japan was slightly higher than Japanese direct investment in the United States in 1980, by 1994 Japanese direct investment in the United States was nearly 2.8 times as large as American direct investment in Japan.

The broad trend from the early 1980s to the mid-1990s was that firms based in the advanced countries expanded their investments greatly in other advanced countries. But while American direct investment in Japan and Europe was higher than Japanese and European investment in the U.S. in 1980, by 1994 that had changed, most dramatically in the case of Japan, but also in the case of Europe. In 1980, combined American direct investment in Japan and Europe totalled US$102 billion, while combined direct Japanese and European investment in the U.S. was US$60 billion. By 1994, combined American direct investment in Japan and Europe had climbed to US$347 billion. But combined Japanese and European investment in the U.S. had risen to US$416 billion.10 By 1994, only in Canada and the Third World did the United States still enjoy an edge as a direct foreign investor.

As a long-term development, the change in the deployment of direct foreign investment reflects a fundamental shift in economic power away from the United States to Japan and Europe. Over the long term, it has been the great creditors who have always stood at the apex of global capitalism and have held the whip hand. For those who deploy it, direct foreign investment is a form of credit, while for those who are the recipients of it, foreign investment represents indebtedness.

This point needs to be underlined for Canadians, who have listened for so long to proselytization extolling the benefits of American investment in Canada that they have become mired in confusion. When a country's investors have large direct investments abroad, the advantage is a constant flow of dividends to the home country. On the other hand, a country that is a large-scale recipient of direct foreign investment experiences a constant outflow of dividends to the countries where the investors are based—as Canadians ought to know better than most.

The Canadian current account, which most years is in deficit, features a large surplus on the merchandise trade side: this results from a deficit in trade on manufactured goods that is more than offset by a huge surplus in trade on primary and semi-fabricated products. On the other side of the account—the services side—which features the balance among countries in dividends, interest payments and tourism, Canada always runs a huge deficit. Responsible for this is the cost of foreign investment, both direct (equity) investment and indirect investment—through the holding of Canadian corporate and government bonds by foreigners.

Unlike its post-war predecessor, the third American empire does not rest on a solid foundation of U.S. superiority in industrial productivity or in the deployment of foreign investment. But today's American empire does have an economic foundation. In place of the superior production techniques that worked so well in the past, the secret of the new empire can be summarized in a single term—cost cutting. Against its Japanese and European competitors, the United States has benefited from relatively low labour costs. In Japan between 1980 and 1994, hourly compensation for production workers in manufacturing soared from 56 percent of those in the United States to 125 percent. In Germany (West Germany before 1990), hourly wages in manufacturing increased from 125 percent of those in the U.S. in 1980 to 160 percent in 1994.[11]

In the early 1990s, a cheap American dollar against the yen and the deutschmark held down the cost of American labour and increased the international competitiveness of U.S. products. In 1985, it took 238 yen or 2.94 deutschmarks to purchase one U.S. dollar. By 1994, it took just 102 yen or 1.62 deutschmarks to purchase one U.S. dollar.[12] Over this nine-year period, the yen had appreciated by more than 230 percent against the dollar, while the deutschmark had risen by more than 180 percent.

The depreciation of the dollar sheltered American industry against Japanese and German imports. Although Americans, as avowed free traders, have been loath to admit this fact, the recovery of U.S. industry relative to that of the Japanese and the Germans in the 1990s was much more the consequence of the old-fashioned protectionism afforded by the depreciation of the dollar than of the widespread corporate restructuring that has been hyped so much.

Aided by the protectionism provided by the cheap dollar, American industry revived in the 1990s in comparison with industry in Japan and Europe. While industrial output contracted in Japan and Europe in the early 1990s, it expanded in the United States. With 1990 as a base year (rated at 100.0), industrial production in the U.S. shrank slightly in 1991, but then expanded strongly in 1992 and 1993, so that by 1993 industrial production was up to 105.7. In the same years, industrial production in Japan declined from 100.0 in 1990 to 92.0 in 1993, and German industrial production contracted from 100.0 in 1990 to 93.6 in 1993.[13]

During 1997, when American commentators were waxing eloquent about the global economic ascendancy of the U.S., the American dollar was rising against the yen and the deutschmark. By early November, the yen had fallen to 120 to the dollar and the deutschmark had dropped to 1.72 to the dollar.[14] But while the dollar was staging a significant recovery against the yen and the deutschmark, it remained far below its 1985 value. The rising dollar reflected the success of the United States in achieving modest, but singularly unspectacular, economic growth with very low inflation, a reduced rate of unemployment, and above all else, a soaring stock market—the most spectacular bull market in American history.

The lengthy, indeed historic, decline of the dollar against the yen and the deutschmark from the mid-1980s to the mid-1990s made it far more difficult for Japanese and German industry to compete for American markets. Indeed, the protectionism accomplished by the cheap dollar was a major reason for the huge rise in Japanese and European direct investment in the U.S. during these years. Instead of simply exporting to the United States, the Japanese and the Europeans found it highly expedient to establish branch plants there, from which they could access the American market. One consequence of what we can call exchange-rate protectionism was the strong revival of the American automobile industry against its Japanese competitors in the 1990s.

If domestic labour costs relative to foreign were held down by the cheap dollar, U.S. corporations were also reaping huge dividends from the fact that the real pay of most American wage and salary earners was actually falling. In 1980, workers in the U.S. manufacturing sector were paid, on average, us$8.49 an hour (in constant 1982 dollars); by 1994, the hourly rate of pay in this sector had fallen to us$8.02 (in constant 1982 dollars). Looking at wage and salary rates across the whole spectrum of the U.S. resource, manufacturing and service sectors, we see the same picture. In 1980, the average hourly rate of pay in this broad swath of the American economy was us$7.78 (in constant 1982 dollars); by 1994, the average hourly rate of pay in these sectors had fallen to us$7.40 (in constant 1982 dollars). Take-home pay for employees in these industries, again in constant 1982 dollars, declined from an average of us$275 a week in 1980 to us$256 a week in 1994.[15]

Despite the fact that American workers have seen their paycheques shrink, they have been loath to mount strikes against their employers. In comparison with the 1960s and 1970s, there has been a steady decline in the number of days lost to U.S. industry as a result of strikes during the 1980s and 1990s.[16] Alan Greenspan, chairman of the Federal Reserve Board, has regarded the reluctance of American workers to push for higher wages as his ace in the hole in preventing a resumption of inflation. Labour's deep insecurity and fear of job loss, even in an economy in which unemployment has declined significantly, has become an important part of the calculation in the setting of U.S. monetary policy.[17] It is no exaggeration to say that the foundation of the new American empire has been the taming of U.S. labour and the confident belief that American wage and salary earners will stay tame for a long time to come. When they talk of restructuring and hector the Japanese and the Europeans to follow in their footsteps, American business and political leaders really have in mind subduing U.S. labour.

Today's American triumphalists are confident that the United States has learned the lessons of globalization better than anyone else and will grow stronger against its competitors as the globalization agenda unfolds. Indeed, the third pillar on which the present American empire stands is globalization. Those who proclaim that this is a new age of American supremacy believe that the United States is better suited than any other country to prosper in a truly global economy. At heart, globalization is about the corporate management of assets and markets on a world-wide scale. In a setting in which the particular adaptations of societies to the pressures of modern industrialism are thought to be less important than the single quality of universal adaptability, the United States is seen as having the edge.

At work here is the revival in a new form of two old American ideas. The first idea is that the United States as a new society, indeed a "new world," is more able to adapt to new conditions than are older nations that are more set in their ways. The second idea is that laissez-faire capitalism, combining the maximum of free market with the minimum of state intervention, is the best way to maximize economic output and efficiency. In fact, both of these notions are mere axioms, self-proclaimed truisms, for which no serious proof is ever offered.

The notion that the United States is a new society and therefore more adaptable than older societies can easily be challenged. The United States Constitution and its system of government are among the oldest in the world. Since the Americans cut themselves loose from Europe in the eighteenth century, the United States has had less exposure to new ideas than have most other countries, certainly European countries. With its narrow range of legitimate ideological options, which excludes socialism as well as traditional conservatism, the United States has been a remarkably intolerant society. The fact that some ideas have been seen as "un-American" as recently as the 1950s, that a congressional committee could have dedicated itself to rooting out un-American activities, makes the point. It is unimaginable that any other contemporary Western country would engage in such official witch hunts whose purpose is to guard the national belief system against foreign concepts.

Few Americans speak foreign languages and, compared with other peoples, Americans have little knowledge of the ideas, literature, films and customs of other countries. When I lived in France (for nearly four years between the mid-1980s and the mid-1990s), I was impressed by the way French newspapers and television treated American films, books and societal trends with passionate interest, if sometimes with evident incomprehension. After long stays in Europe, I have always experienced culture shock on returning to North America, not least because of its deeply parochial exclusion of ideas from the outside. It is certainly true that the United States has a powerful culture and has an enormous impact on other societies. However, the idea that the United States is highly adaptable in a changing world strikes me as a non-starter.

The second idea, that unimpeded free enterprise works better than interventionist Japanese or European approaches to the economy, is also based more on myth than on fact. Although it is true that the American economy has grown more rapidly for parts of the 1990s than have the Japanese and European economies, to draw far-reaching conclusions based on such a short time span is likely to lead to a sharp surprise when the next downturn occurs in the U.S. economy. If we take a longer time span—either the past thirty or forty years—the nod goes to the Japanese and the Europeans, whose economies have outgrown the American economy. (For good measure, it is worth making the same point about the British economy, since boosters of the American model also claim that a British miracle has been under way in the 1990s. Over the past three or four decades, British average growth has been significantly lower than growth in Japan and Europe.) Furthermore, there is plenty of evidence that the interventionist model has been much better at applying major technological breakthroughs than has the free enterprise model. And it appears that the interventionist model makes for a society with a more egalitarian sharing of income and a more effective network of social programs, both with pronounced effects on quality of life and even on overall life expectancy.

Much of the current crowing in the United States and Britain about the advantages of the Anglo-American model has to do with the problems that Japan and Europe are now passing through. In the late 1980s, it was fashionable in the English-speaking world to wonder whether Japan had discovered a superior form of capitalism that would leave the

United States in the dust. Today, it is even more fashionable in the Anglo-American world to think that Japan has foundered. The current received wisdom is that the Japanese need to learn the truths that have been revealed to the Americans and the British if they are to resume their forward economic march.

In 1998, Japan's economic problems, which had been accumulating for close to a decade, became much more serious as a consequence of a wider Asian economic crisis that devastated Thailand and South Korea, damaged Indonesia's economy and slowed growth in China.

Japan has suffered from two self-inflicted economic wounds in the 1990s. The first is the bursting of the speculative bubble in both the real estate and stock markets, and the second is the fallout from the corruption scandals that tarnished the lustre of governing and corporate elites, hobbling the Japanese leadership in taking economic decisions.

With the sanction of key government ministries, Japanese business pushed up property values to levels that were the most excessive in the world during the 1980s. By the end of the decade, on paper at least, the islands that make up Japan were worth twice as much in their notional land value as the entire United States. The value of commercial land in Tokyo quadrupled in just a few years, reaching its peak in 1990 and then collapsing in 1991. In the most desirable commercial districts of Tokyo, property values ultimately declined by a devastating 80 percent. (The rest of the industrialized world was also involved in land speculation in the 1980s. From Beverly Hills to Toronto to the Côte d'Azur, property values soared and then crashed.)

The Japanese stock market took off like a rocket during the same years. In Tokyo, stocks went up and up in a bull market in which the relationship between economic fundamentals and the value of shares seemed to disappear altogether. As the price-to-earnings ratio for shares climbed ever higher, investors were paying very dearly for the dividends they could expect. What drove them on was not the meagre dividends but the speculative return they hoped to reap from constantly rising share prices. The Japanese market had become a giant casino where the frenzy to win had departed from reality. As with all such speculative bubbles, there were more than a few credible analysts around who were willing to explain why this boom market could go on indefinitely, warning signs to the contrary notwithstanding. But finally, as all bubbles will, this one burst. As the stock market plunged, Japanese banks were thrown into a crisis in which their profitability, and in some cases their survival, was threatened by the torrent of bad debts.

By the late 1990s, although it had recovered from some of the consequences of the collapse of the bubble economy, Japan faced formidable new economic difficulties. In 1997, Japanese real estate prices reached pre-bubble 1984 levels and were beginning to firm and even climb, making real estate once again an attractive investment.[18] But this positive development was more than offset by the financial turmoil in Asia that posed new threats to the viability of Japanese banks and the Japanese economy. In the summer and autumn of 1997, as currency and stock market turbulence spread from Thailand and Indonesia to Hong Kong, the Japanese stock market began a new downward slide. Because Japanese banks depended heavily on equity participation in industrial corporations, the falling market cut away at their asset base, seriously narrowing their capacity to lend. The collapse of a number of Japanese banks was a distinct possibility. Moreover, the Japanese economy, along with that of much of Asia, was poised on the edge of a possible deflationary contraction. The prospect of a sharp reduction in economic growth in Asia, the destination of 44 percent of Japanese exports, threatened Japanese producers with a serious loss of markets. And since domestic consumption has been virtually flat, exports have been carrying the Japanese economy. The paradox of a nation of savers endangering their own well-being through underconsumption confronted Japan in late 1997. And since Japan is the world's most important creditor nation, the dangers its financial institutions face could also hurt financial markets in London, Frankfurt and New York. The Asian economic crisis had the potential to slow economic growth in Europe and the United States.

The Asian crisis highlighted the risk of deflation throughout the industrialized world. Investors around the world have focused on the perils of inflation for so long that they have scarcely considered the even greater devastation that can be the consequence of deflation. General deflation involves falling prices and salaries. As in the extreme case of the 1930s, a deflationary spiral feeds on itself, driving down the output of goods and services and depressing the value of real estate, stocks and bonds. Signalling the risk of a descent into deflation not only in Asia but in the global economy are a number of warning signs. Chief among them is the emergence of global overcapacity in key sectors including automobiles, chemicals, electronics, computer software and hotels. The world's auto companies, for instance, now have the capacity to produce nearly eighty million cars a year, even though global annual sales are fewer than sixty million cars. On top of that, consumers are strapped with excessive levels of debt. In the United States in 1997, household debt reached 91 percent of disposable personal income, compared with 65 per cent in 1980. With real wages flat or growing only modestly and consumer debt extremely high, there is a real risk of a sharp global economic downturn driven by overcapacity.

Despite the grave problems now faced by Japan, the strengths its economy has acquired over the past several decades remain intact. Japan's industrial base is formidable, and as an export engine it is still second to none. In 1996, Japan enjoyed a us$83.7 billion surplus in merchandise trade and a us$66 billion surplus on its current account. (The flipside of these Japanese surpluses, of course, was huge American deficits. In 1996, the U.S. had a us$186.1 billion deficit in its merchandise trade—the highest in its history—and a us$153.5 billion deficit on its current account.[19] The U.S. net debt relative to the rest of the world could be expected to reach us$1 trillion by the turn of the century.) Indeed, while U.S. GDP grew by 2.4 per cent in 1996, Japan's grew by a much more robust 3.6 percent, the highest in the G-7.[20] Those intent on showing the superiority of the Anglo-American economic model in comparison with that of Japan need to grapple with the fact that for decades Japan has consistently achieved more rapid economic growth than the U.S. and Britain, as the following statistics show: from 1961 to

1969, average real GDP growth in Japan was 10.2 percent, while in the U.S. it was 4.3 percent and in Britain 2.9 percent; from 1970 to 1979, average real GDP growth in Japan was 5.1 percent, while in the U.S. it was 2.8 percent and in Britain 2.4 percent; from 1980 to 1989, average real GDP growth in Japan was 4.0 percent, while in the U.S. it was 2.5 percent and in Britain 2.4 percent; from 1990 to 1994, average real GDP growth in Japan was 2.1 percent, while in the U.S. it was 2.0 percent and in Britain 0.8 percent.[21]

And despite the strain on Japanese banks as a consequence of the twin blows of the collapse of land values and stock prices, they remain the world's largest. In December 1996, Japan had the world's biggest foreign reserves, which totalled US$217 billion. By contrast, U.S. foreign reserves were about US$70 billion.[22] And perhaps most significant of all, through the years of lagging economic growth and persistent difficulties in the mid-1990s, Japan managed to maintain what would have been described as full employment in any other industrialized country. While the Americans celebrated their achievement in reducing unemployment—it was 4.9 percent in September 1997—Japanese unemployment was 3.4 percent, the lowest in the G-7.[23]

A further word needs to be said about U.S. unemployment. As in other industrialized countries, it pays to read the fine print where official American statistics are concerned. In 1994, there were 6.2 million American adults who were not officially in the labour market but nonetheless desired employment. For various reasons—they were discouraged from seeking employment, they were not currently looking for a job but wanted work, they were encumbered with family responsibilities or, in the case of about 2 percent, they were ill—these people were not counted among the officially unemployed.[24] If these Americans are added to the ranks of those who ought to be considered unemployed, the actual U.S. unemployment rate doubles to about 10 percent.

It is also worth noting that nearly 31 million Americans were employed part-time in 1994. Of this number, more than 4.5 million were working part-time because they were unable to find full-time work or because of the conditions in the firm where they were working.[25] These

Americans are underemployed. Meanwhile, 1.4 million Americans were behind bars in jails or in state or federal prisons in 1994. This matters because the American incarceration rate is far higher than that in other industrialized countries and has been increasing dramatically over the past quarter century. (In the early 1970s, about 350,000 Americans were behind bars.)[26] And though it would be unreasonable to include among the ranks of the unemployed or underemployed those locked up, it is not at all unreasonable to question the social policies that have led to imprisonment on such a scale that it removes close to 1.5 million adults from American society and, as a consequence, from the U.S. labour force.

Like Japan's, Europe's economic problems are serious. At the heart of Europe's economic doldrums in the 1990s is a severe unemployment crisis. France's unemployment rate stood at 12.7 percent in the winter of 1997. Italy and Germany had only marginally lower rates at 11.9 percent and 11.3 percent respectively.[27]

In France, the unemployment crisis has become a social crisis as well. In the winter of 1997, there was immense dissatisfaction with the neo-Gaullist government of President Jacques Chirac. Public opinion polls revealed that the French were in a morose mood, believing that their children faced a difficult future of declining opportunity. Discontent led to a sharp rise in the popularity of left-wing ideas, although it was not clear that the political left understood how to deal with the fury that was building in France. The sociologist Emmanuel Todd explained the renewed popularity of left-wing thought this way: "In the mid-1980s, 80 percent of the French believed their lot would improve in the near future. Today, studies show that 80 percent of the French fear unemployment and forced 'downlifing.' It is no wonder there is such a renewed demand for more equality."[28]

One sign of the mood in France was the astounding sale of 200,000 copies of a polemical book by the novelist Viviane Forrester entitled *L'Horreur Economique* (The Economic Horror). The title was inspired by the exclamation "The horror! The horror!" in Joseph Conrad's *Heart of*

*Darkness.* In the book, Forrester decries the tendency of the private market economy to relegate the majority of the population to a position of marginalization. Meanwhile, opinion polls showed that a majority of the French population thought that firms could employ more people if they wanted to. Likewise, a majority opposed further privatization of public sector companies and a surprising 40 percent wanted to see whole industries renationalized.[29]

The unemployment crisis was also creating a new opening for the extreme right-wing Front National led by Jean-Marie Le Pen, who, as we have noted, ascribes the unemployment problem to the presence of foreigners in France. From the hoardings in French towns, Front National posters displayed the threatening message "When we take power, they [the foreigners] will leave."

Since the early 1980s, the Front National has presented itself as the alternative to the governing elites, whether of the traditional right or the left. In the winter of 1997, the Front National won the mayoral election in the southern municipality of Vitrolles, the fourth city hall the extremist party has won in recent years. The backdrop to the electoral victory in Vitrolles, with its unemployment rate of 22 percent and its high immigrant population, was the crisis of joblessness.

Both the receptiveness of the French people to left-wing ideas and the continued advance of the extreme right were key factors in the outcome of the legislative elections called by President Jacques Chirac in April 1997. Legislative elections were not required until the following spring, but Chirac and his neo-Gaullist prime minister, Alain Juppé, made the grave miscalculation that the traditional right could win a surprise election in 1997. They believed this would put them in the driver's seat for the difficult task of making further cuts to French government spending to qualify France for admission to the single European currency, the euro, scheduled for introduction in 1999. Instead, the discontent of the French people with chronic unemployment boiled to the surface, and to the surprise of almost everyone, Lionel Jospin's Socialists, who had formed an electoral alliance with the Communists and the Greens, won the legislative elections.

In Germany as well, unemployment reached crisis proportions in the winter of 1997. While jobless levels inside Germany were the highest since the 1930s, German industrial firms were creating hundreds of thousands of new jobs in cheap labour areas such as Eastern Europe, and German trade unions and wage and salary earners were forced to defend the gains they had made in the past. Meanwhile, high unemployment rates provoked a nativist anti-immigrant backlash, which in the early 1990s resulted in horrific outbursts of violence against Turkish migrant workers and other non-Germans. A marginal, but highly noisy, extreme right, made up of neo-Nazis, white supremacists and skinheads, made their presence felt. In the winter of 1997, five thousand neo-Nazis staged a march through Munich to protest a public exhibition in the city devoted to documenting the crimes of the regular German army, and not just the Gestapo and the SS, during the Second World War.

At the root of Germany's economic problems in the 1990s has been the challenge of unification, the integration of the former East Germany into the Federal Republic. Indeed, the economic problems experienced by all of Europe in the 1990s can be traced back to the crucial decisions that were made in the months following the opening of the Berlin Wall in late 1989.

The idea that unification could be a gradual process was scrapped within weeks of the opening of the Wall when German Chancellor Helmut Kohl made himself the man of the hour by playing to the fervent desire of the East German population to put as much distance as possible as quickly as possible between themselves and the collapsing Soviet empire. Kohl offered the East Germans the prospect of immediate economic union, to be quickly followed by political union. And he attached a huge bribe to that offer, the conversion of East German ostmarks for deutschmarks on extremely favourable terms, most of them at a rate of one to one (a gross overvaluing of the ostmark).

Monetary and economic union preceded political union by three months, coming into effect on July 1, 1990. On that day, East German retail outlets were completely outfitted with Western products. Not surprisingly, as easterners switched from their own domestic products, the economy collapsed in eastern Germany, with thousands of enterprises going bankrupt, and unemployment rates soaring. Total collapse was prevented only by the expenditure of billions of deutschmarks by the Bonn government to rebuild the Federal Republic's new eastern region. By the autumn of 1992, when I drove across eastern Germany from east of Frankfurt to Berlin, the autobahn was being completely rebuilt for hundreds of kilometres. There was a vast army of construction workers all along the route. In addition to the large public sector investment, there was also very considerable private sector investment. On the perimeters of eastern towns and cities, new plants and office buildings were springing up.

Both Westies and Osties (western and eastern Germans) disliked the way the great undertaking was unfolding. Westerners resented paying the bills for the reconstruction of the east, financed in part by a special unification tax. Meanwhile, easterners hated being poorer than their western neighbours, and resented their seemingly helpless dependence on Bonn. And matters were not helped by the fact that the Bundesbank, the powerful and highly autonomous German central bank, disapproved of the terms of economic union right from the start. The Bundesbank feared that the buyout of ostmarks at such a favourable rate and the failure to raise taxes high enough to reflect the true cost of rebuilding the east would threaten the soundness of the deutschmark and generate inflation. Constitutionally entrusted with the job of preventing inflation, the Bundesbank reacted to unification by running a very tight monetary policy, which pushed up interest rates. Indeed, it was the high interest policy of the Bundesbank that drove Europe into the economic doldrums in the early 1990s. The Bundesbank's high-interest-rate policy compelled Germany's close economic partners to pursue similar monetary policies. High interest rates reduced economic growth in both Germany and France, destroying hundreds of thousands of jobs, reducing tax revenues, forcing increased outlays of social benefits and pushing the welfare state in both countries into crisis.

In the summer of 1992, Britain bailed out of this high-cost strategy when the Conservative government pulled the pound sterling out of the exchange rate mechanism of the European Monetary System (EMS). The consequence was a sharp decline in the value of the pound against the deutschmark, but Britain was thus able to regain control over its monetary policy. A devalued pound and lower British interest rates were crucial to the success Britain subsequently enjoyed in generating economic growth and lower unemployment. It was the British version of the success the Americans had experienced as a consequence of exchange-rate protectionism.

Eventually the Bundesbank eased German interest rates, and Germany's monetary partners were enabled to follow suit. By then, however, Europe's economy was mired in recession and high unemployment. Lamentably, high interest rates and a tight money supply are much better at triggering recession than a return to low interest rates is at restoring economic growth. By itself, a resumption of low interest rates does little to restore economic demand in an economy where high unemployment and job insecurity act as severe restraints on consumer spending.

From the frying pan of high interest rates in the early 1990s, Europe's economy was thrown into the fire of the approaching launch of the single European currency later in the decade. In the 1980s, the European Community's strategy for competing with the United States and Japan was the single European market, a vast reform that was largely completed on schedule on December 31, 1992. The next great hurdle, aimed at allowing European business to invest, produce and market its goods and services on a continent-wide scale, was to be the creation of the single currency.

For the Germans, the single currency was to confirm their position as the financial power at the heart of the new Europe. For the French and the other members of the European Union, the single currency represented a shared responsibility. Once it was launched, they believed, the single currency would end the ability of Germany's central bank, the Bundesbank, to set French monetary policy for them singlehandedly.

To get the Germans to sign on to the single currency, which would require them to give up their formidable deutschmark (their most successful post-war creation), the members of the EU had to go along with stringent rules dictated by the Bundesbank. Since its establishment in 1957, the Bundesbank had always been dedicated to values dear to the heart of bankers. The Bundesbank cared about sound money, achieved through zero inflation. Its directors—the most retentively compulsive of central bankers—believed in the proposition that creditors should be repaid in currency that was as sound as the money they lent in the first place. And throughout its forty-year history, the German central bank has let nothing stand in its way. To avoid inflation and to keep the deutschmark rock solid, it has been prepared to raise interest rates even at the cost of sharply reduced economic growth and higher unemployment.

According to the 1991 Maastricht Treaty on European Union, countries wanting admission to the single currency had to ensure that their annual rate of inflation was less than 3 percent, that their public sector deficit did not exceed 3 percent of GDP, that their public sector debt did not exceed 60 percent of GDP and that they had managed to remain within the inner circle of the European exchange rate mechanism for two years prior to the creation of the single currency.

These rules forced EU member countries to run highly restrictive monetary and fiscal policies. If Italy, France or other EU countries, including Germany itself, were to qualify for the single currency, they had virtually no room to manoeuvre in using the major levers of macro-economic policy. This meant that France, Italy and the others could do little to foster economic recovery, large-scale job creation and the reduction of unemployment. To gain admission to the single currency, with its hope for increase in their decision-making power, EU member countries were forced to don an economic straitjacket at a time of serious economic difficulties.

This predicament was revealed in the efforts of the Chirac regime in France to appear to be grappling with the unemployment crisis, without actually making use of monetary or fiscal policy to encourage greater job creation. In a country where 600,000 people under the age of twenty-five were unemployed, President Jacques Chirac was reduced to acting like a cheerleader on the issue of jobs. On one absurd occasion in March 1997, Chirac starred in a two-hour live public forum on national television devoted to dealing with the problems of young people. He assumed the role of an upbeat pedagogue, advancing his theories on how French children could overcome their literacy problems by the time his seven-year term was up. He enthused about computers and CD-ROMs and promised that by the year 2000, every French secondary school would be online. What he did not do—and this flowed from his commitment to European monetary union—was to announce any concrete measures aimed at actually creating jobs for young people.[30]

Despite the seriousness of Europe's economic problems, it would be easy to exaggerate them. Advocates of the Anglo-American model have done precisely this to make the case for the inherent superiority of their socioeconomic model. And yet Europe's economic strengths are formidable. The single market has been a considerable success, giving European producers the world's largest single economy as their launchpad for international competition. Europe's social and infrastructure spending has created an environment in which business can operate without leading to the urban problems and violence that are so much a part of the American scene. But Europe has reached a dead end. On one side, its economic policies are highly favourable to bankers; on the other side is a politically conscious working class/middle class that, particularly in France and Germany, has shown itself ready to defend itself in difficult times. The impasse will end with either the success of the single currency, or with the modification or collapse of the project and the reassertion of an economic strategy that reflects a much broader range of social interests.

Europe's economic problems, like Japan's, are capable of solution over the middle-range future. Similarly, it can be concluded that what currently appear to be America's major advantages are unlikely to endure. Beneath the surface of American success, there lurk the fundamental social problems that the country has failed to grapple with. The crisis of the inner cities, the growing problems generated by the rise of the new urban poor, the pandemic of violence that sets the United States apart from other advanced countries, the malaise of the public school

system, the widening gap between rich and poor and the enduring fact
of racism at the heart of American life—this Gordian knot of interre-
lated predicaments exceeds the challenges facing Japan and Europe.


Emanating as they do from the world's only superpower, American ideas
and values have a hegemonic force in our time. American ideas are the
ruling ideas against which all others must contend if they are to survive.
Indeed, it is natural enough in our time that it is the American view of
how the economy should be run and how labour should relate to management that has pride of place at Davos, the IMF and the World Bank,
as well as in the policy ideas of the OECD. In the nineteenth century, the
ideas of the British ruling class seemed similarly permanent and unchal-
lengeable. But empires come and go.

As we have seen, the first American empire was short-lived. It was the
adolescent empire of a rising world state. The second American empire
arose at the end of the greatest war in history. It was the mature empire of
a country at the height of its powers. The third American empire arose
following the collapse of the Soviet system. As a consequence of its self-
destructive elements and the huge potential of its likely challengers, it is
an empire with an uncertain future.

Those who live in the outlying regions of the empire, Canadians
among them, have to find ways to console themselves. If we do not live
in a time of great art, we can at least be thankful that we reside in a peaceful and comparatively affluent corner of the empire. The downside for
Canadians has been that our country has ceded much of its ability to
grapple with the social and economic consequences of being drawn more
closely into the heart of the American empire. There is genuine and
increasing suffering in our day in class-divided Canada. There is also the
despair of living in a time when money and power are so overwhelmingly
devoted to bowing to the thin accomplishments of American civilization
and the comforts, baubles and amusements it provides.

Chapter 12

# The Whirlwind

Orthodox Anglo-American opinion was scandalized in June 1997 when the people of France elected the Socialists to power, in an alliance with the Communists and the Greens. The *Washington Post* delivered an editorial lecture to the uppity French: "In today's world, technology and capital are increasingly mobile; businesses can set up shop wherever profits will be greatest. . . . Thus, nations find their own political possibilities limited; if they set taxes high to fund a generous social safety net, businesses will move away, shrinking the tax base and requiring even higher taxes. . . It is safe to say that wishfulness, which seems to be the underlying mood in the French electorate, won't repeal the new laws of global economics."[1]

The *New York Times* columnist Thomas L. Friedman echoed those sentiments: "The French seem to think they can . . . still enjoy the best of all worlds. They actually believe that they can still be a world power and have their truck drivers retire at 55 with nearly full pay, work a 35-hour week and close their shop for two hours every afternoon. . . . France has no realistic alternative . . . and the markets will soon hammer home that reality." But then Friedmann softened his tone and admitted that "there is something appealing about the French struggle to maintain their lifestyle and to resist the constraints, and one-size-fits-all sterility, of the golden strait jacket [the laws of the new global economy] . . . It's Don Quixote versus the bond market. You've got to admire it."[2]

The French have always gotten under the skin of the Anglo Americans. France is the one large country in the West that has never bowed to the superiority of the Anglo-American way of life. Sustained by a past when France was Europe's leading power and by the great revolution that did more than any other event in history to usher in political and social modernity, the French have always assumed that they have as much right as the Americans and the British to be regarded as the founders of the contemporary West.

In the spring of 1997, President Jacques Chirac and his neo-Gaullist prime minister, Alain Juppé, were planning a year of harsh cuts in government spending to get France ready for integration into the single European currency. Believing that the French left was in disarray, the French conservatives planned to win an early legislative election before inflicting yet more pain on a society already distressed as a consequence of an unemployment rate of 12.7 percent in the early months of 1997. Their electoral campaign presented them as the apostles of economic restructuring that would prepare France for the rigours of globalization. They did what parties of the right have done everywhere for the past fifteen years: they accused the left of being hopelessly stuck in the past.

But things did not go according to plan. French wage and salary earners were not buying the argument that they ought to make further sacrifices at a time when stock markets everywhere, including France's, were marching from triumph to triumph. Instead of reelecting a government that had won a crushing legislative majority in 1993, wage and salary earners turned in huge numbers to the Socialists, Communists and Greens, whose campaign for a government of the left was based on the notion that jobs ought to take precedence over the creation of the single European currency. At the other end of the spectrum, the extreme right Front National increased its share of the national vote to 15 percent, its highest ever in a legislative election. The conservative government was left with almost no support from wage and salary earners.

While keeping the support of business, it had been abandoned by the populace as a whole in the worst showing by the mainstream right in the history of the Fifth Republic. It was the first time a major electorate had rejected a rigorous policy to prepare for globalization in an election in which this was unquestionably the overriding issue. To the annoyance of orthodox believers in the system, the French said no.

Not everyone was annoyed with the results, however. The week after the Socialist victory, the Paris stock market rallied strongly, in part because French retailers and manufacturers sensed that the election of a non-monetarist government signalled hope for economic expansion and for a more buoyant domestic market. The true significance of the election was that wage and salary earners were no longer willing to believe that a government that preached capitalist orthodoxy had their interests at heart.

The French election was not the only sign of the changing political behaviour of wage and salary earners. In just one year, 175 million Europeans in three countries had thrown out governments of the right and had opted instead for governments of the left. A year earlier, Italians elected a truly left-wing government for the first time ever—the Olive Tree Alliance with Romano Prodi as prime minister. All previous Italian governments since the end of the Second World War had been coalitions designed around the objective of keeping the Communists out of power. The Olive Tree was a new departure for an Italian government because the largest group in Romano Prodi's coalition was the former Communists. In addition, a month before the French chose a government of the left, British voters elected a Labour government with Tony Blair as prime minister.

In each case, wage and salary earners were the essential constituency to support the winners, though the results of each of these elections owed much to particular conditions in Italy, Britain and France. And the governments that came to power differed significantly from one another. Tony Blair was much more of a market enthusiast than was French prime minister Lionel Jospin. Romano Prodi's highest priority was to ensure that Italy qualified for entry into the single European currency. Blair remained standoffish about the single currency, and Jospin, while favouring it, insisted that the single currency had to be tied to making job creation the leading European economic priority. But beyond the differences, Italian, British and French wage and salary earners were moving in the same direction. They wanted governments concerned about their economic problems, not about the global dreams of bankers and multinational corporations. Their top priorities were job creation and the protection of social programs, not public sector budget cuts and privatization of state-owned firms.

When we step back from these three elections, we see that the heightened class conflict of our time is transforming the way the political systems of the advanced industrialized countries work. To appreciate the nature of the transformation, it helps to grasp how different the political system is today from the way it was in the post-war decades.

Following the military victory over Nazism and Fascism in the Second World War, the working class was accorded a share of power within the system. To be sure, that share—embodied in the Great Social Compromise—was a distinctly inferior share, and its extent varied considerably from country to country. The Great Social Compromise, with its growing real incomes and expanded social programs, arose out of a broad societal consensus underpinning the political systems of the advanced countries. In practice, if not necessarily in theory, centrist political parties that promulgated the main tenets of the Great Social Compromise were predominant. While power sometimes alternated between a party on the right and a party on the left, a wide base of support for the main features of the social consensus ensured that changes in governments did not lead to drastic shifts in policy.

The British case provides a clear illustration of such alternation between two more or less centrist parties, one on the left and the other on the right. The Labour Party stormed to power in the summer of 1945, when the British people turned out wartime hero Winston Churchill and made Clement Attlee prime minister. In theory, the Labour Party was committed to a quasi-revolutionary program that included the nationalization of most of the major industries of the country. What Labour actually did in power, however, was very different from its stated program. While indeed there were some significant nationalizations in the coal and later the steel industries, Labour's main achievement was to launch the welfare state, most notably the National Health Service (NHS). Most of the economy remained in private sector hands. Labour had crafted the British version of the Great Social Compromise.

When the Conservatives returned to office in 1951, they privatized the steel industry, but they retained the Labour Party's welfare state. Under several prime ministers, the Tories held on to power until 1964, continuing to espouse support for centrist policies. Similarly, when Labour regained power in 1964 under the leadership of Harold Wilson, a major shift in policy did not occur. The steel industry was renationalized and Britain took some small steps in the direction of a Continental-style industrial policy, but the post-war consensus remained in place.

It was not until the the Great Social Compromise began to disintegrate everywhere during the 1970s that the pattern of British politics shifted dramatically. A severe new right-wing agenda was developing among those close to the business class at a time when the economy was stalling, unemployment was rising and the fiscal crisis had begun. To Margaret Thatcher, the new Tory leader who became the chieftain of the new right, the post-war compromise was an abomination—"Compromise is the language of the devil," she loved to say. She wanted victory over her social democratic and trade union foes, not compromise. And the tailwinds of the new financial capitalism enabled Thatcher to do just that. As the Tories moved to the right before and after the 1979 election, the age of consensus in British politics came to an end. Anyone with any first-hand knowledge of British politics in the Thatcher era knows that people either loved or detested Thatcher. The middle ground was gone.

Throughout the West, similar political developments occurred as the balance within capitalism shifted from industrialists to globalizing financial capitalists, and the parties of the right moved further right.

American Republicans, Canadian Progressive Conservatives, French neo-Gaullists and German Christian Democrats all developed monetarist enthusiasms to a greater or lesser extent. With relish they tore up their versions of the Great Social Compromise, just as the Thatcherites had done in Britain.

In the post-war decades, the working class of Continental Western Europe had won a much more far-reaching welfare state, job security and remuneration regime than their counterparts in the United States, the most market-centred of Western countries. Although the French and German systems differed significantly, with the French system operating more through the power of the state and the German functioning more through worker representation on the boards of large companies, both France and Germany evolved models that accorded substantial recognition to the working class. In Scandinavia, Austria and the Benelux countries (Belgium, Holland and Luxembourg), regimes similar in their effect to those in France and Germany were established. Indeed, the most advanced welfare state in the world, and the country with the most egalitarian income distribution, was Sweden. In Britain and Canada on the other hand, the Great Social Compromise resulted in a system that lay between that of the United States and that of Continental Western Europe. In the British and Canadian cases, while a more advanced welfare state was established than in the U.S., the power of workers was much less enshrined in the remuneration and job security regimes than in Western Europe.

The Great Social Compromise was certainly in decline before the end of the Cold War, but the "end of history" mentality that grew out of the collapse of the Soviet bloc speeded its demise. Empowered by new technology and a new global division of labour, capitalists could see no reason at the end of the Cold War for not realizing themselves, psychically and materially, in every possible way. They had always chafed at any sort of partnership with labour and at the idea that market relations had to be limited by the state to achieve social policy goals. When the opportunity to advance their interests presented itself, the response of the capitalists was to abandon the Great Social Compromise, in more or less triumphalist fashion, depending on the circumstances in particular countries.

Discarding the Great Social Compromise turned out to be much more difficult in France, Germany, Italy and other countries in Continental Western Europe than in the English-speaking countries—the United States, Britain, Canada, Australia and New Zealand—where capitalists won a string of major victories. The national particulars aside, capitalism has reverted to type. Even in Europe, where working-class resistance has prevented the crushing of the welfare state and the kind of wholesale economic restructuring that has occurred in the English-speaking countries, the remains of the Great Social Compromise are merely tolerated. In the present climate and balance of power between capital and labour, the working class/middle class has been reduced to a defensive posture.

With the demise of the Great Social Compromise, the system has become more homogeneous, its features of genuine plurality sharply attenuated. Neoliberals like to think it is a great virtue that capitalism promotes individual choice in all realms of existence, believing this allows individuals to become autonomous actors as never before. There is considerable irony in the fact that the return to unfettered capitalism has generated increasing sameness rather than a diversity of social and cultural forms.

Unfettered capitalism has promoted a "one-myth" ethos in which the pursuit of profit is paramount. And rather than wealth being produced for the use of individual citizens to pursue their dreams in a myriad ways, profit is the one objective that subsumes all possible others. When art, literature, medicine, architecture and the sciences are captured by the drive for the bottom line, whether directly in the case of the private sector or less directly in the public sector, the consequence is a narrowing, not a broadening, of options. Contemporary capitalism embodies the ultimate reversal of means and ends. In a class-divided society, the vast majority of the population becomes the means by which the profit-making ends of the minority are realized.

Social explosion never has a simple cause. But one is coming. In launching the new class war, business has sowed the wind. It will reap the whirlwind. Where the social explosion will first occur or over what specific issue, no one can tell. It may show its full force first in France as in 1968—when a strike by ten million workers and students against the government of Charles de Gaulle galvanized the new left throughout the industrialized world—or it may begin elsewhere.

Anger toward the current corporate self-interest is becoming more intense and widespread, no longer the outrage of specific groups against specific wrongs. We are seeing the first signs of a general repudiation of a whole system and its values. What is coming is a movement as profound as any in the past that have advanced the cause of human freedom. It will have its own character, absolutely unto itself, but it will also be linked to the movements for change that can be traced back two or three centuries, past the French Revolution all the way to the English Civil War of the mid-seventeenth century.

The market-centred global capitalism of our age has advanced swiftly over the past two decades. In its early days, it was not clearly understood, and when it reached high tide, for a time it swept all before it. Those who were in its path stood alone during those days. Indeed, many of those who were being pushed aside by the global offensive of the new capitalism were distracted by quarrels with each other—workers against the poor, those with jobs against those without, men against women, whites against blacks, native-born against immigrants.

Today's capitalism preaches a new version of the perilous doctrine that might is right: the idea that the world should put its future in the hands of entrepreneurial saviours who have risen through the ranks of private corporations.

When several hundred salaried employees occupied the Crédit Foncier offices in Paris in 1997, American observers asked themselves in exasperation how a country with workers like that could ever expect to produce a Bill Gates. The advice from America was that they should abandon their fight to defend their own interests and put their faith in the corporate man on horseback—or, to update the metaphor, the man from cyber capitalism. And yet to watch, as I did, these employees develop personally and in their relationships with one another over the course of the three-week occupation left me with hope for the future of democracy. Hundreds of them engaged in round-the-clock cultural activities. They formed musical groups and performed for the public; Parisian musicians came in to lend them support. They read aloud, made speeches, learned from each other, grew as human beings. They brought in children, opened up their offices to the community and talked about how their bank could serve the population at large. The occupation of the offices of the bank was nothing less than an intensive school for the development of an alert, socially aware citizenry.

At the dawn of the twenty-first century, the defenders of today's predatory capitalism have to contort themselves to make the claim that the system they advocate is the best way to meet the needs and aspirations of humanity. Today's capitalism is much like the Ptolemaic idea of the solar system, which, although it was exactly wrong in its depiction of the relationship between the earth and the sun, was vociferously defended for centuries against all evidence to the contrary. Capitalism works best for a small minority of the world's people, condemns hundreds of millions to exploitation and a stunted existence, and leaves billions, particularly in the Third World, in a state of poverty or near-poverty. And yet, the hoary idea persists that the pursuit of profit, regardless of the people who arc in the way, is the best means to meet the needs of the human race and to broaden its potential for the future.

The proponents of the market system have always maintained that they have unlocked the essential secret of human motivation. All the complex mathematics used by the wizards who promulgate contemporary economics is still based on the simple eighteenth-century notion that human beings are rational economic actors, motivated by the quest for what economists call "marginal utility." At base, theoretical economics is a school of psychology perched on a theory of human motivation. Considering the immense authority of economics, which rationalizes capitalist practice, it is worth considering that the theoretical edifice rests on notions about human beings that would be rejected as simplistic in any other context. What gives mainstream economics its authority is not its completely outdated conception of human nature, but the fact that its practitioners guard the intellectual temple that protects the power of the capitalist class.

Capitalist economics blithely overlooks the purpose of the economy. The economy exists to provide the means to meet the needs and wants of people and their families. But capitalist economics is premised on the idea that the economy exists to satisfy the drive of private businesspeople and private corporations to make a profit. To that end, human want, hunger, unemployment and environmental degradation do not come into the equation. If the hungry have no money to purchase food, their hunger does not register as an economic fact. The longing of the unemployed for the self-worth that goes with a job is not an economic fact. And the natural systems of the planet that we depend on for survival do not show up in an economic equation. These are dismissed as mere externalities. Capitalist economics, we must conclude, is designed precisely to keep a small minority rich and powerful at the expense of all the rest. And yet, despite its conceptual shortcomings, the capitalist paradigm is firmly entrenched, in some ways more firmly than ever before. Entrenched yes, but entrenched beyond challenge?

The working class/middle class is already caught up in endless battles with today's capitalism, battles that are bound to grow in intensity and in coherence as well. Some observers in our seemingly disordered epoch, with its multiple identities, would object that the notion of a social class (in this case the working class/middle class) as an agency of change is wrongheaded. And I would agree that any concept of social class as a kind of absolute, which shuts out perceptions of the vast diversity that makes up the working class/middle class of our period, would be erroneous.

But I am convinced that it is a grave error to imagine that "new social movements," valid though many of them are, have replaced the working class/middle class as the crucible of change. While it has recently been fashionable for some intellectuals to refuse to consider capitalism as a system, for fear of falling into the trap of constructing "grand narratives" of the kind that are so offensive to post-modernists, I believe that the failure to recognize capitalism, with all its diversities, as a system is short-sighted. The denial of social class is not some liberation from the false categories of the past, but rather a failure to analyse an oppressive system as an essential step toward changing it.

It is not fashionable in our age to draw broad conclusions about the course of history. Indeed, I am not enamoured of the idea of history as a purposeful sequence of events leading to steady improvement over long periods of time. Any such "progressive" interpretation of history has surely been laid to rest by the unequalled carnage and inhumanity that have characterized the twentieth century.

That said, it seems to me that it is possible to draw some broad conclusions about the course of human experience over the long term, even if these conclusions are of a negative sort. When we consider the human journey over thousands of years, the domination of the many by the few stands out as being as close to a constant as there is. Societies in which a dominant class exploits a dominated class have been the rule since slave owning emerged thousands of years ago. The human story, whatever else it has involved (and it has involved much), has perennially featured the exploitation of one group by another. Benign regimes have been tiny in number in comparison with malevolent ones. But must we assume that this situation is fundamental to human experience and therefore unalterable? Should we draw the conclusion that we would be better advised to turn our attention to minor ameliorations of the condition of those around us than to confront and challenge the idea of class-divided society?

In an age of vast technological prowess and puny expectations about what can be done about human inequality, many have come sadly to this conclusion. There is very wide acceptance in the world today that predatory capitalism is a given, and that there is no more point questioning it than debating the weather. Since the end of the Cold War, capitalism has come to be seen by many as a virtual fact of nature and has therefore dropped away from the realm of discourse, at least as far as its essentials are concerned.

Indeed, in the United States, Britain and Canada, the idea of an alternative to capitalism was only ever a tenuous part of the political and intellectual agenda in the past. Today in the English-speaking world, we are experiencing an era of capitalist triumphalism. Here, more than anywhere else, the "end of history" idea—that the system we have today is the system we will have for the long term—goes unquestioned.

Suppose we accept that a very large part of the misery, exploitation and marginalization of people over many centuries has been the consequence of class-divided societies, and that class division retains its pernicious character at the dawn of the new millennium. Some may ask, what is the point of making the case that we live in a society riven by the deep divisions that are the consequence of one social class exercising dominance over another. If there is no alternative, then why bother?

The problem with ignoring the most central of all social realities is precisely that it will not go away. In today's class war, the capitalist class is steadily expanding the material and ideological terrain it occupies. The welfare state we thought we had won is disintegrating. The right to a decent education for our children is being compromised. Universities, which were opened up to much of the working class/middle class in the 1960s, are becoming elitist institutions once again. The principle that governments can intervene to promote economic growth and the creation of jobs—accepted in the West in the post-war decades—has been trashed. In its place is the notion that the market must be allowed to operate untrammelled. The very concept of the mixed economy, in which there are distinct roles for the private and public sectors, has disappeared.

Now, everyone acknowledges that the income gap and especially the wealth gap between the rich and the rest of the population is growing wider. Never in the history of humanity has there been such an immense concentration of wealth in the hands of the super-rich of the planet as there is today. Does anyone discuss doing anything about the fact that in our midst there are individuals with the wealth and power of potentates? Instead of debating the way this extraordinarily powerful minority sets priorities in democratic countries, governments of all political stripes vie for the favour and largesse of these princes of the capitalist realm. We look to capitalist exemplars the way our ancestors once looked to dukes and viscounts.

The reader may think I am indulging in a rhetorical flourish when I make a comparison between today's super-rich and the princes of old. If anything, the comparison understates the case. Imagine a country in which the wealthiest three individuals have more financial assets than the poorest one-third of the population. There is such a country—the United States. Bill Gates and Warren Buffett and John Walton have personal financial assets worth as much as the combined assets of one hundred million of their fellow Americans.

Small wonder there is such an inclination in our age to petition the super-rich to solve our problems rather than to expect anything of the governments we elect. The consequence is that the notion of a society in which all citizens enjoy real influence and an important degree of equality is enfeebled. Indeed, the majority of the 100 million Americans whose combined assets are less than those of the Big Three never even vote in their country's elections.

In Canada, where most cultural offerings are imported, domestic cultural institutions, such as public radio and television, community ballets and orchestras and domestically owned publishing companies are falling by the wayside as government assistance falters. The word is now out that if those running cultural institutions want them to survive, it is time to go cap in hand to business, and to trim sails as necessary. A generation ago in Canada, there was strong political support for the idea that more of the national economy, which was owned and controlled to a unique extent by foreign corporations, should be owned and controlled by Canadians. Programs to achieve that goal were launched by federal and provincial governments in the 1970s. In almost all cases, those programs have been scrapped and their initiatives reversed. Today, no political party in Canada talks about Canadians owning their own economy. The idea has slid away as the major political parties have accepted the notion of a globalized economy.

There is a tendency among some social democratic political leaders, like British prime minister Tony Blair, to proclaim that the discussion of questions of this sort has no place at the dawn of the new millennium. For the new Labour government of Britain, the fundamental inequalities bequeathed by the Thatcher-Major governments that preceded it are accepted as unchangeable realities. Gone from the agenda of the Blair government is the central principle on which the Labour Party was established at the end of the First World War, that the running of the country by a wealthy, privileged minority had to end in favour of power for those who work, whether that work be physical or mental.

Is a society of greater equality possible in the advanced countries? Even by contemplating it, we open the way to further steps. Must we accept that at the apex of society there will always be tycoons whose individual ownership of capital gives them an immensely disproportionate say in human affairs? Is it impossible to imagine a future in which no one is allowed to own assets on such a scale? Is it not conceivable that we can limit the power of financial markets to decide how many people will work and how many will be left on the margin? Can we not figure out how to turn around our present Ptolemaic conception of the economy so that the goals of the people at large set the agenda and financial markets are reduced to serving those goals? This is a time for thinking in large, even utopian, terms.

The principles are simple enough: the highest priority should be meeting the needs of wage and salary earners, and this should be achieved via the transfer of power from the members of the dominant capitalist class—they have far too much power—to the members of the dominated wage and salary earning class.

One obvious step, which should have been taken years ago, is the international imposition of a small tax on every foreign-exchange transaction, the so-called Tobin tax, named after its Nobel Prize–winning original advocate, the Yale economics professor James Tobin. The purpose of the tax is to discourage purely speculative currency transactions. Because the rate of the tax would be so low, it would have no impact on foreign-exchange transactions that are undertaken for the purpose of engaging in real commerce. It would limit transactions whose aim is to reap large profits from very small margins through currency trading that is often under-taken for very short periods of time (a few hours, or even a few minutes).

Countries should tax businesses and wealthy individuals according to the amount of income they actually make in the country doing the tax-ing. If tax haven jurisdictions refuse to assist in making it possible for countries to collect from their absentee wealthy, those tax havens should be blacklisted—countries should ban all financial transactions with tax haven residents.

In recent decades, tax rates for the wealthy have been reduced, while those of wage and salary earners have been increased. This trend needs to be reversed. Wealthy individuals and profitable businesses should pay higher taxes, while wage and salary earners should pay lower taxes. Con-sumption taxes like the GST, which hit the poor much harder than the rich, should be sharply reduced, which would promote the expansion of economic demand. Personal income and corporate income taxes should be raised at the high end.

Wealth taxes are a good idea, and the principle is already estab-lished in some countries. The United States has a wealth transfer tax, and a number of European countries have wealth transfer taxes and annual levies on net wealth. Canada has neither of these taxes. (A wealth transfer tax is levied when wealth moves from one owner to another. An annual wealth tax is levied, at a low rate, on a person's net wealth.) A longer-term goal should be to apply a wealth tax sufficiently high at the top end that it effectively prohibits the accumulation of personal fortunes in the range of several hundred million dollars and higher. As we have seen, the billionaire subclass is rapidly expanding. The existence of billionaires is not consistent with the functioning of a democratic society.

Legislation should be passed to levy a steep surtax on any firm cut-ting its workforce in a year in which the company has declared a profit.

Measures should be adopted to encourage wage and salary earners to acquire ownership of the businesses they work for. If the future is to be different from the past in ending the dominance of the many by the few, a large part of the answer must be for people to own and control the firms where they work. There are many possible means to implement ownership of firms by wage and salary earners. The pension funds of wage and salary earners can be used for that purpose. Legislation could be passed to earmark a fixed proportion of the net income of a firm to go into an equity fund, owned by the wage and salary earners, which would eventually give them a majority of the voting shares in the firm. (For a time in the 1980s, this idea was a part of the program of the Swedish Social Democratic Party.) Most currently planned privatizations of publicly owned firms should be stopped, and in some cases privatized firms should be renationalized.

Governments should announce targets for the reduction of unemployment and underemployment so that the goal of a decent job for all who can and wish to work can be realized. Since the rules of regional trade pacts and of the World Trade Organization and the impending MAI are powerfully biased against such government action, these trade deals must be renegotiated to include the achievement of employment, labour, social and environment goals, or they should be abrogated.

Taking these steps would not create a world with no rich and no poor. It would, however, reverse the present and pronounced trend toward much greater inequality. It would move us a long way toward full employment. The fiscal crisis of the state would be alleviated and social programs and public education systems would be reinvigorated so that they could do the jobs that now exceed their capacities.

Today, no government in the world has as its goal the achievement of this kind of agenda. The program outlined here is eminently practicable, but only a democratically energized citizenry can achieve it—wage and salary earners will need to summon up their immense potential power. These steps will not end the dominance of society by the capitalist class, but they are a beginning. Taking them will point the way to further steps, bringing into view the achievement of a society that at long last will transcend the rule of class by class.

# Notes

Chapter 1

1 Statistics Canada, *Canada Year Book*, 1997 (Ottawa: Department of Industry, 1996), p. 215.
2 *Ibid.*, p. 214.
3 Statistics Canada, *Income Distribution by Size in Canada*, 1995, Table 8.
4 *International Herald Tribune*, January 22, 1997.
5 *Ibid.*
6 *Globe and Mail*, December 23, 1997.
7 *Ibid.*
8 *Ibid.*
9 *Forbes, The Richest 400 People in America*, 1997 edition, pp. 152, 153, 162, 163.
10 Andrew Hacker, *Money: Who Has How Much and Why* (New York: Scribner, 1997), p. 86.
11 *International Herald Tribune*, January 14, 1997.
12 *International Herald Tribune*, April 8, 1997.
13 *Globe and Mail*, September 17, 1997.
14 *International Herald Tribune*, April 8, 1997.
15 U.S. Department of Commerce, *Statistical Abstract of the United States*, 1995, p. 436.
16 *Libération*, January 8, 1997.
17 Charles Handy, *Inside Organizations* (London: BBC Books, 1990), p. 204.
18 *Ibid.*, pp. 204, 205.
19 *Ibid.*, p. 205.
20 *Ibid.*, p. 206.

21 *Ibid.*

22 Hacker, *Money*, p. 83.

23 Donald L. Bartlett and James B. Steele, *America: What Went Wrong?* (Kansas City: Andrews and McMeel, 1992), p. 47.

24 U.S. Department of Commerce, *Statistical Abstract of the United States*, 1995, p. 860.

25 *Monitor* (Ottawa: Canadian Centre for Policy Alternatives, October 1997).

26 *Ibid.*

27 *New York Times*, February 25, 1996.

28 *International Herald Tribune*, April 23, 1997.

29 *Ibid.*

30 *Ibid.*

31 *Monitor*, April 1996.

32 *Libération*, January 20, 1997.

33 *International Herald Tribune*, January 21, 1997.

34 *Ibid.*

35 *Libération*, January 20, 1997.

36 *International Herald Tribune*, April 17, 1997.

37 *International Herald Tribune*, February 3, 1997.

38 *International Herald Tribune*, April 1, 1997.

39 *International Herald Tribune*, April 17, 1997.

40 *Ibid.*

41 *International Herald Tribune*, April 1, 1997.

42 *Ibid.*

43 *Guardian Weekly*, July 13, 1997.

44 *International Herald Tribune*, January 21, 1997.

45 *International Herald Tribune*, January 22, 1997.

46 *International Herald Tribune*, April 7, 1997.

47 Statistics Canada, *Canada Year Book*, 1978–79 (Hull, Quebec: Supply and Services Canada, 1978), p. 154.

48 Statistics Canada, *Canada Year Book*, 1997 (Ottawa: Minister of Industry, 1996), p. 67.

49 Statistics Canada, "Computer literacy—a growing requirement," *Education Quarterly Review*, 1996, p. 9.

50 *Ibid.*

51 Statistics Canada, *Canadian Social Trends*, Autumn 1995, p. 6.

52 Statistics Canada, "Computer Literacy—a growing requirement," *Education Quarterly Review*, 1996, p. 10.

53 Statistics Canada, *Canadian Social Trends*, Autumn 1995, p. 6.

54 *Guardian*, January 9, 1997.

55 *Observer*, January 26, 1997.

56 *International Herald Tribune*, June 20, 1997.

57 *Vanity Fair*, January 1998.

58 *International Herald Tribune*, January 2, 1998.

59 U.S. Department of Commerce, *Statistical Abstract of the United States*, 1997, p. 223.

60 *Vanity Fair*, January 1998.

61 Canadian Broadcasting Corporation, "Ideas," November 21, 1996.

62 U.S. Department of Commerce, *Statistical Abstract of the United States 1995*, pp. 849, 850.

63 *Ibid.*

64 Margaret Whitehead, *The Health Divide*, 1988, p. 352, as cited in David Smith, *North and South* (Harmondsworth: Penguin Books, 1989), p. 33.

65 David Smith, *North and South* (Harmondsworth: Penguin Books, 1989), p. 32.

66 Canadian Broadcasting Corporation, "Ideas," November 21, 1996.

67 *Ibid.*

## Chapter 2

1 OECD, *United States*, 1996, p. 87.

2 *New York Times*, February 25, 1996.

3 *International Herald Tribune*, April 5–6, 1997.

4 *International Herald Tribune*, February 4, 1997.

5 *Challenges*, July–August 1997.

6 Daniel Bell, "On Meritocracy and Equality," *The Public Interest*, Autumn 1972, p. 30, as cited in John H. Goldthorpe, "Problems of 'Meritocracy,'" in A.H. Halsey et al., eds., *Education: Culture, Economy and Society* (New York: Oxford University Press, 1997), p. 665.

7 *Globe and Mail*, October 25, 1997.

8 Conrad Black, *A Life in Progress* (Toronto: Key Porter Books, 1993), p. 175.

9 *Ibid.*, p. 1.

## Chapter 3

1 *International Herald Tribune*, January 24, 1997.

2 Terry Eagleton, *The Illusions of Postmodernism* (Oxford: Blackwell, 1996), p. 63.

3 A summary of the argument, which is encountered in many post-modernist writings, is to be found in Barrie Axford, *The Global System: Economics, Politics, and Culture* (Cambridge, U.K.: Polity Press, 1995), p. 162.

4 Anthony Giddens, *A Contemporary Critique of Historical Materialism*, 2nd ed. (London: Macmillan, 1995), p. xi.

5 Thomas Carlyle, *The French Revolution* (1837) (London, 1930), p. 29, as cited in Norman Davies, *Europe: A History* (New York: Oxford University Press, 1996), pp. 693, 694.

Chapter 4

1 U.S. Department of Commerce, *Statistical Abstract of the United States*, 1997, pp. 838, 847.

2 *Ibid.*, p. 847.

3 *Ibid.*, pp. 855, 864.

4 *Forbes, The Richest 400 People in America*, 1997 edition, p. 183.

5 *International Herald Tribune*, September 25, 1997.

6 *Globe and Mail*, January 24, 1998.

7 U.S. Department of Commerce, *Statistical Abstract of the United States*, 1997, pp. 401, 406.

8 *Ibid.*, p. 485.

9 *Ibid.*

10 John H. Goldthorpe, "Problems of 'Meritocracy,'" in A.H. Halsey et al., eds., *Education: Culture, Economy and Society* (New York: Oxford University Press, 1997), p. 666.

11 Lester Thurow, "Education and Economic Inequality," in *The Public Interest* (Summer 1972), p. 79, as cited in John H. Goldthorpe, "Problems of 'Meritocracy,'" in Halsey et al., eds., *Education: Culture, Economy and Society*, p. 667.

12 A.H. Halsey, "Towards Meritocracy? The Case of Britain," in J. Karabel and A.H. Halsey, eds., *Power and Ideology in Education* (New York: Oxford University Press, 1977), p. 184, as cited in Goldthorpe, "Problems of 'Meritocracy,'" in Halsey et al., eds., *Education: Culture, Economy and Society*, p. 663.

13 Goldthorpe, "Problems of 'Meritocracy,'" in Halsey et al., eds., *Education: Culture, Economy and Society*, p. 673.

14 R.J. Herrnstein, "IQ," *Atlantic Monthly*, September 1971, as cited in Goldthorpe, "Problems of 'Meritocracy,'" in Halsey et al., eds., *Education: Culture, Economy and Society*, p. 668.

15 Jeremy Rifkin, *The End of Work: The Decline of the Global Labor Force and the Dawn of the Post-Market Era* (New York: Tarcher/Putnam, 1996), p. 173.

16 Ferdinand Lundberg, *The Rich and the Super Rich* (New York: L. Stuart, 1968), p. 129.

17 *Financial Times*, February 3, 1995.

18 *Sunday Times*, April 6, 1997.

19  *Ibid.*

20  U.S. Department of Commerce, *Statistical Abstract of the United States*, 1995, p. 855.

21  *Sunday Times*, April 6, 1997.

22  *Fortune*, June 28, 1993.

23  *Newsweek*, March 31, 1997.

24  *Forbes, The Richest 400*, pp. 162, 163.

25  *Sunday Times*, April 6, 1997.

26  *Forbes, The Richest 400*, pp. 152, 186.

27  *Sunday Times*, April 6, 1997.

28  *Fortune*, April 14, 1997.

29  *Sunday Times*, April 6, 1997.

30  *Fortune*, April 11, 1988.

31  *Forbes, The Richest 400*, pp. 154, 156, 158.

32  *Financial Post Magazine*, January 1996.

33  *Sunday Times*, April 6, 1997.

34  *Ibid.*

35  *Ibid.*

36  *Forbes, The Richest 400*, p. 312.

37  Andrew Hacker, *Money: Who Has How Much and Why* (New York: Scribner, 1997), p. 74.

38  *Sunday Times*, April 6, 1997.

39  *Forbes, The Richest 400*, pp. 214, 366.

40  *Ibid.*, p. 230.

41  *International Herald Tribune*, 10 February 1997.

42  *Globe and Mail*, January 13, 1997.

43  *International Herald Tribune*, May 12, 1997.

44  *Metropolitan Home*, May/June 1996.

45  *Forbes, The Richest 400*, p. 152.

46  *International Herald Tribune*, May 12, 1997.

47  *Fortune*, May 26, 1997.

48  *Ibid.*

49  *Economist*, May 24, 1997.

50  *Fortune*, May 26, 1997.

51  Associated Press, March 4, 1998.

52  *Fortune*, April 14, 1997.

53  *Forbes, The Richest 400*, p. 182.

54  *Sunday Times* Rich List 1997, April 6, 1997.

55  Lester Thurow, *Dangerous Currents: The State of Economics* (New York: Vintage Books, 1984), p. xviii.

56 U.S. Department of Commerce, *Statistical Abstract of the United States*, 1995, p. 414.

57 *International Herald Tribune*, February 3, 1997.

58 *Ibid.*

59 *Atlantic Monthly*, February 1997.


Chapter 5

1 *Newsweek*, July 14, 1997.

2 *Ibid.*

3 William Greider, *One World, Ready or Not: The Manic Logic of Global Capitalism* (New York: Simon and Schuster, 1997), p. 309.

4 *Ibid.*, p. 32.

5 *International Herald Tribune*, November 17, 1997.

6 OECD, *Banks Under Stress* (Paris: OECD, 1992), p. 90.

7 OECD, *The New Financial Landscape: Forces Shaping the Revolution in Banking, Risk Management and Capital Markets* (Paris, 1995), p. 13.

8 *Ibid.*

9 OECD, *Banks Under Stress*, p. 59.

10 OECD, *The New Financial Landscape*, p. 15.

11 Christel Lane, *Industry and Society in Europe: Stability and Change in Britain, Germany and France* (Aldershot, U.K.: Edward Elgar, 1995), p. 30.

12 *Ibid.*

13 OECD, *The New Financial Landscape*, p. 15.

14 Collin Randlesome, "The Business Culture in Germany," in Collin Randlesome, William Brierley, Kevin Bruton, Colin Gordon and Peter King, eds., *Business Cultures in Europe*, 2nd ed. (Oxford: Butterworth-Heinemann, 1993), p. 25.

15 *Ibid.*, pp. 25, 26.

16 *Fortune*, April 1972.

17 Collin Randlesome, "The Business Culture in the United Kingdom," in Collin Randlesome et al., eds., *Business Culture in Europe*, p. 230.

18 Quoted in *ibid.*, p. 213.

19 *Ibid.*, p. 216.

20 OECD, *The New Financial Landscape*, p. 347.

21 Martin Mayer, *The Bankers: The Next Generation* (New York: Truman Talley Books/Dutton, 1997), p. 281.

22 *Sunday Times*, April 6, 1997.

23 *Nouvel Observateur*, July 23, 1997.

24 *International Herald Tribune*, January 24, 1997.

25 William Greider, *One World, Ready or Not*, p. 32.

26 Martin Mayer, *The Bankers*, p. 78.

27 *Ibid.*, p. 79.

28 *Ibid.*

29 *Ibid.*, p. 76.

30 Catherine Caufield, *Masters of Illusion: The World Bank and the Poverty of Nations* (London: Macmillan, 1996), p. 262.

31 *Ibid.*

32 William Greider, *One World, Ready or Not*, p. 296.

33 *Ibid.*, p. 300.

34 Linda McQuaig, *Shooting the Hippo: Death by Deficit and Other Canadian Myths* (Toronto: Viking, 1995), p. 85.

35 *International Herald Tribune*, March 29–30, 1997.

36 Martin Mayer, *The Bankers*, p. 361.

37 William Greider, *One World Ready or Not*, p. 292.

38 *Ibid.*

## Chapter 6

1 *The Economist*, April 5, 1997.

2 OECD, *Historical Statistics 1960–1994* (Paris: OECD, 1996), p. 42.

3 *Ibid.*

4 *Ibid.*, p. 43.

5 Statistics Canada, *Canada Year Book 1978–79* (Hull, Quebec: Supply and Services Canada, 1978), p. 267.

6 OECD, *Historical Statistics 1960–1994* (Paris: OECD, 1996), p. 39.

7 Martin Mayer, *The Bankers: The Next Generation* (New York: Truman Talley Books/Dutton, 1997), p. 141.

8 Jeremy Rifkin, *The End of Work: The Decline of the Global Labor Force and the Dawn of the Post-Market Era* (New York: Tarcher/Putnam, 1996), p. 88.

9 OECD, *Historical Statistics 1960–1994*, p. 39.

10 *Ibid.*

11 *Ibid.*

12 *Ibid*, p. 40.

13 *Ibid.*

14 *Ibid.*

15 *Ibid*, p. 43.

16 *Ibid.*

17  OECD, *Main Economic Indicators: Historical Statistics: Prices, Labour and Wages* (Paris: OECD, 1993), pp. 19, 20.

18  OECD, *Historical Statistics 1960–1994*, p. 42.

19  *Ibid.*

20  *Ibid*, p. 43.

21  Jeremy Rifkin, *The End of Work*, pp. 181–97.


Chapter 7

1  *Challenges*, July–August 1997.

2  *Ibid.*

3  Roger Scruton, *The Conservative Idea of Community* (London: The Conservative 2000 Foundation, 1996), pp. 17, 18.

4  Richard Hoggart, *The Way We Live Now* (London: Pimlico, 1995), p. 1.

5  *International Herald Tribune*, April 8, 1997.

6  *Sunday Times*, April 6, 1997.

7  David Willetts, *Why Vote Conservative?* (Harmondsworth: Penguin, 1997), p. 7.

8  Collin Randlesome, "The Business Culture in the United Kingdom," in Collin Randlesome et al., eds., *Business Cultures in Europe*, 2nd ed. (Oxford: Butterworth-Heinemann, 1993), p. 208.

9  *Ibid.*, p. 70.

10  William Brierly, "The Business Culture in Italy," in Collin Randlesome et al., eds., *Business Cultures in Europe*, p. 153.

11  *Economist*, November 8, 1997.

12  *Globe and Mail*, August 14, 1997.

13  Collin Randlesome, "The Business Culture in the United Kingdom," in Collin Randlesome et al., eds., *Business Cultures in Europe*, pp. 208, 209.

14  Sigmund Freud, *Standard Edition of the Complete Psychological Works of Sigmund Freud*, ed. James Strachey (London: Hogarth Press, 1953–74), vol. 22, p. 221, as cited in Richard Webster, *Why Freud Was Wrong* (London: HarperCollins, 1995), p. 319.


Chapter 8

1  *European*, January 9–15, 1997.

2  Gallup Poll Canada, Inc., *The Gallup Poll*, Thursday, January 23, 1997.

3  Gallup Poll, Thursday, April 14, 1997.

4  Gallup Poll, Thursday, January 23, 1997.

5 Gallup Poll, Thursday, May 20, 1997.

6 *Gallup Poll Monthly*, November 1995.

7 *Gallup Poll Monthly*, October 1995.

8 Ruy A. Teixeira and Joel Rogers, "Who Deserted the Democrats in 1994," in Robert Kuttner, ed., *Ticking Time Bombs* (New York: New Press, 1996), p. 4.

9 *International Herald Tribune*, June 5, 1997.

10 *Economist*, June 7, 1997.

11 *Challenges*, July–August 1997.

12 Jeff Faux, "How to Rebuild the Democratic Party," in Robert Kuttner, ed., *Ticking Time Bombs*, p. 34.

13 *Economist*, March 8, 1997, p. 75.

14 *Ibid.*

15 *Ibid.*

16 *Libération*, March 17, 1997.

17 *Ibid.*

18 *Ibid.*

19 *International Herald Tribune*, February 25, 1997.

20 *International Herald Tribune*, March 25, 1997.

Chapter 9

1 *International Herald Tribune*, April 2, 1997.

2 *International Herald Tribune*, April 7, 1997.

3 Paul Harrison, *Inside the Inner City: Life Under the Cutting Edge* (Harmondsworth: Penguin, 1983), p. 49.

4 Ronald B. Mincy and Susan J. Wiener, *The Under Class in the 1980s: Changing Concepts, Constant Reality* (Washington, D.C.: Urban Institute, 1993), as cited in Tom Wicker, *Tragic Failure: Racial Integration in America* (New York: William Morrow, 1996), p. 127.

5 Wicker, *Tragic Failure*, p. 127.

6 U.S. Department of Commerce, *Statistical Abstract of the United States*, 1995, p. 480.

7 OECD, *Lone-Parent Families: The Economic Challenge* (Paris: OECD, 1990), p. 29.

8 U.S. Bureau of the Census, *Statistical Abstract of the United States*, 1995, p. 470.

9 OECD, *OECD Economic Surveys* (Paris: OECD, 1996), p. 89.

10 Arloc Sherman, "Rescuing the American Dream: Halting the Economic Freefall of Today's Young Families with Children," *Children's Defense Fund*, 1997, p. 3.

11 *Ibid.*

12 *Ibid.*

13 *Ibid.*

14 *Ibid.*

15 Robert B. Reich, "Why the Rich Are Getting Richer and the Poor, Poorer," in A.H. Halsey et al., eds., *Education: Culture, Economy and Society* (New York: Oxford Unversity Press, 1997), p. 165.

16 *Ibid.*

17 *New York Times*, February 25, 1996.

18 Robert B. Reich, "Why the Rich Are Getting Richer," p. 165.

19 Statistics Canada, *Canada Year Book*, 1997, p. 197.

20 Tom Wicker, *Tragic Failure*, p. 124.

21 *Ibid.*, pp. 124, 125.

22 *Ibid.*, p. 125.

23 *International Herald Tribune*, April 1, 1997.

24 Charles Murray, *Losing Ground: American Social Policy 1950–1980* (New York: Basic Books, 1986).

25 R.J. Herrnstein and Charles Murray, *The Bell Curve: Intelligence and Class Structure in American Life* (New York: Free Press, 1994).


Chapter 10

1 U.S. Bureau of the Census, *Statistical Abstract of the United States,*1996 (Washington, D.C.: Department of Commerce, 1996), p. 153.

2 Statistics Canada, *Canada Year Book*, 1978–79, p. 285.

3 *Ibid.*

4 *Globe and Mail*, November 1, 1997.

5 U.S. Department of Commerce, *Statistical Abstract of the United States*, 1995, p. 413.

6 OECD, *Main Economic Indicators 1962–1991*, p. 41.

7 U.S. Department of Commerce, *Statistical Abstract of the United States*, 1995, p. 411.

8 Andrew Hacker, *Money: Who Has How Much and Why* (New York: Scribner, 1997), pp. 124, 126.

9 *Ibid.*, p. 125.

10 *Ibid.*

11 *Ibid.*, p. 124.

12 Statistics Canada, *Canada Year Book*, 1997, p. 101.

13 Statistics Canada, 1991.

14 E.J. Dionne Jr., *They Only Look Dead: Why Progressives Will Dominate the Next Political Era* (New York: Simon and Schuster, 1996), p. 120.

15 Andrew Hacker, *Money: Who Has How Much and Why*, p. 124.

16 Statistics Canada, 1991.

17 William Kristol, "The Politics of Liberty, the Sociology of Virtue," in Mark Gerson, ed., *The Essential Neo-Conservative Reader* (Reading, MA: Addison-Wesley, 1996), p. 439.

18 U.S. Department of Education, National Center for Education Statistics (NCES), *Digest of Education Statistics*, 1996, Table 79. Bank of Canada, ETS Date Management System, Data Report B4300. Reports from Provincial Departments of Education.

19 Statistics Canada, 1991.

## Chapter 11

1 U.S. Bureau of the Census, *Statistical Abstract of the United States*, 1995, p. 805, and U.S. Bureau of the Census, *Statistical Abstract of the United States*, 1997, p. 791.

2 U.S. Bureau of the Census, *Statistical Abstract of the United States*, 1997, p. 791.

3 U.S. Bureau of the Census, *Statistical Abstract of the United States*, 1995, p. 880.

4 U.S. Bureau of the Census, *Statistical Abstract of the United States*, 1997, p. 791.

5 *Ibid.*

6 U.S. Bureau of the Census, *Statistical Abstract of the United States*, 1995, pp. 806, 809.

7 *Ibid.*, p. 809.

8 U.S. Bureau of the Census, *Statistical Abstract of the United States*, 1996, p. 788, 791, and U.S. Bureau of the Census, *Statistical Abstract of the United States*, 1997, p. 795.

9 U.S. Bureau of the Census, *Statistical Abstract of the United States*, 1995, p. 806, 809, and U.S. Bureau of the Census, *Statistical Abstract of the United States*, 1997, p. 795.

10 U.S. Bureau of the Census, *Statistical Abstract of the United States*, 1996, pp. 788, 791, and U.S. Bureau of the Census, *Statistical Abstract of the United States*, 1997, p. 795.

11 U.S. Bureau of the Census, *Statistical Abstract of the United States*, 1995, p. 865.

12 *Ibid.*, p. 879.

13 *Ibid.*, p. 863.

14 *International Herald Tribune*, November 3, 1997.

15 U.S. Department of Commerce, *Statistical Abstract of the United States*, 1995, p. 431.

16 *Ibid.*, p. 442.

17 *International Herald Tribune*, March 1, 1997.

18 *Economist*, March 22, 1997, p. 109.

19  *Economist*, March 1, 1997, p. 123.

20  *International Herald Tribune*, March 14, 1997.

21  OECD, *OECD Economies at a Glance: Structural Indicators* (Paris: OECD, 1996), p. 17.

22  *Economist*, March 1, 1997, p. 123.

23  *Economist*, November 8, 1997, p. 114.

24  U.S. Department of Commerce, *Statistical Abstract of the United States*, 1995, p. 410.

25  *Ibid.*, p. 409.

26  *Ibid.*, p. 217.

27  *Economist*, May 24, 1997.

28  *European*, January 10, 1997.

29  *European*, January 9–15, 1997.

30  France 2, telecast, March 10, 1997.

Chapter 12

1  *International Herald Tribune*, June 5, 1997.

2  *International Herald Tribune*, June 6, 1997.

# Index